THE RULES OF THE GREEN

The Rules
of the Green

A History of the Rules of Golf

Kenneth G. Chapman

This edition first published in Great Britain in 1997 by
Virgin Books
an imprint of Virgin Publishing Ltd
332 Ladbroke Grove
London W10 5AH

First published in the United States by
Triumph Books
644 South Clark Street
Chicago, Illinois 60605

A catalogue record for this book is available from the British Library.

ISBN 1 85227 711 4

Printed in the United States of America.

The meeting, considering that before the Cup is played for, the Rules of the Green and other Regulations ought to be more definitively fixed than at present, expressed a wish that the Committee appointed on 14 July last to revise the Laws should hold a meeting.

MINUTE OF MEETING OF THE MUSSELBURGH GOLF CLUB
13 MARCH 1829

Contents

Foreword from USGA and R&A

One of the undisputed pleasures of golf lies in the comforting knowledge that all golfers around the world play the same game. Imagine the chaos that would exist if there were, as some have suggested, different Rules for professional and amateur golf or if each country had its own unique code of Rules. It is the uniformity and world-wide acceptance of the Rules that allows us to compare our rounds to those of the top players and to appreciate a tournament played on the other side of the world. There are some necessary differences in Local Rules, but we will still take the same relief from casual water as a player will on the final hole of the U.S. Open.

In the history of the Rules of Golf there are three landmark years: 1744, when the first code was written; 1952, when the USGA and R&A first issued a uniform set of Rules for the world; and 1984, when the Rules were reorganized. The 1952 date is even more significant today as international competition has increased dramatically. It would be asking too much of today's globe-trotters to adjust their knowledge of the Rules as well as their games from country to country. The vision of the two bodies in 1952 should be applauded.

Golfers should rest easy knowing that the Rules of Golf may be changed only every four years. This revision schedule assures that the Rules will not be changed on a whim. Rather, the Rules change process is an involved, laborious one which must end in an agreement between the USGA and R&A. If one body is not in favor of a particular proposed amendment, that Rule will not be changed. There have been exceptions, as in 1960 when the USGA obstinately went off on its own in search of a better penalty for a ball lost or out of bounds, but the quadrennial schedule has provided uniformity as well as continuity to the game.

It is the hope of the USGA and R&A that this book will shed some light on how and why the Rules have evolved into their present form and demonstrate the progress made in writing and interpreting the Rules.

David B. Fay
Executive Director
United States Golf Association

Michael Bonallack
Secretary
Royal and Ancient Golf Club
of St. Andrews

Research in the Kingdom of Golf

It was late in the afternoon of a day in October 1992. I was standing on the fifteenth tee of the ancient golf course on the parkland area called the North Inch in the city of Perth in Scotland. According to tradition, King James VI of Scotland, son of Mary Queen of Scots, played golf here four centuries ago. This circumstance in itself is enough to impress any golfer with an interest in the history of the game, but what was really impressing me was the prospect of the drive I was about to hit: to a narrow fairway, mounded on the right and bordered on the left by the most threatening body of water I had seen since the last time I stood on the eighteenth tee at Pebble Beach.

The broad Tay River flows swiftly along the entire length of the 373-yard hole, its dark surface only a yard or so below the level of the fairway. I suddenly realized as I stood there why two golf clubs that played on the North Inch during the 1860s and 1870s had special lateral water hazard rules. This adaptation dated from the time when there was no official rules-making body, and each club drew up its own rules. The Royal Perth Golfing Society (the first golf club in the world to become a royal club) and the King James VI Golf Club (named after that fellow who played there so long ago) both had special rules to cope with the situation before me. They involved either the problem of being able to see the ball go into the river or whether it went in on the fly or on the bounce. (The details of these rules are discussed in the section on Rule 26: Water Hazards, later in this book.)

As I stood there, the sun was setting, the shadows were lengthening, and the mist was beginning to rise off that huge sweep of dark water. I was face to face with the same conditions that had plagued those golfers more than a century ago. I understood better than ever before an important truth: golf rules aren't an abstract set of injunctions designed to punish the player. They're practical reflections of playing conditions designed to aid the golfer in his game.

What happened when I finally stopped musing on historical matters and hit my drive? I have to admit I held back a bit to keep my usual draw from getting out of control and pushed the ball onto the mounds on the right. But a good four-wood off a fluffy lie in the short rough and a lucky chip that found the hole on a green sloping sharply toward the water gave me a birdie. I was left wondering whether old King James had ever played so well—or been so lucky—on that time-honored piece of golfing land. It was a great end to a great day of research.

Research? Yes, it was actually research that I had been doing. I had spent the day studying the old minute books containing, among many other interesting things, those old water hazard rules. Then the time had come to do a little on-course research. My experience that day left me wondering why I hadn't thought of doing this sort of research years ago, instead of spending my professional life in libraries. For that matter, I've had to spend a lot of time in libraries as well doing research for this book.

Not every bit of information about golf can be found on the course. My main library sources have been the wonderful collections of golf material of the National Library of Scotland in Edinburgh and the United States Golf Association in Far Hills, New Jersey. I've also found a great deal of material in the archives of many golf clubs, especially those of the Royal and Ancient Golf Club of St. Andrews, and other royal and nonroyal clubs in Britain. Many days spent going through old minute books, followed by rounds of golf on the actual playing grounds concerned, have made research for this book a true pleasure. I've also had the pleasure of being in contact with golf club secretaries and historians in all corners of the world and have received much valuable information from them, for which I'm extremely grateful.

I should note that I mean to discuss only the rules for playing the game. While regulations governing the design and performance of equipment, along with the rules of amateur status, are included in the rulebook, they remain outside the scope of this book.

It would be impossible to make an exhaustive survey of the history of the rules of golf in a single book of reasonable and manageable size, so I've had to condense the material considerably and leave out many interesting details. The book is divided into four parts. The first part is an introductory chapter on why the rules of golf change. Part II presents a historical overview of the entire process. Part III traces the evolution of individual rules and definitions, organized in the same order as they're found in the current rule book. Part IV contains the appendices. This structure should make it easy for the reader to locate the discussion of any particular rule of interest. Probably the best way to use the book is to read the introduction and historical survey first, then browse through the rest as your interest dictates.

It seemed unnecessary to include the texts of the rules. Every golfer interested in the evolution of the rules must certainly own a copy of the current code. A copy of *Decisions on the Rules of Golf* (the official rulings published by the USGA and the R&A) is also always good to have on hand.

Acknowledgments

In addition to the many golf club secretaries and historians who have helped me in my search for information on early rules, I'm especially indebted to a number of rules and golf history experts on both sides of the Atlantic who saw the manuscript at various stages in its development and have given me valuable criticism and suggestions for improvement.

Frank Hannigan, a former executive director of the United States Golf Association, and Bill Williams, a former USGA president who served as chairman of its Rules of Golf Committee in 1984, gave me both valuable criticism and encouragement at the early stages of my work. John Glover, Rules Secretary of the Royal and Ancient Golf Club through 1995, Bill Bryce and Denis Hayes, chairmen of the R&A Rules of Golf Committee in, respectively, 1988 and 1984, as well as John Pasquill, deputy chairman of that committee in 1984, all were kind enough to read the manuscript carefully and share their opinions with me.

I have also benefited greatly from discussions with Stewart Lawson of the R&A and Peter Lewis, Director of the British Golf Museum in St. Andrews. Bob Sommers, former editor of the USGA *Golf Journal*, did a careful job of editing the manuscript and greatly enhanced its read ability. The great knowledge of the rules of golf and the eagle eyes of all these experts truly freed me "frae monie a blunder . . . an' foolish notion" in the words of that wise auld Scot Robert Burns. Any remaining blunders and foolish notions are, of course, solely my own.

I would like to extend special thanks to David Fay, Executive Director of the USGA, whose constant support and enthusiasm for this project made it possible to carry it through to completion.

—Ken Chapman

PART I

Introduction

Why the Rules of Golf Change

*Nobody is ever satisfied with the rules
of golf as they may happen to stand.*

—H. S. C. EVERARD, 1907

More than two hundred fifty years have passed since the first written code of golf rules appeared in 1744. During this time the rules have changed frequently and extensively. There are good reasons for this.

- Conditions of play have changed greatly. Organized golf as we know it today began as a diversion for a small group of gentlemen sportsmen in eastern Scotland in the eighteenth century.
- Now the game is an obsession for millions of people from all stations in life in all parts of the world.
- Golf equipment—the clubs and the ball—has undergone immense development.
- Commercialization has accompanied the explosive evolution of professional golf since the end of the Second World War.

All these factors have combined to bring about fundamental changes in attitude toward the game and how it should be played.

In his 1972 study, *Muirfield and The Honourable Company,* George Pottinger summed up the first two points:

> Inevitably, the rules have had to be modified to cope with the vast growth in the number of players and the extension of the game to more exotic conditions and diverse countries.

A direct relationship exists between the growing number of golfers and the degree of change in the rules. The greatest changes have coincided precisely with periods of the game's most rapid expansion.

The first period of expansion occurred in Britain, where more than a thousand golf clubs were founded during the 1880s and 1890s. A similar period, accompanied by radical changes in the rules, followed the end of the Second World War. Most recently, the 1980s and 1990s show noticeable growth and change.

EQUIPMENT CHANGES

Starting with the switch from the feather ball to the gutta percha ball in the middle of the nineteenth century, the game's equipment began changing. The rate of change has increased enormously during the twentieth century, but changes in the rules due to equipment changes have been relatively few. There are two reasons for this. First, the basic nature of golf has remained unchanged through the hundreds of years people have been playing it. The situations a player might meet during a round—various types of hazards, lost balls, extraneous inanimate objects and living things, the effect of weather— have always been with us, and throughout the years the rules have handled them in basically the same way. Without these elements, golf isn't golf.

Second, many of the radical changes in equipment have been subject to rigid limitations and standardization by the governing bodies of golf—the United States Golf Association (USGA) and the Royal and Ancient Golf Club of St. Andrews (R&A). For example, any ball approved for competition must have passed a strict test of its performance. Its size is limited as well, and since 1 January 1990 no ball can be smaller than 1.68 inch in diameter. Many older players from outside North America mourned the passing of the small ball with its 1.62-inch diameter. They felt it flew farther than the larger ball, especially into the wind, but now its day is gone for good. The larger ball has been mandatory under the rules of the USGA since 1931.

ATTITUDES CHANGE

To see how fundamentally attitudes toward golf have changed, even somewhat recently, we can look at what Robert Harris wrote in 1953:

> Golf is a game of the people. It is played by the Common Man as a sport and a relaxation from the worries of life rather than used as an exhibition for onlookers, to which it is not suited.

This point of view might strike the modern golfer as a bit quaint. Harris held a generally conservative attitude toward the rules and the changes made in them. He wrote passionately against abolishing the stymie in 1952, and he would have been astonished, if not appalled, at the conditions of a modern professional tournament, with grandstands filled with cheering and shouting spectators, venues selected with an eye to space for gallery movement and corporate tents, and course design influenced by the demands of golf as a spectator sport.

DISTINCTIVE VENUES

Golf differs from other sports played on regularly defined areas, like tennis courts, billiard tables, or football fields. Relatively few unpredictable events occur in these games, so a relatively modest code of rules assures that they can be played fairly. Golf has a great accumulation of rules (a bulk many people believe to be quite immodest) because the game is played on an area that can-

Robert Harris stood among the leading figures in golf of his day. He won the 1925 British Amateur Championship, played on British Walker Cup teams in 1923 and 1926, and served more than twenty years on the R&A Rules of Golf Committee during the 1920s, 1930s and 1940s. He made a significant contribution to golf throughout his career.

not be strictly defined. A golf course is a slice of nature itself. Although marked by many artificial features, it's bound to be full of natural phenomena that lead to unpredictable events which plague the golfer. The rules have to be so extensive to cover the unlimited number of contingencies that crop up in nearly every round.

AN ADVENTURE OF THE SPIRIT

This perspective, of course, is a modern one. Nowadays we expect rules to cover every problem. Our golf-playing forefathers were much more willing than we to accept a bit of bad luck as a part of the game. Robert Browning pointed out this fact in his 1955 book, *A History of Golf.* He noted that

> we have been so anxious, in the sacred name of fair play, to take all the element of luck out of the game, that we have to a proportionate extent destroyed its value as a test of each man's ability to stand up to bad luck. Modern golf is a stiffer test of a player's skill, but it has robbed the game of its charm as an adventure of the spirit.

It's amazing, actually, to think that the game was played for more than three centuries without a written code of rules, but what was involved at that time was a considerably different sort of activity from the game we play today. It was a much sterner business then; occasional chance difficulties were part of the game and nobody thought much about it. The rough character of the playing fields and the primitive equipment ensured that golf at that time was a true "adventure of the spirit."

EVOLVING ATTITUDES

Writing in 1912 of conflicting attitudes toward the rules at the beginning of the twentieth century, John Low, chairman of the R&A Rules of Golf Committee for many years, said

> During the past five and twenty years, men have been looking at the rules of the game from two very distinct points of view. We may style the opposing forces the Conservative Party and the Party of Equity. The doctrine of the Conservative Party is easily understood; it lies round one fundamental principle: it makes golf a game of two sides and two balls and demands that every ball shall be played from the place where it lies. The Party of Equity holds that golf should be ruled by laws which mete out to each offense an absolutely just and properly proportioned punishment: it cannot bear that a man suffer unjustly or that the wicked appear to prosper while the slightly erring are discomfited. The Conservative Party holds that golf is a game of risks and hazards, a game in which a man distinguishes himself by his steady progress around the course, a progress which should not be needlessly interrupted.

It was a much sterner business then; occasional chance difficulties were part of the game and nobody thought much about it.

Low was accurate in his historical evaluation of the situation: the principle of equity first appeared in the rules of golf in the 1891 code of the R&A. Ever since then it has played a more and more dominant role in determining the form of the rules and has become enthroned as one of the basic principles of the game (Rule 1-4). Low's early twentieth century Conservatives must be gnashing on their mashies as they look down on us from the Ultimate Bunker.

GROWTH AND CHANGE

Since the Honourable Company of Edinburgh Golfers set down the first written rules in 1744, later codes have taken many different forms. Although those who look closely can detect a certain arbitrariness now and then in their evolution, in general the changes in the rules carried out at different periods have been motivated by a genuine attempt to improve them:

- to organize them more logically,
- to make them more consistent, and
- to write them more clearly and precisely.

A joint USGA-R&A press release announcing the 1996 code explained the rationale behind the process:

> Modifications come about as a result of actual on course situations which expose minor weaknesses or omissions in the Rules and the continuing effort by both the R&A and the USGA to make the Rules as clear and concise as possible.

Even though the basic character of golf has remained constant over the past two and a half centuries, the rules of the game have evolved significantly. Because we can anticipate that conditions of play will continue changing, we can assume that the rules will continue changing as well. We have no way of knowing, however, just how they will change.

The rules of the game have evolved significantly.

PART II

Historical Survey

SHINTY, AN EARLY SCOTTISH BALL-AND-CLUB GAME.

*The first rules must have been
very simple, for the manner of play
is not complicated; but we do not
have those earliest rules, which were
probably more or less a code
of honour for men who knew nothing
of golfing sin or golfing law.*

—JOHN LOW, 1912

The Prehistory

CHAPTER 1

"UTTERLY CONDEMNED"

The origins of both the rules of golf and of golf itself are hidden from us by the mists of time. We do know, though, that by the middle of the fifteenth century the Scots were playing some sort of game in Scotland. We also know that King James II of Scotland issued a decree in 1457 that "ye fut bawe and ye golf be uterly cryt done and not usyt," which Olive Geddes has translated as "football and golf be utterly condemned and stopped."

James was annoyed. During this period of persistent wars with the English, his soldiers' enthusiasm for these games was taking too much time away from archery practice, which was more important for the defense of the realm. His grandson, James IV, continued the tradition in 1491, when he decreed that "in na place of the realme be usit fut bawis, gouff or uthir sic unproffitable sports" (try your own translation).

MAJESTY RELENTS: FIRST RECORDED MATCH

As may happen on occasion, time and the bonds of marriage worked their magic. Early in 1502, James became engaged to the English princess Margaret Tudor, whose brother was soon to become Henry the Eighth, and for a time peace reigned between Scotland and England. The effect on golf was immediate and decisive. The next year we find this same James IV ordering clubs from a Perth bowmaker, who now could apply his talents to implements other than weapons of war. James seems to have set to work practicing with great industry. Within a year we find him taking on the Earl of Bothwell in what was the first recorded match in the history of golf.

BEYOND SCOTLAND

Things took a definite turn for the better when James, son of Mary Queen of Scots, ascended to the thrones of both Scotland and England and, as James I of England, brought the game south to London in 1603. This most famous of all King Jameses made a lasting contribution to more than one aspect of world culture. The bible translation that he commissioned remains to this day

The name of the game of golf has been variously spelled in documents from earlier times.

Goff	Gowff
Goufe	Goulf
Goofe	Golff
Goiff	Golfe
Gauff	Golf

The First Lady Golfer

A couple of generations further down the royal line we find Mary Queen of Scots, James the IV's famous granddaughter, being criticized for her golfing activities. She left Edinburgh only a "few dayes eftir the murther" of her husband, Lord Darnley, in 1567, according to a deposition filed against her on 6 December 1568. Her reputation had already been sullied by her dalliance with the Earl of Bothwell, and it didn't help that she was spotted whacking the ball around the fields of Seton when pious Scots felt she should still be in mourning. The Scottish writer Lewine Mair wittily reminds us that Mary's golf career was "dramatically cut short when she failed to maintain that relationship between head and shoulders which all the game's great teachers have deemed essential."

MARY QUEEN OF SCOTS DEPICTED PLAYING GOLF AT ST. ANDREWS.

the standard version used throughout most of the English-speaking world. It's one of the foundation stones of the modern English language, and therefore of the language of the rules of golf as well. The game that James and his Scottish courtiers made popular in England has spread even further than the limits of the English-speaking world. It is played today by millions of people on every continent.

A LUCRATIVE GAME

Toward the end of the seventeenth century we come across yet another King James practicing the royal and ancient game—James II of England, grandson of Mary's golfing boy. Tradition has placed him on the links of Leith in 1681, when he was still Duke of York, playing a foursome match with a poor shoemaker named John Patersone as his partner. The cobbler may have been poor, but he could really play golf. He and the Duke won the match and split the winnings. With his share Patersone built a house in Edinburgh bearing his coat of arms and the inscription "Far and Sure," a good description of how he could belt the ball. A replica of this coat of arms can be seen in the Canongate in Edinburgh. It decorates the wall of the modern building that occupies the site where the shoemaker's house was supposed to have stood. While there are unfortunately no deeds or other records to substantiate this tale, a good golf tale always deserves repeating.

RULES, ANYONE?

We know, then, that golf was being played during those early centuries, but we know nothing about how it was played or what rules were used. Perhaps written rules weren't necessary because early golf seems to have consisted of informal, friendly games. We have generally assumed that golf at that time was a match play game, and since it was played mainly by gentlemen, they could settle disagreements amicably. This explanation is as good as any. We do know that the first written codes of rules followed the formation of the earliest golfing societies, but we don't know the precise relationship.

THE NINETEENTH HOLE

Many early Scottish golfers were also Freemasons. It seems that golf served primarily to whet their appetites for the gluttonous feasts laced with the liberal amounts of drink so important to their meetings. For them the main purpose of the game was what we know today as the nineteenth hole—as it is for many modern players as well. Once again, the more things change, the more they stay the same.

UNCOMMONLY CLEVER

The seventeenth century gives us a glimpse of commoners involved with the game. One David Wedderburn, an inventive schoolmaster in Aberdeen, gave the world its first sketchy description of golf in 1636 when he hit upon the bright idea of translating golf terms into Latin. Apparently he hoped in this way to trick his golf-playing pupils into learning a bit of that most ungolfish language.

"IN TYME OF SERMONS"

*The ancient rules of golf if read aright,
and honestly carried out, will be found
in every respect all that is required
in regulating the noble game.*

—"OLD ENGLISH GOLFER" 1888

The Thirteen Articles

The following notice appeared in the April 1744 number of the *Scots Magazine:*

Domestick History
EDINBURGH

On application of several persons of honour, skilled in the ancient and healthful exercise of the goff, an act of the town council of Edinburgh was passed on the 7th of March, appointing their Treasurer to cause make a silver club, of 15 l. value, to be played for on the links of Leith the first Monday of April annually. The act appoints, That the candidates names be booked some day of the week preceding the match, paying 5 s. each at booking: That they be matched into parties of two's or of three's, if their number be great, by lot: That the player who shall have won the greatest number of holes, be victor; and if two or more shall have won an equal number, that they play a round by themselves in order to determine the match: That the victor be stiled Captain of the Goff; that he append a piece of gold or silver to the club; that he have the sole disposal of the booking-money, the determination of disputes among goffers, with the assistance of two or three of the players, and the superintendency of the links,—Accordingly, the first match was played on the 2d of April, by the Gentlemen, and won by Mr. John Rattray Surgeon of Edinburgh.

The conditions for this match, the first organized tournament we know of, have caused justifiably puzzled commentary. Historical records tell us ten players participated, each of them paired with one other player. The victor was to be "the player who shall have won the greatest number of holes," but it's not clear exactly how holes were won. Was the competition played as match against some standard (another one hundred fifty years or so were to pass before the concepts of par and bogey originated), or was it some sort of Jacobite skins game? It's hard to say, but the good gentlemen of Edinburgh seem to have known what they were up to because they were able to produce an undisputed winner year after year.

A NEED FOR RULES

The minutes of the Edinburgh Town Council meeting of 7 March 1744 provide some additional information of special interest to us:

> *That the player who shall have won the greatest number of holes, be victor.*

As many Noblemen or Gentlemen, or other Golfers, from any part of Great Britain or Ireland, as Shall Book themselves eight Days before, or upon any of the lawfull Days of the Week Immediately preceeding The Day Appointed by the Magistrates and Council for the Annual Match, Shall have the Priviledge of playing for the said Club . . .

Apparently those who organized the match felt that because the tournament was open to other than local players, it would be best to publish, if not the rules of play commonly followed by the Gentlemen Golfers of Leith, at least a version of them suitable for this kind of competition. The original copy of those rules still exists; it is in the archives of The Honourable Company of Edinburgh Golfers, the direct descendant of the Gentlemen Golfers.

In 1984 the city of Edinburgh erected a small monument on the western edge of the present city park that incorporates the original Leith links. The inscription on the monument's northern face reads:

Leith Links

THE HOME OF GOLF

Historical home of The Honourable Company of Edinburgh Golfers. The game was played over a five hole course, each hole being over 400 yards long. In 1744 the first official rules were drawn up for a tournament on Leith Links and these rules, 13 in all, formed the basis for the modern game of golf.

THE ORIGINAL RULES OF GOLF

The thirteen rules of this oldest code read as follows:

Articles & Laws in Playing at Golf

1. You must Tee your Ball, within a Club's length of the Hole.

2. Your Tee must be upon the Ground.

3. You are not to change the Ball which you Strike off the Tee.

4. You are not to remove, Stones, Bones or any Break Club for the sake of playing your Ball, Except upon the fair Green/& that only/ within a Club's length of your Ball.

5. If your Ball comes among Watter, or any Wattery Filth, you are at liberty to take out your Ball & bringing it behind the hazard and Teeing it, you may play it with any Club and allow your Adversary a Stroke for so getting out your Ball.

6. If your Balls be found anywhere touching one another, You are to lift the first Ball, till you play the last.

7. At Holling, you are to play your Ball honestly for the Hole, and, not to play upon your Adversary's Ball, not lying in your way to the Hole.

8. If you shou'd lose your Ball, by its being taken up, or any other way,

you are to go back to the Spot, where you struck last & drop another Ball, And allow your Adversary a Stroke for the misfortune.

9. No man at Holling his Ball, is to be allowed, to mark his way to the Hole with his Club or, any thing else.

10. If a Ball be stopp'd by any person, Horse, Dog, or any thing else, The Ball so stop'd must be play'd where it lyes.

11. If you draw your Club, in order to Strike & proceed so far in the Stroke, as to be bringing down your Club; If then, your Club shall break, in, any way, it is to be Accounted a Stroke.

12. He, whose Ball lyes farthest from the Hole is obliged to play first.

13. Neither Trench, Ditch, or Dyke, made for the preservation of the Links, nor the Scholar's Holes or the Soldier's Lines, Shall be accounted a Hazard; But the Ball is to be taken out/ Teed/ and play'd with any Iron Club.

The last of these Thirteen Articles is clearly what we nowadays call a local rule, but the twelve that precede it pertain to the general principles of how the game was played at that time. Considering how long ago these Articles were written and how different the playing conditions were, it's striking how little the basic idea of the game has changed. Essentially identical then and now are the rules governing the order of play, interference by an outside agency (although not referred to in those terms), holing out, making a stroke, and the contingency of a lost ball. The articles that surprise us most are the first two.

ARTICLE 1

The thought of driving from within a club-length of the hole shocks the modern golfer, accustomed as he is to meticulously manicured greens and spacious teeing grounds. Clearly, greens in the eighteenth century had none of the luxury we expect of greens nowadays. This fact is confirmed by any number of famous paintings of early golf matches, as well as by photographs of playing conditions even in the late nineteenth century. In truth, the condition of the area close to the hole was, in early times, barely of higher standard than the rest of the playing area.

In this connection we should remember that the term *green* originally was applied to the entire playing area. Our modern expressions *through the green*, *rub of the green*, *Green Committee*, *Green Fee*, and *Greenkeeper* reflect this. Actually, in the eighteenth century, and far into the nineteenth as well, the only "greenkeepers" on most courses were sheep and rabbits. Mechanical methods of cutting grass were not adopted until the last decades of the nineteenth century. *(See Rule 11: Teeing Ground.)*

It's striking how little the basic idea of the game has changed.

15

ARTICLE 2

The short sentence "Your Tee must be upon the Ground" has caused much puzzled commentary. Its exact significance is not immediately apparent, but the rule probably meant neither more nor less than what it says. A "tee" at that time was a pile of sand that the ball was placed on, and this rule seems to say that the sand had to be formed directly on the ground and not on anything else placed on the ground. It's the forerunner of our present Rule 14-3 which bans the use of artificial devices and unusual equipment. An eighteenth-century golfer would probably look with great disapproval on our modern wooden, plastic or rubber tees and point out that their use was strictly against the rules of the game. *(See Rule 11: Teeing Ground.)*

ARTICLE 3

Rule 15-1 in our modern code corresponds most closely to the 1744 categorical prohibition: "You are not to change the Ball which you Strike off the Tee," although we choose to look at the matter from a positive point of view:

> A player must hole out with the ball played from the teeing ground
> unless a Rule permits him to substitute another ball.

Our Rule 5-3 sets precise conditions for replacing a ball unfit for play, but balls simply weren't replaced in the eighteenth century, though certainly not because the feather balls of that time were impervious to damage. Quite the contrary. They were very susceptible to splitting open, to becoming waterlogged, and to being damaged in myriad ways. Being allowed to replace a damaged ball would thus have given the player an undue advantage. Damage to the ball was to be expected and to be borne. In addition, since balls were frequently and extensively damaged, it was difficult to define exactly what constituted damage sufficient to justify replacement.

ARTICLE 4

This article deals with what we nowadays call loose impediments. Our present definition includes a number of things (leaves, twigs, and such) that sound quite harmless compared with the ominous-sounding "Bones and Break Clubs" that our eighteenth-century forefathers had to contend with. This article serves to remind us of the primitive conditions they played under and the relative frailty of their equipment. *(See Rule 23: Loose Impediments.)*

ARTICLE 5

This article, with its reference to "Watter" and "wattery filth," is clearly the forerunner of both Rules 25 and 26 in our modern code because no clear distinction is made between water hazards and casual water. A clear-cut distinc-

**FEATHER BALL
CIRCA 1840.**

tinction is made between water hazards and casual water. A clear-cut distinction between hazards in general and abnormal ground conditions was slow to develop.

The colorful expression "Wattery Filth" probably referred to generally sloppy conditions that golfers nowadays expect to be allowed to drop clear of without penalty. This sort of playing situation may be what P. G. Wodehouse had in mind when he hit upon his most entertaining golf course name: "Squashy Hollow." *(See Rule 25: Abnormal Ground Conditions and Rule 26: Water Hazards.)*

ARTICLE 6

Nowadays it's very rare that two balls come to rest touching one another, but in the eighteenth century it was common enough to rate a separate rule. The old feather balls must have behaved quite differently from modern balls. They were perhaps more inclined to snuggle up to each other, especially if their leather covers were wet and they happened to meet at the bottom of one of the innumerable small depressions that still make up the uneven surfaces of Scottish links.

This article eventually developed into something of great significance in the history of the rules of golf. The very next code adopted by The Honourable Company, in 1775, redefined the conditions under which the ball closer to the hole was to be lifted:

> If your Balls be found anywhere touching *or within six inches* of one another, you are to lift the first Ball until the other is played. [Italics added.]

The stymie was born. *(See Rule 16: The Putting Green, page 128)*

ARTICLE 7

By insisting that the ball "be played honestly for the hole," this article states in simple and unequivocal terms that golf is not croquet. However, this principle doesn't seem to have been universally accepted in the early days of the game. Playing on your adversary's ball (in order to knock it away, as in croquet) was expressly allowed at Bruntsfield Links, in Edinburgh, as late as 1814. This practice would seem to have been an earlier one that was on the way out at the time the earliest codes were written down.

Playing on an adversary's ball wasn't tolerated in the eighteenth century at most of the important golfing centers: not at St. Andrews, nor at Aberdeen, Glasgow, or Leith. The relationship of this article to Article 6 is clear: if your adversary's ball lay in your way to the hole—after 1775 at a distance of more than six inches—you were stymied. In this single case you were allowed to play upon the adversary's ball. *(See Rule 16: The Putting Green, page 127.)*

ARTICLE 8

The contingency of a lost ball is the most complex issue in the history of the playing rules of golf. It has been the source of more dispute and more frequent change than any other issue. Finally, in 1968, the conflict surrounding it was happily resolved. In 1744 The Gentlemen Golfers applied the concept of a lost ball somewhat more broadly than we do now (our present Rule 18-1 allows us to replace a ball that is "taken up"), but they correctly perceived the principle. In this they showed great foresight, and later rules-makers could have avoided years of unnecessary conflict if they hadn't chosen to experiment with penalties that were less wise and less equitable than what we now call stroke and distance. *(See Rule 27: Ball Lost or Out of Bounds.)*

ARTICLE 9

This ban on "marking the way to the hole" tells us the temptation to improve one's chances of sinking a putt by all means possible was apparently as strong in the eighteenth century as it is today. This principle has remained essentially unchanged through more than two hundred fifty years of written codes of rules. *(See Rule 8: Indicating Line of Play.)*

ARTICLE 10

This rule stating that the player must play the ball as it lies if it hits "any person, Horse, Dog, or anything else," reminds us once again that the conditions under which our forefathers played golf were less than ideal. There was a great deal of traffic on the links, not only at Leith, but everywhere that golf was played. The links were public areas where the townspeople engaged in all sorts of activities, including "playing at golff, futball, shuting at all gamis with all other maner of pastime" to quote a grant to the people of St. Andrews from 1552. Rubs of the green were certain to abound, although that term had not yet emerged. *(See Rule 19: Ball in Motion Deflected or Stopped.)*

ARTICLE 11

This article implies a definition of the stroke, but places the emphasis on the tendency of wooden-shafted clubs to break. Many players still alive today who learned to play golf with such clubs can attest to how fragile they were. The switch to steel shafts during the 1920s and 1930s solved the problem to a great extent, but even modern clubs occasionally break. This contingency is no longer specifically mentioned in our rule, but our definition of the stroke covers it adequately. *(See Rule 14: Striking the Ball.)*

The links were public areas where the townspeople engaged in all sorts of activities.

ARTICLE 12

The wording of this basic rule of golf has remained virtually unchanged through more than two hundred fifty years. Our present Rule 10 is much wordier, but nothing essential has been added. All that's really important is that "the ball farthest from the hole shall be played first." *(See Rule 10: Order of Play.)*

ARTICLE 13

This article is the first recorded local rule in the history of golf. No one has ever been able to determine what "the Scholar's Holes" or "the Soldier's Lines" were. The former may have been a short course for pupils of a nearby school. The presence of soldiers in the vicinity of a golf links should surprise no one because the links of Scotland were used as practice grounds for archery in early times. The excessive amount of time that his soldiers were spending playing golf and football led King James II to issue his famous edict of 1457 to the effect that they'd better stop wasting time on silly games and get back to work. Even today you can occasionally hear small arms fire near Scottish golf links, most noticeably at Carnoustie.

When the Society of St. Andrews Golfers adopted these articles in 1754, they took over this local rule verbatim, so presumably they knew what sort of things "Scholar's Holes" and "Soldier's Lines" were (they even corrected the spelling to "Scholars' holes" and "Soldiers' lines"). It's perhaps significant that these obstacles are mentioned only in these first two codes of rules. The next set of rules adopted by the Honourable Company, in 1775, omits all reference to them, although mention is still made of "Water tracks for draining the Links." Perhaps the scholars and soldiers had been forced to move out. Crowding was beginning to be a problem on some links at that time. This may have been why the number of putting areas at St. Andrews was reduced from twelve to ten in 1764. At about that time the expansion of the town into the area now known as The Scores brought about the elimination of two of the original putting areas.

WHY EIGHTEEN?

Why eighteen holes makes a full round of golf: In the eighteenth century, the putting areas at St. Andrews were played to twice, from opposite directions: once on the way out from town, and once again on the way in. The first hole was started by driving from the putting area closest to town and continuing to that farthest away. After 1764, when there were ten putting areas, this made nine holes out. Then nine holes in made a total of eighteen, still the standard for a full round of golf.

GOLFERS AT ST. ANDREWS.

It would seem that the 19th century marked the gradual formation of what may be called the modern rules . . . . Golf Clubs had their own sets of rules which often differed one from the other . . . . With score competitions becoming more and more a feature of the game, it became more and more necessary to provide for all possible contingencies which might arise in stroke play.

—C. B. CLAPCOTT, 1952

Adaptation: 1750-1850

The more than two hundred fifty years during which the rules of golf evolved into their present form divide themselves naturally into four distinct periods. The first of these, which was a period of adaptation, lasted approximately one hundred years. The following three were, in order, periods of consolidation, divergence, and uniformity. They lasted about fifty years each. Both the beginning and end of each of these periods coincided with some technical advance or economic factor that either influenced the development of the game or contributed to its spread.

ORDER OUT OF CHAOS

The first period, lasting from the middle of the eighteenth until the middle of the nineteenth century, was characterized by relatively stable political and economic conditions, at least compared to the turmoil of the preceding hundred years. It's tempting to say that that turmoil began on the golf course. At least tradition tells us that Charles I, as ardent a golfer as his grandmother, Mary Queen of Scots, was playing golf on the links at Leith on 27 October 1641 when a messenger informed him of the outbreak of the Irish Rebellion. This was the beginning of a long period of civil war, revolution, and rebellion that for Scotland's part lasted more than a century, coming to its final, bitter end on the bloody fields of Culloden in 1746.

SCOTTISH RITES

The subsequent period of relative peace and economic growth favored the development of golf on a more organized basis. By 1850, twenty-three golf clubs or golfing societies had been formed in Scotland and two in England (at Blackheath and at Manchester). This type of social club had its origins in the political clubs that had taken root in the England of Charles II in the 1670s and was easily applicable to the organization of leisure activity among the gentry. There was a great deal of communication between all these newly formed golf clubs. Many of the players were members of more than one club, and frequent matches were arranged between them. They observed for the most part the same rules, but there were many exceptions. The rules drafted for the competition for the Silver Club at Leith in 1744 served as basis for all the codes during this period, but many clubs adapted them, often radically, to suit their particular conditions.

The first adaptation was made on 14 May 1754, when a group of twenty-two St. Andrews gentlemen formed a golfing society and instituted their own competition for a Silver Club. With only one minor change, they adopted the 1744 Leith code word for word. Instead of teeing the ball behind water in taking relief, as provided in Article 5, the St. Andreans threw it at least six yards behind the hazard. This difference is thought to have its origins in differing playing conditions. The links at Leith are said to have been wet and soft, those at St. Andrews relatively dry and firm, as they still are.

INCREMENTAL CHANGE

The Gentlemen Golfers made an adjustment to their own code in 1758, which they appended to their original copy of the 1744 Articles and Laws. It will be seen from the wording that this adjustment was the first (informal) Decision in the history of golf:

> The 5th and 13th Articles of the foregoing Laws having occasioned frequent Disputes It is found Convenient That in all time Coming the Law shall be, That in no case Whatever a Ball Shall be Lifted without losing a Stroke Except it is in the Scholars holes When it may be taken out teed and played with any Iron Club without losing a Stroke—And in all other Cases The Ball must be Played where it lyes Except it is at least half Covered with Water or filth When it may if the Player Chuses be taken out Teed and Played with any Club upon Loosing a Stroke.

Considering the later history of continual change in the rules, the optimism of the Gentlemen concerning the duration of their code "in all time coming" is touching, but how could they possibly have foreseen how their congenial athletic pastime would eventually develop?

PRETTY BASIC

In addition to clearing up questionable points in the Laws relating to hazards, this addendum drew attention to one of the most vexing problems in the history of the rules: the question of "playing the ball as it lies." This principle is one of the most sacred underlying doctrines of golf as we play it today, but there's no evidence of this in the early codes. This principle is mentioned only in connection with exceptions to it. There are strong indications that the opposite principle was the rule: that the ball could at any time be lifted and dropped or teed upon loss of a stroke. *(For more detailed discussion see Rule 13: Ball Played As It Lies and Rule 28: Ball Unplayable.)*

JOHN RATTRAY'S
CLOSE CALL

It's a curiosity of history that John Rattray, the first "Captain of the Goff," winner of the Silver Club in the inaugural match at Leith in 1744, was directly and dramatically involved in the final crushing of Scotland's aspirations. A physician, he was pressed into service as a medical officer with the army of Bonnie Prince Charlie when it occupied Edinburgh in the fall of 1745, and was with it on its march to destruction. He was captured at Culloden and imprisoned, but a fellow Gentleman Golfer, Duncan Forbes, Lord President of the Court of Session, secured his release. Rattray's golfing ability survived this ordeal unscathed; he won the Silver Club again in 1751.

WHAT, NO PENALTIES?

The failure to specify penalties for breaking rules is a peculiarity of these original articles. A stroke is assessed for dropping or teeing a ball under certain circumstances, but this isn't a penalty for breach of a rule. Everyone today assumes there must have been a general penalty, but there's a difference of opinion over whether it involved a stroke or loss of hole. Frequent mention of penalties in rules in force at various clubs during the first half of the nineteenth century indicates that this general penalty probably was loss of hole. Failure to mention it in the earliest codes was perhaps just an omission of the obvious. All these rules applied to match play, where no difficulty was involved in applying this general penalty. The advent of stroke play, however, changed the situation and led to the gradual inclusion of penalty statements. Although the first stroke play tournament was held at St. Andrews as early as 1759, match play continued to be the most common form of play all through the eighteenth and nineteenth centuries.

SPATE OF CODIFICATION

During the hundred years following the first written code of rules, more than thirty codes were adopted by different clubs. *(See Appendix 4.)* Of these, the most important by far were those of the Honourable Company of Edinburgh Golfers, as the Gentlemen Golfers came to be known, and those of the Society of St. Andrews Golfers. Most of the codes adopted by other clubs followed these quite closely, but original contributions were made in some cases. Such innovations characterize, in particular, the codes of the Edinburgh Burgess Golfers, who played over Bruntsfield Links and made major contributions to the rules governing the lost ball contingency, and the codes of the Aberdeen golfers. In 1783 Aberdeen introduced the five-minute time limit on the search for a lost ball.

THE ST. ANDREWS IMPRIMATEUR

The Honourable Company adopted revised codes of rules in 1775, 1809, and 1839, while the dates of the St. Andrews codes were 1812, 1829, and 1842. By the time this last code was adopted, the St. Andrews club had become the Royal and Ancient Golf Club and was well on its way to becoming the leading authority in matters pertaining to the rules. The St. Andrews code of 1812 had been based on the Honourable Company code of 1809, which had served as model for most of the codes of that time. Thirty years later, however, the tables had been turned, and the 1839 code of the Honourable Company was based on the 1829 St. Andrews code. By mid-century other Scottish clubs that

The Royal and Ancient Golf Club was well on its way to becoming the leading authority in matters pertaining to the rules.

ST. ANDREWS CLUBHOUSE AND HOME GREEN, 1933

had based their earlier codes on those of the Honourable Company now also chose to follow the R&A.

TOP DOG

Two examples illustrate the R&A's primacy. At a general meeting on 26 April 1830, The Montrose Golf Club (founded 1810) adopted a code of rules for play on its links clearly modeled after the 1809 code of the Honourable Company, although the Montrose version exhibited some surprisingly original features. *(See Appendix 4.)* However, in 1851, when this same club, now called The Royal Albert Golf Club, Montrose, adopted a new code of rules, it was a word-for-word copy of the R&A code of 1842, omitting only a few sentences referring to local conditions at St. Andrews. In 1824 the Leith Thistle Golf Club (founded 1815) also adopted the 1809 code of the Honourable Company, which is only reasonable since both clubs played over the same links. By 1866, however, Leith Thistle had switched its allegiance to the R&A and adopted a close copy of the R&A code of 1858.

ONLY ONE NUMBER ONE

There's a very good reason for this development. At the beginning of the 1830s the Honourable Company found itself in financial difficulties and was forced to curtail activity for several years. At the same time, crowding on Leith Links was beginning to be a problem. When the Honourable Company finally resolved its difficulties, in 1836, it moved its entire operation to the links at Musselburgh. During this same period, golf at St. Andrews was on the ascent: two separate holes on the putting areas were taken into use in 1832 and the club obtained royal patronage in 1834.

The formation of the St. Andrews Railway Company in 1850, with inauguration of rail service in 1852, was one of the factors that marked the beginning of the next period in the evolution of the rules of golf.

A JOLLY PARTY OF GOLF PLAYERS POSING
FOR THE PHOTOGRAPHER, CIRCA 1895.

The need of codes of rules, in the grandiloquent sense of the words, was not felt until golf became the popular game it now is, not until railways began to beguile players away to distant greens.

—WALTER G. SIMPSON, 1888

Consolidation: 1851-1899

The expansion of the Scottish railway system, not only to St. Andrews but throughout the entire country during the middle of the nineteenth century, was a major factor contributing to the spread of golf during this period. Between 1837 and 1870 the number of miles of railway line increased by more than tenfold.

EXPLOSIVE GROWTH

According to the most recent statistics compiled at the British Golf Museum in St. Andrews, the increase in the number of golf clubs between 1850 and 1880 was still quite modest in both Scotland and England, but from 1880 to the end of the century the growth was explosive. During those first thirty years sixty-two new clubs were founded in Scotland—about two per year. The rate of development quadrupled during the 1880s, when eighty new clubs were formed, and the 1890s saw three hundred sixty new clubs founded in Scotland alone, with similar rapid development in England.

O CALEDONIA!

All the new Scottish courses built were meant to serve not only the rapidly increasing number of Scottish golfers, but also English tourists who began to spend their holidays in Scotland at this time. The economic upswing brought about by the Industrial Revolution was the most important factor in this development, but there were other, more subtle, factors as well. In 1852 Queen Victoria purchased Balmoral Estates (where a private nine-hole golf course was eventually built), and her regular visits there drew Scotland to the attention of the English. The expanded Scottish railway system made travel to golf courses much easier than it had been. Many Scottish golfing centers, from Troon and North Berwick in the south to Nairn and Dornoch in the north, benefited from this and grew into vacation spots for English golfers. They've remained so ever since.

GREENKEEPER

In the nineteenth century the "keeper of the green" was not only the equivalent of a modern greenkeeper. He was also club and ball maker, professional and general handyman.

THE NEW GUTTA PERCHA BALLS THAT CAME INTO USE AROUND 1848 WERE EXTREMELY DURABLE.

The early British Open Championships were played according to the "Rules for the Game of Golf as it is played by the Prestwick Golf Club over their links."

NEW AND BETTER

There was another important factor in the spread of golf in the second half of the nineteenth century—the development of the gutta percha ball. The old hand-made feather balls were very perishable and in limited supply. The new gutta percha balls that came into use around 1848 were extremely durable and could easily be remolded and repainted as they wore out. After 1880, when new and better methods of molding them came into use, they were even more durable and inexpensive. The combined effect of all these factors was the first golf boom during the 1880s and 1890s.

INCREASING INFLUENCE

The importance of St. Andrews as rules-making authority continued to grow. The example set by Prestwick Golf Club founded in 1851, the very first year of this period, was of great importance. The club adopted "the St. Andrews rules of playing," according to the minutes of the first meeting held on 2 July 1851 at the Red Lion Inn, which still stands only a good brassie shot up the road from the present Prestwick clubhouse. One reason for the club's adoption of the R&A rules was that the newly formed club hired Tom Morris of St. Andrews as Keeper of the Green. It was he who laid out the original twelve-hole course at Prestwick and who was a major factor in its development as one of the most important golfing venues in Scotland. His stay at Prestwick lasted fourteen years, a period that saw the initiation of the British Open Championship. The first twelve, of which Morris won four, were held at Prestwick.

A LITTLE FRIENDLY COMPETITION

These early British Open Championships were played for a challenge belt offered by Prestwick Golf Club acting alone. The contestants played by "the

rules of Prestwick Golf Club," according to the minutes of a club meeting on 16 October 1860, the day before the first contest. The club had adopted these rules in July 1858 and printed them as "Rules for the Game of Golf as it is played by the Prestwick Golf Club over their links." A copy of these rules is on display in the smokeroom of the clubhouse. They are in all essential respects the code of rules adopted by the R&A on 5 May 1858, omitting only local references to the Swilcan Burn, the Eden River, and the North Sea.

In 1870 "Young Tom" Morris, who had been born in 1851 and had grown up at Prestwick, won the British Open for the third time in succession, retiring the Challenge Belt. With no trophy to play for, the championship wasn't played in 1871. When it was taken up again in 1872, both the R&A and the Honourable Company joined Prestwick in setting up a silver claret jug as the trophy. This jug is still the trophy of the British Open. The championship was from then on played on a rota, until 1894 circulating among the venues of the three sponsoring clubs: Prestwick, St. Andrews, and Musselburgh, where the Honourable Company played between 1836 and 1891, when it moved to its present home at Muirfield. During these years the British Open was always played under the rules of the R&A when it was held at Prestwick (1872, 1875, 1878, 1881, 1884, 1887, and 1890) or at St. Andrews (1873, 1876, and so on).

When the British Open was held at Musselburgh in 1874, 1877, and 1880, it was probably played under the rules of the Honourable Company, a code adopted in 1866, which was a modest revision of their 1839 code. At the Annual General Meeting of the club on 5 April 1883, however, the Honourable Company voted to play from then on by the rules of the R&A. The club issued a code of rules on July 19 of that year entitled "Rules of Golf as played by The Honourable Company of Edinburgh Golfers on Musselburgh Links adapted from the Rules of the Royal and Ancient Golf Club of St. Andrews." The few adaptations made were due to local conditions. Thus from 1881 on, the British Open was always played under the rules of the R&A. This was a major factor in the establishment of the authority of the R&A in matters concerning the rules throughout Scotland.

The situation was not so simple in England. Several leading English clubs played under their own rules throughout most of the nineteenth century. Of these, Royal Blackheath was the most influential, because it was the oldest club in England. It had its origins in the playing of golf in London by the Scottish courtiers of King James I at the beginning of the seventeenth century, so naturally, Blackheath played by Scottish rules. The earliest extant code of Blackheath rules dates from 1828 and is an adaptation of the rules drawn up in 1783 by The Society of Golfers at Aberdeen. Following several revisions of this code, Royal Blackheath formally adopted R&A rules on 4 April 1889.

During the second half of the nineteenth century the number of English clubs began to grow, though slowly at first. Only nineteen new clubs had been founded by 1879, but from 1880 on the tempo picked up considerably. The period between 1880 and 1889 saw the founding of eighty new English clubs,

Several leading English clubs played under their own rules throughout most of the nineteenth century.

the same number as were founded in Scotland in that decade. The real explosion came during the 1890s, though, when 522 new clubs were founded in England.

QUITE COMPLEX

The rules situation at the English clubs founded in the 1860s and 1870s was extremely complex. Some of them adopted rules of other English clubs, usually Royal Blackheath, while others adopted the R&A code current at the time they were founded. The popularity of the rules of the R&A grew during the 1880s. John T. Milton, in his history of the Royal Eastbourne Golf Club, sums up the situation as it was in 1887:

> The R&A Club had established a leading position in the government of the game and its rules, although designed specifically for local conditions, were generally adopted wherever the game was played.

Nevertheless, a surprising number of exceptions to this hegemony existed. Two can be mentioned as examples. The Wallasey Golf Club, founded in 1891, adopted "Hoylake Rules"; those of their close neighbors, the Royal Liverpool Golf Club. These rules were, in turn, a quite original adaptation of the R&A code of 1875. When the Epsom Golf Club was founded in 1888, it adopted the rules of nearby Royal Wimbledon Golf Club.

MORE THAN JUST A TENNIS CYNOSURE

The founding of the Royal Wimbledon Golf Club, in 1882, was of special importance in the history of the rules of golf. As Milton points out, R&A rules were designed specifically for St. Andrews conditions, with no provisions made for non-St. Andrews conditions. The R&A code of 1882 was an extensively rewritten version of the code of 1875, but there were still references to local conditions, such as the River Eden and the Station-Master's Garden, in the body of the rules themselves.

It was to correct this, and what they considered to be other weaknesses in the new R&A code of 1882, that the Wimbledon golfers developed their own rules. These were basically a rather close adaptation of the principles of the new R&A code, but the Wimbledon code was original in that it combined the rules for match play and stroke play, and in many instances set different penalties for breaches of rules. The refined rules were adopted by the Royal Wimbledon Golf Club in 1883. The main architects of this new code were the Honorary Secretary of the club, Henry A. Lamb, and Dr. William Laidlaw Purves.

Continually Seeking Improvement

The next rules-reforming initiative by the Wimbledon golfers came in the form of a letter sent in March 1885 suggesting that the R&A call a conference of golf clubs to establish uniformity of the rules. Unfortunately, no copy of this letter exists today, but the minutes of the Spring General Meeting of the R&A on 5 May 1885 give an impression of its contents:

> A communication from the Honorary Secretary of the Royal Wimbledon Golf Club was read, stating that that Club had instructed their Committee to urge the Royal and Ancient Golf Club to take steps for the formation of an association of Golf Clubs, bound to accept one uniform Code of Rules.

Wimbledon's appeal was, unfortunately, not positively received by the R&A membership, and no change in the situation came about. This rejection was, however, far from the end of the matter. Widespread dissatisfaction with the St. Andrews rules existed among English golfers, and a flood of letters to newspapers dramatized the situation. A lively debate ensued in the pages of the English country life journal *The Field* between 1886 and 1888, with more than twenty correspondents participating. One of the early letters set the tone of the debate:

> During the last few years golf has grown much as a pastime in popular favour, and numerous golf clubs have been established throughout the country, to become at once flourishing institutions. The greater the pity, then, that there should be, as your columns prove, a serious drawback to this prosperity—a condition detrimental to the interests of the game. There is no authoritative code of general laws. Practically, each club makes its own code—a mischief apt to spread. The best code—that known as the St. Andrews Rules—is the source from which the other codes are derived; but it cannot be universally adopted and accepted as authoritative for at least two reasons: it contains many rules which are in no sense general rules, but are of purely local application; and, as to other rules, while it may be possible to improve them, the golf world possesses no facility for proposing, much less seriously discussing or carrying out, any modification or alteration.

The writer of this letter chose to sign it only with his initials (W. R.), as did many other correspondents, while some employed fanciful pseudonyms: Old English Golfer, A Bunker, A Fossil, Hoylake, Wimbledon Hal, White Flag.

A ROBUST, HEARTY CONTROVERSY

White Flag, who later dropped his disguise and identified himself as Sir Walter G. Simpson, Captain of the Honourable Company, also published a long article on the subject in the first issue of *The Golfing Annual* in 1888, to which the letters in *The Field* during the previous two years were appended. Sir Walter presented a stirring defense of the St. Andrews rules. Other well-

---

AN EARLY REFORMER

A Scot by birth, Dr. William Laidlaw Purves played an important role in more than one aspect of the history of golf. He provided crucial support and encouragement to Issette Pearson, both in her playing at Wimbledon and in her successful efforts to found the Ladies Golf Union in 1893, and he was instrumental in the development of many golf courses during the 1880s and 1890s in the southeast of England. Many years passed, however, before his incessant agitation for reform of the rules of golf was to bear real fruit.

known golfers who took part in the debate in *The Field* were Henry Lamb, of Royal Wimbledon; Hall Blyth, of Royal Liverpool (Hoylake); and Horace Hutchinson, of Royal North Devon (Westward Ho!), who was at that time the British Amateur Champion. Laidlaw Purves held his fire for a long time, but finally answered Simpson in a long article of his own in *The Golfing Annual* in 1889, writing in his capacity as Captain of the St. George's Golf Club at Sandwich which he had helped found in 1887.

This entire debate is one of the most entertaining and informative episodes in the history of golf. It included a great deal of discussion and comparison of details of the various codes in use at different clubs and is a major source of our knowledge of some codes that haven't survived in extenso.

LOCAL ACCIDENTS

All this discussion didn't go unnoticed by those toward whom it was directed, and it led to revision of the R&A code in 1888. This advance was brought about by a motion made by Horace Hutchinson at the Spring General Meeting of the R&A on 1 May 1888. He proposed that they

> extract from the main body of their rules those relating to such local accidents as the Swilcan Burn, the Eden and the Station Master's Garden, and so group these under a separate heading, so that the main body of the Rules may be used wherever the game of Golf is or shall be played.

Seconded by Hall Blyth, this motion was adopted unanimously by the meeting. The new code was, in all essential respects, identical to the 1882 rules, but the collection of what Hutchinson termed "local accidents" under a separate section entitled "Local Rules for St. Andrews Links" made it easier now for other clubs to adopt the general rules and append to them their own local rules.

EVENTUAL COOPERATION

The early British Open Championships, begun in 1860, had, as we've already seen, considerable influence on the development of the rules. Thirty years later the British Amateur Championship played a similar role. The first was held at Hoylake in 1885. When it was held there again in 1890, the delegates of the clubs represented in the championship appealed to the R&A for a revision of the rules. The matter was taken up at the Autumn General Meeting of the R&A on 23 September 1890, resulting in the unanimous approval of a resolution that "a Special Committee of members thoroughly qualified to carry out a careful revision of the whole Rules of Golf, be appointed."

Four of this committee's "thoroughly qualified" seven members are by this time familiar to us: Henry Lamb, Hall Blyth, Horace Hutchinson, and

Some of those critiquing the inconsistency of golf rules employed fanciful pseudonyms: Old English Golfer, A Bunker, A Fossil, Hoylake, Wimbledon Hal, White Flag.

Laidlaw Purves, who were all members of the R&A as well as other clubs. The result of their work was the code adopted by the R&A on 29 September 1891. Although this code was substantially revised and more easily applicable to many different playing conditions, the R&A was still not formally recognized as a rules-making authority.

YET ANOTHER OPTION

The next step in the long, slow ascendancy of the R&A as a rules-making authority was a slight temporary sidestep. Hall Blyth informed the Spring General Meeting of the R&A on 4 May 1896 that he was circulating a motion to be considered by the delegates to the British Amateur Championship at Sandwich later that month. His motion called for them to consider the advisability of forming a Golf Union.

Not an Option

The delegates at Sandwich were not, however, in favor of establishing a Golf Union. They were of the opinion "that no support should be given to any scheme tending to set up, or to attempt to set up, an authority rival to the Royal and Ancient Club." They called upon the R&A "to evolve some scheme that would enable important Clubs to explicitly recognise the authority of the Royal and Ancient, instead of only tacitly as at present." They also proposed that the R&A appoint a committee to act in matters of interpretation of the rules. These opinions and proposals were communicated to the R&A in a letter from the Honorary Secretary of St. George's Golf Club, W. Rutherford. *(The complete text of this letter is found in Appendix 5.)*

These proposals were duly considered by a special joint committee consisting of the Committee of Management of the R&A plus the club members on the R&A Green Committee, one of whom was Hall Blyth. On 10 July 1896, the results of their deliberations were forwarded to Mr. Rutherford. *(The text of this communication also appears in Appendix 5.)* They proposed that the new committee should be composed of seven members of the R&A and seven members from other clubs, specifically one each from The Honourable Company, Prestwick, Royal Blackheath, Royal North Devon, Royal Liverpool, St. George's, and Royal Portrush. When Mr. Rutherford informed the clubs represented at the Amateur Championship of these proposals, he received positive replies from each of them.

BIT OF A MISSTEP

Subsequently, when the Autumn General Meeting of the R&A, held on 29 September 1896, approved the scheme, a special committee was appointed to work out the details and report to the next general meeting. It appeared that the problem was solved. The report of the special committee was presented to the Spring Meeting of the R&A in May 1897, but a difficulty arose. Two letters were read: one from the Edinburgh Burgess Golf Club and the other from the Royal Albert Golf Club, Montrose. These clubs objected to the proposal. They felt that the R&A should retain full authority in rules matters, but if there was to be a committee including representatives from other clubs, then they also should be represented because of their great seniority. *(See Appendix 5 for the full texts of these letters.)*

This may seem to us nowadays to be a rather petty reason to block what was a very necessary reform, especially in light of the present broad representation on the Rules of Golf Committee, but the question of seniority bore great weight at that time. The reaction of these senior clubs was not really so unreasonable. St. George's and Royal Portrush, two of the clubs proposed as members of the new committee, were not even ten years old, and Royal North Devon and Royal Liverpool, two others proposed, were barely thirty years old.

THERE'LL BE RUCTIONS

The minutes of the Half Yearly Meeting of the Edinburgh Burgess Golfing Society on 14 October 1896 provide some insight into their way of thinking. The proposer of the motion to object to the proposed committee stated that "the Burgess Society, like other Scottish clubs, was perfectly content under the control of the Royal and Ancient, but they would not be disposed to tolerate the supremacy of minor clubs." The seconder of the motion "protested strongly against clubs which were comparatively mushroom clubs being co-operated in the fashion proposed by the Royal and Ancient." They could hardly have stated their objections more pithily.

Unconscionable Insult

Even though protests were sent to the R&A only by the Edinburgh Burgess and the Montrose Royal Albert clubs, the matter was taken under consideration by other societies. On 8 October 1896 the Royal Musselburgh Golf Club met and discussed the R&A proposal. The minutes of that meeting report they preferred that no change be made and that "the older recognized Golf Clubs some of which have been in existence for more than a century should be consulted before any change in the present mode of management is again proposed." The minutes conclude: "the matter was remitted to the Council who were authorized to act along with other Clubs and to report to the next Meeting."

WHISKEY GALORE

Unfortunately, those words were all that was written concerning the R&A proposal in the minutes of the Royal Musselburgh Golf Club. The next meeting, on November 4, was devoted exclusively to the question of obtaining a "supply of whisky at wholesale prices for one year." The Council met frequently during November 1896, but the minutes of those meetings report nothing concerning the matter uppermost in our minds. The minutes of one of those meetings reports, in its original form, that all the whisky samples submitted for consideration had been "carefully and soberly tested," but a later hand had, apparently in the name of strict truth, crossed out the words *and soberly*. It would seem that the sample testing of different whiskies made sober reflection on other matters difficult.

A WICKED CONTRETEMPS

As a result of the letters received from the Edinburgh Burgess and Royal Albert clubs, the R&A rejected the proposal to form a rules-making body that included representatives from other clubs at the Spring Meeting in May 1897. This was not unexpected, since word of the revolt had spread. Horace Hutchinson had already raised a warning in an article in the 12 February 1897 issue of *Golf*:

> If the committee proposed by the Royal and Ancient fails to take shape, under stress of the opposition which is threatening it, we shall require a very strong expression of opinion to enable us to move the golfing legislative machinery out of the dead-lock into which it is likely to fall.

Fortunately, a way out of the impasse was found.

PEACE AT LAST

At its next general meeting on 28 September 1897, the R&A adopted an amendment to the original proposal, authorizing the club to appoint a committee to be called the Rules of Golf Committee, consisting of fifteen of its own members. Its power was to be limited to questions of interpretation of the rules, but in this it was to be the final authority. It could also propose changes in the rules, but these changes would have to be approved by two-thirds of the members present at a general meeting of the R&A. This has remained the mandate of the Rules of Golf Committee to this day.

Although the committee's membership has subsequently been broadened to include representatives of many golf unions and associations from throughout the world, any proposed changes in the rules must still be approved by a two-thirds majority at a general meeting. The Committee

The R&A rejected the proposal to form a rules-making body that included representatives from other clubs at the Spring Meeting in May of 1897—word of the revolt had spread.

exercises its authority in matters of interpretation by issuing Decisions on questions put to it by secretaries of golf clubs or golf associations.

Creepy Crawlies

The Rules of Golf Committee didn't delay exercising its authority. At its second meeting, on 10 January 1898, it issued seven Decisions. The first formal Decision in the history of the rules of golf dealt with the problem of worm casts on inland courses. The Committee ruled that it was permissible to remove such loose impediments. In direct response to the query put to it, it added that worm casts could not be treated as dung. This was the rather mundane beginning of what has become a highly developed system of golf "case law" that unifies the interpretation of the rules throughout the world and leads in many instances to changes in the rules.

UNIVERSALITY

The first new code of rules proposed by the Committee was adopted by the R&A on 26 September 1899. It was this code that was the first truly universal code of rules, observed by golfers in all clubs and on all courses in all parts of the world. Its adoption put an end to more than one hundred fifty years of what could be called separatism and anarchy and set the stage for the development of golf in the new century about to unfold.

The first formal Decision dealt with the problem of worm casts on inland courses.

**PROBABLY THE FIRST PHOTOGRAPH OF
GOLF IN AMERICA—THE APPLE TREE GANG
AT ST. ANDREWS, N.Y.**

*The United States of America are
not bothered, as we are, by our golfing
traditions. They are at liberty to adopt
so much of the spirit of these traditions
as seems valuable, and to leave the
rest, unregretted, on one side.*

—HORACE HUTCHINSON, 1897

Divergence: 1900-1950

T he stability brought to the rules of golf during the last decades of the nineteenth century did not last. A new factor was introduced into the equation when golf became established in the United States. Although the game had been introduced there by Scottish immigrants as early as the end of the eighteenth century, golf hadn't survived more than a few years. During the 1880s, however, activity was revived, with those of Scottish background once again prominently involved. Development of golf was now so rapid that by 1894 the formation of a national golf association became necessary.

ALTOGETHER ESSENTIAL

On 22 December 1894, delegates from five of the country's leading golf clubs met to form such an organization. Originally known as The Amateur Golf Association of the United States, the name lasted less than two months. At a meeting on 21 February 1895, it was changed to its present name: The United States Golf Association. This same meeting adopted a set of By-Laws, of which Section 10 provided that:

> The Competitions shall be played in accordance with the Rules of Golf as adopted by the Royal and Ancient Golf Club of St. Andrews, Scotland, with such special rules as are in force and published on the green over which the competition takes place, and with such modifications as the Executive Committee may from time to time adopt.

RAPID ELABORATION

Accordingly, at a meeting on 18 July 1895 the Executive Committee appointed a special committee "to interpret the Rules of Golf." This committee consisted of two members: Charles Blair Macdonald and Laurence Curtis. Macdonald was the chairman of the committee and its most influential member, indeed the most influential member of the USGA in its early years with respect to the development of the rules of golf.

The special committee submitted a code of rules to the USGA on 10 June 1897. Its complete title is worth quoting:

A Grand Gentleman

Charles Blair Macdonald was one of the most colorful and forceful personalities in the history of golf. Born in 1855, he was sent by his father, a native Scot, to live with his grandfather and study in St. Andrews in 1872, when he was 16 years old. As one of his assignments, he was to learn to play golf while there. Although at first it seemed to him to be, in his own words, "a silly game for old men," he quickly became interested in it and quite adept. After his return to America in 1874, Macdonald devoted himself to business and had little time for golf except on occasional business trips to Britain. He took up the game again seriously when he was 38 years old. He helped establish the Chicago Golf Club and succeeded in bringing his golfing skills quickly up to par again. He won the first Amateur Championship sponsored by the USGA in 1895, when he was 40 years old.

C. B. MACDONALD (RIGHT) AND LAURENCE CURTIS (LEFT).

The Rules of Golf as revised by The Royal and Ancient Golf Club of St. Andrews in 1891 with Rulings and Interpretations by The Executive Committee of The United States Golf Association in 1897.

The preface to this code states that

> The Special Committee have made no change in the words of the Rules as they stand in the Code of the Royal and Ancient Golf Club of St. Andrews, revised in 1891; but they have appended to said Rules the rulings of the United States Golf Association, based upon the results of many decisions of committees or experts, or upon customs which have obtained in the best clubs in Scotland and England.

These rulings were, in fact, not any set of formal decisions, since at that time no official committees existed that could make such rulings (more than three months were still to pass before the R&A Rules of Golf Committee was appointed). The rulings were, rather, informal interpretations of the rules as Macdonald and Curtis understood them, based on their own experience and on the opinions of others whom they consulted.

DEALING WITH THOSE RUGGED INDIVIDUALISTS

One of those consulted was Horace Hutchinson, who reported on a letter from Macdonald in the article "An Appeal from America" in the 12 February 1897 issue of *Golf* (which has appeared as *Golf Illustrated* since 1899).

In his letter to Hutchinson, Macdonald explained the crux of the problem for American golfers and rules-makers:

> We find in America that it is necessary to have rules more clearly defined, as people are inclined to play more by the letter than the spirit.

The form Macdonald and Curtis gave to Rule 16 can serve as an example of their approach:

> Rule 16.—A player, or a player's caddie, shall not press down nor remove any irregularities of surface near the ball, except at the teeing ground, under the penalty of the loss of the hole.
>
> *Rulings of the U.S.G.A.*
>
> Penalty for breach of this rule:
>
> > In Match Play, loss of the hole.
> >
> > In Medal Play, disqualification. "Near the ball" shall be considered within a club length. Pressing down the surface near the ball by prolonged or forcible soling of the club shall be deemed a breach of this rule.

Converging Lines

Although the basic R&A organization of the rules is observed in the USGA code, with rules for match play and stroke (medal) play grouped separately, the penalties for both match play and stroke play are included in each USGA ruling. This seems to indicate there was already at that time an interest in America in combining the rules of match play and stroke play, but it wasn't until 1946 that such a merger was carried out in the USGA code.

THE KINGPINS

After the Rules of Golf Committee of the R&A issued its first code of rules in September 1899, the USGA appointed a new special committee consisting of Macdonald and Curtis, along with Alfred M. Coats, to prepare a new American code. This was submitted and adopted on 28 February 1900. It, too, was a word-for-word version of the R&A rules, plus rulings.

A third such special committee was appointed in November 1902 to prepare an American version of the new R&A code that had been adopted on 23 September. Macdonald was once again chairman, joined this time by G. Herbert Windeler and Walter J. Travis, a man who was soon to play a central role in a major rule dispute. Travis had won the U.S. Amateur Championship in 1900 and 1901 and was to win it again in 1903. He shocked the British in 1904 by becoming the first non-British player to win *their* Amateur Championship. And he did it with the aid of an unconventional club: a center-shafted putter.

The codes of the R&A and the USGA remained nearly identical for many years.

41

PLAYING ALONG

The USGA continued to adopt the rules of the R&A plus rulings, which were called interpretations from 1909 on. The codes of the R&A and the USGA remained nearly identical for many years, despite growing dissatisfaction with many aspects of the St. Andrews rules. It wasn't only golfers in the United States who were dissatisfied. Golf was played in many parts of the world under conditions differing greatly from those in Britain. C. B. Macdonald waxed rather poetic when he described this dissatisfaction in his book of reminiscences, *Scotland's Gift: Golf*, published in 1928. He wrote of the situation as it was in 1907:

> The rules of golf as applied to St. Andrews worked out well enough with golfers born and bred there who intuitively absorbed the spirit and traditions of the game, although they might know really little about the letter of the law. Custom made the law and so St. Andrews has ever been a law unto itself in golf. When the myriad of golf clubs sprang up throughout the world, with every variety of golf course, some laid out in the Garden of the Gods in Colorado, others on the torrid lands about Aden, in Arabia, by the rocks, rills, ravines, and woods of Ardsley-on-the-Hudson, or in the cotton fields or amidst the piny woods of Georgia, with their clay and sand putting-greens, and elsewhere, the custom at St. Andrews did not satisfy, nor could it meet the emergencies arising from the new conditions. Then again, in America every person was comparatively a beginner in golf.
>
> St. Andrews had to consent to a revision; otherwise America would certainly have written her own golfing laws.

Daniel Chauncey, the USGA president in 1907, wrote with utmost diplomacy about this matter to the R&A, which responded in kind.

REVISION AS NEEDED

At the Autumn General Meeting, the membership of the R&A voted for a revision of the rules and also, on a motion by Horace Hutchinson, to invite C. B. Macdonald to become a member of the Rules of Golf Committee and serve as liaison on rules matters between the R&A and the USGA. It was natural to think of Macdonald for this position. He was still a member of the R&A (from his student days in St. Andrews) and had always been a champion of playing the game in accordance with tradition. In May 1908 he was formally invited to become a member of the R&A Rules of Golf Committee. He was the first American to serve on the Committee, and although he never actually attended any of its meetings, he was an important link between the governing bodies in the stormy years ahead. He was instrumental in preventing even greater divergence between the rules in Britain and America than actually did develop.

The called-for revision of the rules was carried out in 1908. It was prepared by a subcommittee of the Rules of Golf Committee, whose mandate was to revise the rules "in the light of the decisions given by them." This revision was made with input from the USGA, to C. B. Macdonald's general approval. He wrote a bit wryly about it in his reminiscences:

> There was nothing radical in any of the changes, but the rules were made clearer so a child should know what they meant. Of course, not all of the American suggestions were adopted, but in the main they were, and harmony prevailed for some time to come.

What lack of harmony there was centered around the Schenectady putter that Walter J. Travis had used so effectively during the British Amateur Championship at Sandwich in 1904.

FLATLY INTOLERABLE

In 1909 the Rules of Golf Committee of the R&A banned the use of a croquet mallet as a putter in response to a request for a ruling from the Nga Motu Golf Club in New Zealand. It also took under consideration a proposal to extend the ban to all malletlike clubs. This was not, however, undertaken in retaliation for Travis's use of such a putter five years earlier, as has often been maintained. It came as the result of another request for a ruling during 1909, this time from the Pickeridge Golf Club, asking if it was permissible to use "a putter made in the form of a croquet mallet." The Decision issued by the Committee contained the observation:

> The Rules of Golf Committee is of the opinion that the time has come for the Royal and Ancient Golf Club to decide at a General Meeting whether the various mallet-headed implements at present in use are to be permitted or not.

The R&A proceeded to ban all such clubs at its next General Meeting in May 1910, but with results not entirely satisfactory to everyone. There was considerable dispute over the proper definition of the term *mallet-headed*. By the end of the summer this was resolved by allowing only clubs that had the shaft attached to the heel of the head. All center-shafted clubs were banned.

Violent Discord

C. B. Macdonald was vehemently opposed to a ban on malletlike clubs and to any form of standardization of equipment. He sent a letter from America to all his fellow-members of the Rules of Golf Committee composed equally of reason, indignation, and diplomacy. He expressed the opinion that the Schenectady putter was not a mallet "as universally understood and interpreted in this country." (*See Appendix 5 for the complete text of this letter and the reply to it that the Committee drafted.*) Macdonald's letter was duly entered into

The committee went ahead and in September 1910 banned all clubs "of the mallet-headed type or such clubs as have the neck bent."

43

the minute book of the Rules of Golf Committee, but the committee went ahead and in September 1910 banned all clubs "of the mallet-headed type or such clubs as have the neck bent as to produce a similar effect." This British ban on center-shafted and wry-neck putters lasted 42 years until it was lifted in the first USGA-R&A joint code in 1952.

There was also a certain amount of disagreement between the R&A and the USGA about the penalty for a ball out of bounds. *(See Rule 27: Ball Lost or Out of Bounds.)* Additionally, the USGA legalized steel shafts on 12 April 1924, more than five years before the R&A somewhat grudgingly followed suit on 26 November 1929. The fact that for each passing year manufacturers had more trouble finding first-class hickory contributed to the decision.

PLENTY OF ADVICE

Serious disagreements appeared during the 1930s. A major revision of the rules was carried out in 1933, with input from all the most important golf associations in the world. Minutes of a Rules of Golf Committee meeting on 29 May 1933 mention that suggestions had been received from the USGA, the Royal Canadian Golf Association, the South African Golf Union, the Australian Golf Union, the New Zealand Golf Association, and the Ladies Golf Union. There was certainly no shortage of advice. The new code adopted at the R&A's Autumn General Meeting on 26 September 1933 and by the USGA on 23 November of that year, was as comprehensive a code as it was possible to produce at that time. Nevertheless, during the autumn of the following year the USGA appealed to the Rules of Golf Committee to abolish the stymie and to allow the remittance of the penalty stroke in the case of ball out of bounds. The Committee replied rather testily in a cable received by the USGA on 17 November 1934:

> Rules of Golf Committee regret cannot follow your proposal to eliminate stymie and to alter Rule 23. Also deprecate any change in Rules which were unanimously approved only a year ago.

The stage was set for major conflict.

NOT REALLY THE BAD GUY

It would be wrong, however, to oversimplify the situation by seeing the R&A solely as an inhibitor of change. Although the USGA may have been more inclined than the R&A to propose radical revisions, there were also forces for change in the hallowed halls of St. Andrews. Robert Harris, generally seen as an archconservative in all matters concerning the rules and customs of golf, actually often instigated radical change during his years on the Rules of Golf

Committee. He was the first to attempt to limit the allowable number of clubs to fourteen. In November 1936 he proposed a motion to that effect that was, however, not supported by the membership of the R&A as a whole.

Before the R&A membership had had a chance to reject this proposal, which it did at the Spring Meeting in 1937, the Rules of Golf Committee had already sent a cable informing the USGA and expressing the hope it would adopt a similar rule. The USGA was prepared and willing to do just that. Harris and USGA President John G. Jackson had discussed the matter during the summer of 1936, and Jackson had reported on that discussion to the Executive Committee on 18 September 1936. The USGA included a statement limiting the number of clubs to fourteen in a short preamble to the code of rules they issued in 1938. At the same time it also modified the stymie rule on a trial basis to allow the offending ball to be lifted when it lay closer than six inches to the hole. This trial modification lasted three years, after which it was permanently adopted in 1941. In 1939 the R&A went along with Harris and the USGA on the Fourteen-Club Rule, but it firmly refused to tamper in any way with the stymie. *(For details of the nature and fate of this delightful relic of our golfing past see Rule 16: The Putting Green, page 128.)*

At Least He Tried

In 1936 Robert Harris had also, as Chairman of the Golf Ball Sub-Committee of the Rules of Golf Committee, brought forward the recommendation that the minimum size of the ball be standardized at a diameter of 1.68 inches. He was considerably less successful in this matter than in his efforts to limit the number of clubs. It wasn't until 1 January 1990 that the entire golfing world played with a ball of uniform size, and Harris (1882–1959) had been dead many years by then.

The Timing's Off

Despite continuing communication between the R&A and the USGA, the rules by which golf was played on the two sides of the Atlantic Ocean had begun to diverge seriously by the end of the 1930s. This was the situation when the Second World War broke out and brought controversies about such trivial things as the rules of golf to a standstill.

DEFINITELY ON THE AGENDA

Interest in reforming the rules nevertheless remained high on both sides of the Atlantic during the war, and it quickly found expression when peace came. The USGA was first out of the starting gate. In 1946 it issued a radically modified unilateral code that combined the provisions for both match play and stroke play under the same rule and completely restructured the

The USGA included a statement limiting the number of clubs to fourteen.

order of the rules. The penalty for ball out of bounds was reduced to distance only. In his foreword to this radical new code, John Jackson, at that time chairman of the USGA's Rules of Golf Committee, expressed hope that the R&A would "take like action."

It was 1949 before the R&A took action, but then it went the USGA one better in many respects. An experimental R&A code that went into effect for a two-year period on 1 January 1950 featured extensive reductions in penalties. The penalty not only for a ball out of bounds but also for a lost or unplayable ball, was reduced to distance only, and most formerly two-stroke penalties were reduced to one stroke. *(See Appendix 5 for discussion of the background of these changes in Bernard Darwin's* Preface *to this 1950 R&A experimental code.)* The order of the rules was rearranged, but in a quite different way from that of the USGA. The R&A followed the USGA's initiative in combining the rules of match play and stroke play, but the stymie rule was left intact. Although this code had been adopted on the basis of a referendum among the members of the R&A and only after consultation with other clubs and governing bodies of golf around the world, there was great opposition to it.

A THREAT TO THE GAME

Perhaps the most eloquent opposition was expressed by Robert Harris, who now reaffirmed his conservative point of view of the basic principles behind the rules of golf. He had ceased to be a member of the Rules of Golf Committee in 1946, so he felt free to express himself in no uncertain terms in a pamphlet, *Proposed New Rules of Golf, A Threat to the Game as a Sport,* which he issued at his own expense. He summed up his view of the new experimental code:

> It sets out to modify the sporting aspect in golf by a wholesale reduction of penalties for inefficient play, for carelessness and bad manners, and it will effectively undermine the very fundamentals of the game besides entirely destroying that feeling which inspires all real golfers to exert their best efforts in the face of difficulties.

The adoption by the USGA and the R&A of codes of rules that broke so sharply with tradition, and at the same time differed so greatly from each other, resulted in a situation that threatened the integrity of the game. Once more, golf was in danger of being played by different rules in different parts of the world. Fortunately for the game and for all who play it, such an outcome was avoided.

Revision, Anyone?

Incidents abounded that displayed weaknesses in the new penalty structure of the 1950 experimental R&A code. The one that received the most publicity took place only a few months after the new code went into effect. At Troon, during the third round of the British Open, Roberto De Vicenzo bunkered his tee-shot on the famous par-three eighth hole, The Postage Stamp. Rather than try a difficult bunker shot, he declared the ball unplayable and played a second ball from the tee, under penalty of distance only. He put his second tee-shot close to the hole for an easy par. The shot that he undoubtedly saved by this perfectly legal stratagem allowed him to finish in second place. Under such circumstances the distance-only penalty was clearly too lenient, making it possible for a skillful player to avoid the consequences of a poor shot, or even to test conditions (if he was willing to lose a stroke) when faced with an especially difficult shot.

PETER THOMSON

*Twelve men sat around a large
conference table . . . . They were trying
to develop a code of Rules of Golf
which could be used uniformly
throughout the golf world.*

—JOSEPH C. DEY, JR., 1951

Uniformity: 1951 to the Present

Everyone involved in the rules-making process was interested in preventing further divergence between the two codes of rules—a threat that existed at the beginning of the 1950s. Accordingly, representatives of the R&A and the USGA, plus one representative each from the Australian Golf Union and the Royal Canadian Golf Association, met during the spring of 1951, first in London, then in St. Andrews. Joseph C. Dey, Jr., who attended the conferences as the USGA's Executive Secretary, described the London meeting:

> For four days those twelve men explored every phase of the Rules. There were no axes to grind, no ultranationalistic views. They were just golf-lovers, and they worked together in complete harmony.
>
> They reached full agreement on a uniform code. They had a wonderful experience together, and a memorable one.

Fortunately for the game, those twelve men were congenial and also genuinely concerned about the future of golf. The conference was memorable not only for them, but for the game as a whole. The joint R&A-USGA code of 1952 they produced opened a new era in golf. *(See Appendix 5 for the text of the Preface to this code written by Isaac B. Grainger and Harold Gardiner-Hill, chairmen of the Rules of Golf Committees of, respectively, the USGA and the R&A, who both took part in the conference.)*

UNISON

This new code arrived at a time when the number of golfers was increasing rapidly; the rules in force when these new players learned the game influenced their attitudes toward it. Probably more than 95 percent of those playing golf today took up the game after 1952 and are totally unaware of many of the game's peculiarities before then. The most obvious example is the stymie, abandoned forever in 1952, but many other basic features of the game were also revised at the same time. Among the most important were the definition of the putting green and the rules dealing with provisional balls, unplayable balls, and lifting and cleaning the ball. *(These matters are covered under the appropriate rules in the following section of this book.)*

More than 95 percent of those playing golf today took up the game after 1952.

A CONVENIENT ARRANGEMENT

Since 1952, major changes in the rules have generally been made only every four years, as the result of a conference between the Rules of Golf Committees of the USGA and the R&A that is usually held in connection with the Walker Cup Match when it is played in Britain (that is, in 1955 and every four years since then). There have been some exceptions to this. In 1960 the USGA embarked on another fit of experimentation with the penalties for those old chestnuts: ball lost or out of bounds, once more reducing them to distance only. Joe Dey, by this time USGA Executive Director, gave a playful title to an article describing these changes: "Relaxation in Rules: A New Year's Gift," since they were scheduled to go into effect on 1 January 1960. In reality they were no gift to anyone and only caused confusion. Modified slightly in 1961, and again in 1962 and 1964, they were abandoned completely in 1968. *(See Rule 27: Ball Lost or Out of Bounds, for details.)*

In 1960 the USGA also made unilateral changes in the rules governing the use of a provisional ball. *(See Rule 27: Ball Lost or Out of Bounds, page 183.)* It was 1968 before the R&A had incorporated these changes into their code. Since 1968, however, the main body of the rules of play has been uniform throughout the world. The differences that exist between the rules as they are separately published by the USGA and the R&A are to be found in Appendix I in the rules book, which deals with Local Rules. Over the years the R&A and the USGA have developed distinct attitudes toward local rules and their application. *(For examples, see Local Rules, in Appendix 1.)*

Some Fidgeting

Some minor anomalies have crept in since 1968, however. An important change was made in 1970 by mutual agreement of the R&A and USGA: the rule requiring continuous putting in stroke play that had been adopted in 1968 was abandoned. *(Another short-lived experiment bit the dust: see Rule 16: The Putting Green; pages 124–125.)*

Since 1952, each new code has generally gone into effect on 1 January of the year after its adoption, but there was an exception to this in 1984, when an extensive reorganization of the rules was carried out. The USGA code went into effect, as usual, on New Year's Day, 1984, but the effective date of the R&A code was delayed until 1 April, to give those who translate the rules into various languages time to make all the necessary changes. This meant that for the first three months of 1984 the game was played under different (in some respects very different) rules in different parts of the world. However, no damage was done. Few people were aware of the situation, and those who were wisely kept their peace.

CLEANING HOUSE

The major reorganization of the rules that went into effect in 1984 and the simultaneous consolidation of the Decisions services of the R&A and the USGA opened the latest chapter in the history of the rules of golf. The work involved in both these projects extended over many years.

Issuing Decisions was part of the original mandate of the Rules of Golf Committee of the R&A; in the many decades that had passed since 1897 it had issued hundreds. On 1 February 1922 the USGA had set up its own Rules of Golf Committee, which quickly began issuing Decisions of its own. Over the years differences developed between the Decisions issued by these two bodies, which conflicted with the principle of uniformity.

Lots of Hard Work

At the joint meeting of the USGA and R&A Rules of Golf Committees during the Walker Cup match at Brookline, Massachusetts, in 1973, J. Stewart Lawson of the R&A was asked to analyze the Decisions of the two organizations. In January 1975, Lawson submitted his analysis to the Rules of Golf Committees, leading to the formation in 1979 of a Joint Decisions Committee (JDC). Also in 1979, work on the reorganization of the rules was started. In 1980, the USGA and the R&A issued a booklet titled *Experimental Reorganized Rules of Golf*. It was a word-for-word version of the 1980 rules, but the rules were rearranged, the purpose being to make them easier to find and to learn.

In the January 1981 issue of *Golf Journal*, the USGA's magazine, the USGA's William J. Williams, Jr., architect of the reorganization of the rules, expressed the belief

> that if golf associations and golf unions around the world react favorably to the *Experimental Reorganized Rules*, we could be on the threshold of a period during which progress is made in making the Rules of Golf easier to learn and use. If that could be achieved, it may not be farfetched to hope, then, that more golfers will know the Rules and play by them.

More than five thousand copies of this booklet were distributed to golf associations and unions throughout the world, as well as to especially interested or knowledgeable individuals, with requests for comments. The response was so overwhelmingly in favor of the reorganization that the new arrangement of the rules was incorporated into the code issued in 1984.

In 1979 a Joint Decisions Committee was formed.

CARRYING THE THOUGHT A STEP FURTHER

At the same time, and in connection with this reorganization, there was great interest in rewriting and simplifying the rules themselves. The considerable work this entailed was carried out jointly by the Rules of Golf Committees of the R&A and USGA, chaired respectively by Denis Hayes and William J. Williams, Jr. It was completed in time to incorporate the newly rewritten rules in the reorganized 1984 code. Among the more radical changes made in the rules at this time was the change in the manner of dropping the ball. After more than two centuries of having to drop the ball blind, a much more practical and sensible way of dropping the ball finally saw the light of day, to every golfer's relief. *(See Rule 20: Lifting, Dropping and Placing.)* The new 1984 code also featured further reductions in the differences between match play and stroke play.

**FRED COUPLES AT CASA DE CAMPO, AFTER
LODGING HIS BALL IN A TREE ROOT.**

Linguistic Cobwebs

An important nonsubstantive change, once again to every golfer's relief, involved the updating of the language in which the rules of golf had traditionally been couched. For many years these hallowed rules had been the last refuge of the widespread use of the subjunctive mood in English ("If a ball at rest be moved. . . , If a ball lie. . . , If a player deem his ball to be unplayable. . . ," etc.). In 1984 a firm broom was vigorously applied to these linguistic cobwebs, and the rules of golf were given a form much closer to the everyday speech of the average player.

PULLING IT ALL TOGETHER

While this wholesale revision of the rules was under way, work on producing a consolidated Decisions Service was started. The USGA's chief protagonist in this effort, P. J. Boatwright, Jr., described the process in an article in *Golf Journal* early in 1984:

> Work began on the Joint Decisions Book in 1981. The USGA and R&A agreed that Decisions would be radically rewritten and made as concise as possible; moreover, any Decision dealing with two points would be divided into two Decisions.
>
> The R&A and USGA each rewrote half of the combined Decisions, and drafts were exchanged for comment. Any draft approved by both sides was marked resolved and set aside for final editing and numbering. The JDC discussed unresolved drafts at its meetings, held twice each year. In most cases, these discussions resolved the questions.
>
> A Drafting Committee, consisting of Lawson and Niel Loudon for the R&A, and myself for the USGA, was appointed to: (1) review and edit the resolved Decisions; (2) decide the Rule under which each Decision should be located; (3) decide the sequence for Decisions under a particular Rule; and (4) number each Decision.

Since 1984 a joint Decisions Book has been published by each body. The Decisions are reviewed continuously by the R&A and the USGA working together, and each annual edition of the Decisions book contains some new Decisions and some that are revised. When rule changes are made that incorporate Decisions, those Decisions are then withdrawn. In this way the Decisions are kept uniform and up to date throughout the world.

PROTOCOL

The manner in which requests for a Decision on a matter involving the interpretation of a rule may be submitted to the R&A or the USGA illustrates the differences in the nature and structure of the two bodies. In keeping with traditional practice, the R&A accepts requests for Decisions only from the secretaries of golf clubs and golf associations; requests from individuals must be submitted through these channels. The USGA, however, in addition to accepting requests for interpretations from golfing organizations, also accepts requests from individuals. In spite of this difference of approach, the R&A and the USGA succeed in producing a single, uniform *Decisions on the Rules of Golf* book of great use to golfers in all parts of the world.

TO SUM UP

If we look back over the more than two hundred fifty years since the first code of golf rules was adopted in April 1744, it's easy to see that what's involved is a game played according to the same basic principles as it was then, but with great differences in details of the rules. Most obvious is the enormous expansion in the volume of the text. Through the 1875 code of the R&A, the number and scope of the rules remained quite constant, with only a very modest increase in volume in the course of the preceding one hundred thirty years. The 1882 R&A revision and subsequent codes, however, have involved a great expansion in both the scope and volume of the rules.

An Exceeding Cruel Experiment

Let's try to imagine that John Rattray, the first "Captain of the Goff," winner of the inaugural match at Leith in 1744 was able, through the miracle of time travel, to join us for a round. What would he say if we showed him a copy of our present rule book? He would surely be astonished, perhaps even speechless. A glance at our Decisions book would probably make him head for the Highlands, convinced that late twentieth-century golfers had lost their minds. It would hardly be unreasonable for him to ask the purpose of all this verbosity, when what's involved is such a simple, friendly pastime. The Honourable Company managed to run its inaugural tournament in 1744 with only twelve rules containing a scant three hundred words, plus a local rule of forty words. Why our dozens of rules employing thousands upon thousands of words?

Can't Be Helped

There are many answers to this question, all of them hanging on the fact that playing conditions have changed vastly during the past two hundred fifty

The 1882 R&A revision and subsequent codes have involved a great expansion in both the scope and volume of the rules.

years. If we, too, could travel through time to join our golf-playing descendants for a game two hundred fifty years from now, what would we find? Would conditions have changed by then as much as they have during the past two hundred fifty years, and what form would the rules have assumed? Naturally, there's no way to answer with any certainty. The only thing we can be perfectly sure of is that golf will continue to be played (probably by steadily increasing numbers of people), that playing conditions will continue to change, and that the rules will continue to evolve.

PART III

Individual Rules and Definitions

*The USGA and R&A are uniquely influential and oddly devoid
of actual power. They can only ordain that these Rules be used in their
Championships, such as the U.S. and British Open Championships.*

*All of us who opt to use the Rules of Golf in other competitions and in
everyday golf do so because we respect the USGA and R&A and
because we recognize that uniformity in golf is eminently desirable.
The game is more enjoyable if we all play the same game. There is
a community of golf. It envelops the rawest of beginners, struggling to
get around a course with a minimum of embarrassment but a
maximum of hope, and those of us fortunate enough to play the game on
the loftiest professional level. The Rules of Golf bind that community.*

—TOM WATSON, WITH FRANK HANNIGAN 1992

While a stroke is playing none of the Party shall walk about, make any motion, or attempt to take off the Player's attention, by speaking, or otherwise.

—THE SOCIETY OF GOLFERS AT ABERDEEN, 1783

Etiquette

The conventions of golf etiquette should not be confused with the rules of play, but they certainly are an important part of the game, and their historical development is as interesting as the development of many rules.

The rule quoted above, adopted in 1783 by the Aberdeen golfers, was the only mention of any point of etiquette in any eighteenth-century code. In this, as they did so often, the Aberdonians demonstrated their originality. That they actuallly meant this point of etiquette to be a rule is clear from the form it took in their next code of rules, in 1815:

> The opposite party must not at any time interrupt the player by walking about, speaking to or standing in his way, under penalty of a stroke in the player's favour, or playing the stroke again at his option.

POLITESSE

The next group of golfers to concern themselves with a point of etiquette was the Edinburgh Burgess golfers, who in 1802 adopted six rules as an addendum to their 1776 code of rules. One of these read:

> That in case two or more parties meet at the hole the party who plays first must be allowed to play their second strokes before the party who plays after them shall be allowed to strike off their first balls, and if the first party's ball be in a hazard the said party shall stand aside till the second pass them.

Despite the rather tortured, legalistic early nineteenth-century language in this rule, the intent is clear. The first part is expressed more clearly and generally in our present code: "No player should play until the players in front are out of range." The change from *shall* to *should* is significant. Our modern statements of etiquette aren't rules and carry no penalties. We don't

59

know if any penalties were handed out at Bruntsfield Links early in the nineteenth century for breaches of etiquette rules, but many rules in those days lacked penalty statements. Only the Aberdeen golfers seem to have felt strongly enough about the matter to attach a penalty statement to their rule governing behavior.

WITH DUE CONSIDERATION

Such admonitions to behave in an acceptable manner continued to be incorporated into the rules of a good many golf clubs during the first half of the nineteenth century:

- Glasgow in 1810
- Perth in 1825
- Blackheath in 1828
- Montrose in 1830
- Musselburgh in 1834

Most of them dealt with the two matters covered in the 1802 rule of the Edinburgh Burgess golfers quoted above, plus the question of right-of-way on the course. The 1825 Perth rule stated:

> Parties playing two balls shall be allowed to pass parties playing three, as moving more expeditiously.

Neither the Honourable Company nor the R&A felt it necessary to adopt rules legislating behavior during the eighteenth century or the first half of the nineteenth. In 1851 the R&A added this rule to its code:

> Any party having lost a ball, and incurring delay by seeking it, shall be passed by any other party coming up, and on all occasions a two-ball match—whether by two or four players—may pass a three-ball match.

The use of *shall* in one case and *may* in the other in this rule is interesting. The rule remained unchanged in the 1875 R&A code, but the *shall* changed to *may* in 1882. It was at this point that behavior clearly became recognized as something to be recommended, not legislated.

DECORUM

The explosive increase in the number of players at the end of the 1880s apparently made questions of behavior so important that the R&A devoted an entire separate section to etiquette in its 1891 code of rules. At this point there still seems to have been some uncertainty about what golf etiquette consisted of, because some points in that section dealt with matters of scoring and procedure on the putting green. By 1899, however, this had all been sorted out, and the first list of items devoted exclusively to principles of etiquette appeared:

ETIQUETTE OF GOLF

1. A single player has no standing, and must always give way to a properly constituted match.

2. No player, caddie, or onlooker should move or talk during a stroke.

3. No player should play from the tee until the party in front have played their second strokes and are out of range, nor play up to the putting-green till the party in front have holed out and moved away.

4. The player who has the honour should be allowed to play before his opponent tees his ball.

5. Players who have holed out should not try their putts over again when other players are following them.

6. Players looking for a lost ball must allow other matches coming up to pass them.

7. On request being made, a three-ball match must allow a single, three-some, or foursome to pass. Any match playing a whole round may claim the right to pass a match playing a shorter round.

8. If a match fail to keep its place on the green, and lose in distance more than one clear hole on those in front, it may be passed, on request being made.

9. Turf cut or displaced by a stroke should be at once replaced.

10. A player should carefully fill up all holes made by himself in a bunker.

HAVE A CARE FOR OTHERS

It's quite remarkable that this set of principles of etiquette remained essentially unchanged for so long. There was little change through 1933, but both the USGA and the R&A began to expand it in their independently adopted codes of, respectively, 1946 and 1950. At the same time they moved it to its present position preceding the main body of the rules, then set up the separate section "Priority on the Course" in the first joint USGA-R&A code in 1952. In 1976 they added the section "Care of the Course," followed by the the section "Pace of Play" in 1996.

A careful comparison of the 1899 code of etiquette with our modern code will show how little the basic principles of etiquette have changed over the years.

The Game

P resent Rule 1 was articulated in 1984, during the major reorganization of the rules that was carried out at that time, by collecting in one place several basic principles of the game that had been scattered throughout earlier codes.

RULE 1-1

A definition of the game of golf close to our present formulation in Rule 1-1 first appeared in the 1891 R&A code:

> The game consists in each side playing a ball from a tee into a hole by successive strokes. . . .

Variations of this formulation have appeared in every code adopted by either the R&A or the USGA since. It's a curiosity of the history of the rules that this formulation makes no allowance for the contingency that is every golfer's dream—the hole-in-one. As a matter of fact, this wasn't noticed and corrected until 1984. Since then Rule 1-1 has provided for playing the ball into the hole by means of both "a stroke or successive strokes" from the tee.

It's a further curiosity of the history of the rules that, before 1952, a player who made a hole-in-one but failed to realize it and put another ball into play had to count the score made with the second ball. Decisions issued in both 1910 and 1926 make this clear. The 1926 Decision provides the rationale:

> When the player abandoned the search for the first ball it became a "lost ball," and the second ball played became the ball "in play."

Our present Decisions 1-1/2, 1-1/3, and 1-1/4 (following the lead of a Decision from 1952) are much more player friendly and make it clear that once the first ball is in the hole, nothing done subsequently counts. Decision 1-1/3 states unequivocally:

> The play of the hole was completed when the player holed the original ball (Rule 1-1).

Before 1952, a player who made a hole-in-one and put another ball into play had to count the score made with the second ball.

RULE 1-2

When it was introduced into the rules in 1964, the injunction against exerting influence on the ball was part of the rule covering improving a lie and building a stance (present Rule 13). Now that it has the status of a general principle as Rule 1-2, it has much broader applications than in its previously limited context.

RULE 1-3

Rule 1-3, which forbids agreeing "to exclude the operation of any Rule or to waive any penalty incurred," is also of relatively recent origin. It appeared first as a separate section of Rule 1 in 1933. Between 1952 and 1980 it had the status of a separate rule. (The rules during that period were organized into the relatively large number of 41, many of them quite short.)

RULE 1-4

Rule 1-4—the equity rule—is a rule of the utmost importance. Clearly, one cannot write a code of rules that takes into consideration everything that might take place on a golf course, yet situations not specifically covered by the rules must be dealt with somehow. The principle of equity is applied in these cases. It appeared first in the R&A code of 1891, at which time it was attached to the rule on disputes (present Rule 34). The principle was expressed at that time in the form:

> Should the dispute not be covered by the Rules of Golf, the arbiters must decide it by equity.

This remained part of the rule on disputes until 1984. It was first given its present, more modern, linguistic form in the R&A experimental code of 1950.

Level That Playing Field

That the principle of equity was introduced in the 1891 R&A code is in itself significant. The 1891 code was developed on the basis of a request from the delegates of the clubs represented at the 1890 British Amateur Championship, at Hoylake, who wanted a code that could be applied more easily on a wider range of courses than the 1888 code. The 1888 code had been developed at St. Andrews, where all the players were familiar with traditional interpretations of the rules. *(See also discussion of the background of the 1891 R&A code in Part II, Chapter 4.)*

An appeal to equity is made in more than fifty Decisions in *Decisions on the Rules of Golf.* This indicates how important the principle is. The best way to gain insight into how the concept of equity is applied in golf is to study these Decisions.

They are entirely different games, played in different ways, and with different ends in view. The old game is the match game; the medal game is an innovation of more recent years; and it would be impossible to make the rules for both games the same without spoiling either the one or the other.

—HALL BLYTH, IN *THE FIELD*, 1888

Match Play and Stroke Play

MATCH PLAY (RULE 2)

The original form of competition at golf does indeed seem to have been match play, although Hall Blyth was wrong in assuming that medal (stroke) play was a recent innovation at the end of the nineteenth century, as we soon shall see. All the early games of golf played by the Stuart kings of Scotland that tell us about early traditions were either single matches (King James IV against the Earl of Bothwell in 1503) or foursome matches (the Duke of York, later James II of England, teamed up with the poor Edinburgh shoemaker John Patersone in 1681).

The terms used to refer to match play are a bit confusing. A single match is played by two people (but only a single one on each side), while a foursome match involves only two balls (but four people playing them).

An Inherent Limitation

The great disadvantage with match play is that only two or, at the most, four players can take part at one time, and a tournament run as a knock-out match play competition can take a week or two to complete. This problem was recognized at the very outset of organized golf competition, with the match for the Silver Club set up by the city of Edinburgh for the Gentlemen Golfers of Leith in 1744. It was called a match, but it wasn't a match in the sense of the

64

Whatchamacallit

One source of the confusion over match play terminology is the habit of American golfers using the term *foursome* to refer to what officially is a four-ball. In order to reduce the confusion somewhat, many Americans call the traditional foursome a Scotch foursome. In this way they give recognition to a method of playing the game that is still considered by many Scots to be the finest form of golf. In recent years some American sports commentators have begun to refer to foursome matches as alternate shot matches, which only adds to the confusion.

term as we use it today. We can see this from the terms set out for it in the minutes of the meeting of the Edinburgh Town Council of March 7, 1744:

> 3. After the Figures are drawn, the Set or Match beginning with No.1, &c. Shall go out first, with a Clerk to mark down every Stroke each of them Shall take to every Hole; then, by the Time They are at the Sawmill Hole; the Second Set, beginning with No. 3, or 4 According as the Match Shall be made Shall Strike off; and so all the rest in the same order, Each set having a Clerk; And when the Match is Ended, a Scrutiny of the whole Clerks Books or Jotings is to be made, And the Player who shall appear to have won the greatest Number of Holes, Shall be Declared to be the Winner of the Match, And if there shall be Two, Three or more, that are Equal, then these Two, or Three &c. must play a Round themselves, in the Order of their Figures, before they Go off the Ground, to Determine the Match.

It's not entirely clear to the modern golfer what all this is supposed to mean. The best commentary on this regulation has been made by J. Stewart Lawson in his excellent monograph *The Original Rules of Golf*, published by The Honourable Company in 1981:

> No doubt the gentlemen who drafted this language in Regulation 3 knew what they intended, but it has caused some debate among later commentators. Some have held that only a hole won outright from every other player counted as a hole won; others that a reckoning was made on the basis of a notional match between each player and every other player; others, again, that a player was credited with a win over each player he beat at a particular hole. Whatever system was used, it seems to have been successful, in that there is no record of the tie-break procedure having to be evoked.

Getting the Bugs Out

It would seem that the Society of St. Andrews Golfers also understood what scoring system was employed; when it initiated competition for its own Silver Club, in 1754, it followed the same system. This scoring method apparent wasn't entirely satisfactory, however, because after only five years the Society decided to change it. On 9 May 1759 the society adopted the following resolution:

> In order to remove all disputes and inconveniences with regard to the gaining of the Silver Club, it is enacted and agreed by the captain and the gentlemen golfers present, that in all time coming whoever puts in the ball at the fewest strokes over the field, being 22 holes, shall be declared and sustained victor.

True stroke play, in the modern sense of the word, was born with this resolution although match play continued to be the most common form of golf in organized competitions throughout the rest of the eighteenth and most of the nineteenth century.

STROKE PLAY (RULE 3)

Stroke play is often referred to as "medal play" or "play on medal days," especially in older British sources. This comes from the early practice of awarding a medal commemorating the event to the winner of the day's competition. Such antique medals are now among the most avidly sought collectors' items. The first set of special rules for use during play on medal days was announced by the Edinburgh Burgess Golfing Society on 2 May 1807.

CHUNUKENI CUP MEDAL, 1932.

Lost Ball Problems

The most important difference between these special stroke play rules and the basic rules of the club involved the contingency of a lost ball. The Burgess golfers were at that time playing lost ball–lost hole in match play. *(See Rule 27 for details)*. However, they adopted stroke-and-distance for stroke play:

> That if a ball goes into the whins or is lost, in playing through the Green, the striker goes to the place from whence he struck, drops the ball if it is found, or in case it is lost, another, over his shoulder and loses a stroke.

Other clubs that played lost ball–lost hole in match play quickly followed suit (e.g., Aberdeen in 1815), but such a rule wasn't necessary in the case of clubs that played stroke-and-distance in all forms of play. These included the St. Andrews golfers and the Honourable Company, neither of which had special rules for play on medal days until, respectively, 1829 and 1839, when they both adopted a quite different type of stroke play rule:

> New holes shall always be made on the day the medal is played for, and no competitor shall play at these holes before he starts for the prize.

This was made necessary because all balls had to be holed out on medal days, and the condition of the hole was therefore important. *(See Rule 16: The Putting Green, page 131, for information on the frequently miserable condition of the hole in the early days of golf.)* The form of this rule given above was the St. Andrews 1829 version; the Honourable Company rule added the clause "under penalty of being disqualified for playing for the medal." This penalty is the same that applies today. This restriction on practicing on the course the day of a stroke play competition remains one of the few differences left between the rules for match play and stroke play.

COMPARE AND CONTRAST

Despite Hall Blyth's objections in 1888 to eliminating the differences between the rules for match and stroke play, those differences have gradually shrunk, especially during the past forty years. The crucial date in this respect is 1952, when the first joint R&A–USGA code went into effect. That major revision of the rules involved, among other things, the elimination of the stymie, one of the most distinguishing features of match play. *(See Rule 16: The Putting Green, page 128.)*

The most important differences between the two forms of play have always involved play on the putting green, where the psychological pressures specific to match play come most clearly to the fore. Long after the use of the flagstick as a backstop was outlawed in stroke play (in 1899), it was still permitted in match play. It wasn't banned until 1968, when the general penalty was assigned. *(See Rule 16: The Putting Green, page 122.)* The right of a player to require his opponent to leave his ball in place on the putting green (for use either as a putting guide or as a backstop) lasted until 1984. That there's still no penalty in match play for striking another ball on the putting green when putting is a leftover from the older rule. *(See Rule 19-5.)* It makes little difference, though, since nowadays just about every player marks his ball on the green, whether it's necessary or not.

Other differences between the two basic forms of play do still exist. Perhaps the most important are the rules governing the order of play. In match play, strokes played out of turn may be recalled by the opponent, while this option is lacking in stroke play. *(See Rule 10: Order of Play.)*

Similarly, there's no penalty for playing a ball from outside the teeing ground in match play, but the stroke may be recalled. In stroke play, playing from outside the teeing ground carries an automatic penalty of two strokes. *(See Rule 11: The Teeing Ground.)*

The differences between the rules for match and stroke play have gradually shrunk.

An Important Distinction

The procedure to be followed in cases of doubts and claims is an important difference between the two forms of play.

- In match play the players must either agree or make a claim before playing from the next teeing ground (or before leaving the last green).
- In stroke play a second ball may be played in addition to the original.

This option appeared for the first time in the 1946 USGA unilateral code, and has remained basically the same since, despite some variations in phraseology.

There has been a bit of flip-flopping through the years over whether or not the player must declare ahead of time which ball he wishes to score with ("if the Rules permit"), and also whether the second ball should be called a second ball or an alternate ball, but this was all sorted out in 1980. This rule was part of the rule on Disputes (present Rule 34) in its early years, but it was shifted into Rule 3 during the major reorganization of the rules in 1984.

Taking Turns

The right of a player to recall a stroke made out of turn by his opponent in match play is a rule that many players don't know nowadays, when most tournaments are stroke-play events. A good example of this occurred on the twelfth green on the final day of the 1995 Ryder Cup at Oak Hill Golf Club in Rochester, New York.

Seve Ballasteros, an experienced match player, and Tom Lehman, playing his first Ryder Cup, were both on the green, with Lehman farthest from the hole. He putted to within a few inches of the hole, then walked up and tapped in, as is common in the stroke-play tour events he's used to playing. Seve pointed out to the referee present that Lehman had played out of turn and that he wanted the ball replaced and marked. The position of the marker would give him a good line for his putt. Lehman looked totally confused by it all, and there was even some booing from the spectators, who seemed to think Seve was doing something unsportmanslike. The ball was replaced and its position marked. Seve putted and missed by a whisker (and eventually lost the match 4/3). The referee then explained the situation to the crowd, stressing that nothing unsportmanslike had taken place. A better knowledge of match play rules all around would have made all the confusion unnecessary.

DETAILS: RULE 2-2

Golfers are often puzzled by Rule 2-2, which grants a half in match play when a player might otherwise have lost the hole. There seems to be little justification or application for the rule. This seeming illogic stems from the rule's adoption on the basis of a Decision issued in 1900 that dealt with a rule that has since been changed. In match play at that time, if a player's ball in motion struck either his opponent, or his opponent's caddie, the opponent lost the hole. The Decision describes the situation clearly:

> **Sheringham Golf Club.—A playing the odd* from the edge of the green holes his putt. B in playing the like strikes A's caddie who is standing at the hole. Does A lose the hole? If not, what rule of Golf qualifies Rule 24?**
>
> **A.— No. A does not lose the hole. By holing his putt in the odd he secured the half, at least, and nothing that B does could deprive him of that.**

Since A had already holed out and B was putting for a half, it seemed to many players at that time that it was unfair that A could subsequently lose the hole by an action after he had completed play of the hole. This Decision led in 1902 to the adoption of an earlier version of the second sentence of Rule 2-2:

> When a player has holed out and his opponent has been left with a putt for the half, nothing that the player can do shall deprive him of the half which he has already gained.

The rule governing a player's ball striking the opponent's side was changed in 1980, and the former penalty of loss of hole was cancelled. As a result, the importance of Rule 2-2 has decreased considerably. It may, however, still occasionally be applicable. *Decisions on the Rules of Golf* refers to several possible situations in which the rule can affect the outcome of the play of a hole. A player is penalized loss of hole in match play if he gives advice on the putting line or wrong information about his score to his opponent, but if the opponent is putting for a half and the player has already holed out for a half, he retains that half. *(See Decisions 2-2/1 and 9-2/6.)*

DETAILS: RULE 2-4

Present Rule 2-4 is an extremely clear and detailed statement for concessions in match play, but it's a very recent rule, dating from 1988. It's a peculiarity of the history of the rules of golf that this extremely central aspect of match play was never mentioned in the early rules, probably because it was so basic that it never seemed necessary to state it. Only in 1851 did the rules mention conced-

---

*Playing the odd meant playing one more stroke than your opponent, *playing the like* meant playing the same number of strokes. These terms, and others no longer used, are explained in Rule 9: Information as to Strokes Taken.

What Train?

Sheringham Golf Club, located on England's Norfolk coast, may not be among the best known courses in the golfing world, but in addition to its claim to fame for the origin of Rule 2-2, it also is noteworthy for having been the true venue of one of the most famous incidents in the history of tournament golf.

In 1920, Joyce Wethered won the first of her five consecutive English Ladies' Championships by holing a putt on Sheringham's seventeenth green. As she was putting, a train roared past on the railway bordering the hole. Asked later whether the train had disturbed her, she replied, "What train?"

This story has been retold countless times, usually transferred to other venues—and even ascribed to other outstanding players. The most usual incorrect venue given is St. Andrews' famous seventeenth hole, which was also bordered by a railroad line in 1920, but the incident did in fact happen at Sheringham Golf Club. In any event, it illustrates the extreme powers of concentration that enabled Wethered to become one of the greatest golfers of all time. No less an authority than Bobby Jones said that she had the finest swing of any player of either sex that he had ever seen, and she was one of the few players during the 1920s to achieve a record rivaling Jones's own.

ing a stroke in match play, and then not directly. The following sentence was added to the rule governing stroke play in the R&A code adopted in that year:

> All balls must be holed out on medal days, and no stimys allowed.

Implied here is that stymies were a part of match play and that not all putts had to be holed out in that form of play.

Strike It Away

The first positive reference to conceding a stroke was written into the 1882 R&A code, but even then the concession of the stroke itself wasn't the primary concern:

> When a player's ball rests on the lip of the hole, his opponent, after holing in the "odd" or the "like," shall be entitled to strike away the ball which is at the lip

of the hole, claiming the hole if he shall have holed in the "like" and the "half" if he shall have holed in the "odd."

Here the primary concern was the ball overhanging the hole (present Rule 16-2). A player was allowed to concede a putt by striking away his opponent's ball only after he himself had holed out. Otherwise he might have been able to escape a possible stymie by conceding a putt.

This rule continued in force, with occasional minor rephrasing, until 1956, although the playing of stymies was discontinued in 1952. In the joint USGA–R&A code of 1956 the rule was finally rewritten to take this into account:

> When the opponent's ball has come to rest, the player may concede the opponent to have holed out with his next stroke and may knock away the opponent's ball.

This rule was carried over into the reorganized code of 1984 as a section of Rule 16 (The Putting Green), but was moved to Rule 2 and expanded to its present form in 1988.

With the legalizing of steel shafts there began another flurry and flutter in the game. It was soon realized by players that the rigid steel shaft could not be made to work to the same extent as hickory with its torsion qualities. . . The soullessness of metal took the finesse out of the game—a new, more stereotyped method of hit had to be found.

—ROBERT HARRIS, 1953

RULES 4 AND 5 — Clubs and the Ball

It's fitting to head this section with a quote from Robert Harris, who played an important part in the evolution of the rules dealing with clubs and balls during the 1930s when he was chairman of the Golf Ball Sub-committee of the Rules of Golf Committee of the R&A. As he pointed out in 1953 in his book *Sixty Years of Golf*, the advent of steel shafts changed the game considerably.

The rigidity of steel made it necessary to use more clubs to produce the same result, which "forced the set up to twenty and even twenty-five clubs being carried by some players, in a quest for results which before were obtainable from five or six shafts of hickory." Lawson Little is reputed to have carried as many as thirty-one clubs in his bag in 1934 and 1935 at Prestwick and Royal Lytham and St. Annes when he won his two consecutive British Amateur Championships and his two consecutive U.S. Amateur Championships at The Country Club in Brookline and The Country Club in Cleveland. Harris reported (a bit maliciously) on the state of affairs at the Curtis Cup match at Gleneagles in 1936:

> In 1936 a young "flapper" arrived in the American Women's Team to play against Britain, carrying a bagful of two dozen clubs. In an interview with the Press she remarked: "Yes, I carry twenty-three clubs and, Gee, I need them all."

Why Fourteen?

The question often asked is: Why fourteen? Why not twelve or fifteen, or some other number? Actually, the exact number seems to have been arrived at quite arbitrarily. Harris reports in his book that the matter was settled "without the why and wherefore of only fourteen clubs being questioned or debated." His final remark on the subject is thought provoking:

"It is now apparent that fourteen is too many—these debates with caddies regarding digits, when the player is afraid of the shot, are slowing up the game."

Oh, for the good old days when golfers had to agonize over only "five or six shafts of hickory!"

The advent of steel shafts changed the game considerably.

That's It

Perhaps this was the final straw for Harris. Unfortunately, he doesn't go into the matter in detail in his book, but we know from USGA and R&A records that he and John Jackson, USGA President, discussed the matter during the summer of 1936, and that Harris was the first to propose limiting the number of clubs to fourteen. He did this with a motion before the Rules of Golf Committee in November of 1936, but the R&A membership refused to go along with his suggestion until 1939. The USGA put the fourteen-club limit into effect in 1938.

Once the number of clubs a player might use was limited to "only" fourteen, replacing a damaged club became a concern. This was addressed soon after discussion on the rules of golf was taken up again following the Second World War, in the 1950 R&A experimental code. The rule adopted at that time is in all essential respects identical to our present rule. Borrowing clubs from other players was not permitted. In 1988 the rule was changed to allow borrowing clubs, on the condition that only the borrower subsequently used the borrowed club during the remainder of the round. This proved, however, to be impractical, and the experiment was abandoned in 1992. (*For discussion of the dispute between the R&A and the USGA over the use of center-shafted, mallet-headed, and wry-neck clubs, see Part II, Chapter 5.*)

THE OTHER HALF OF THE EQUATION

Technical aspects of the regulation of both clubs and balls are found in Appendices II and III of the rule book, but a discussion of them is beyond the scope of this study. It's nevertheless difficult to resist the temptation—now that the dust has finally settled around this issue—to mention one aspect of the long dispute about the size and weight of the ball. The question of legislating the dimensions of the golf ball never arose until after Coburn Haskell and employees of the Goodrich Rubber Company developed the rubber-wound ball in the closing years of the nineteenth century. The new ball flew farther than the gutta percha ball, and golf courses began to shrink. Pressure for standardization grew and the R&A Rules of Golf Committee took the problem under advisement in 1902.

Which Shall It Be?

As the years passed, various sizes and weights were proposed, ranging from 1.62 to 1.68 inches and 1.55 to 1.62 ounces. The smaller and heavier the ball, the farther it flew and the better it behaved in wind; the lighter and larger the ball, the shorter the distance it could be driven, but the better it could be maneuvered, which appealed to the quality players. The smaller British ball that eventually came into use (1.62 inches × 1.62 ounces) and the larger American ball (1.68 inches × 1.62 ounces) were compromises suited to conditions in those countries.

Need We Choose at All?

However, many outstanding golfers in the 1920s opposed any such nit-picking form of standardization, among them Bernard Darwin, J. H. Taylor and C. B. Macdonald. They gave their support to a simple and elegant solution to the problem: a floating ball. It could be small and very light, or larger and heavier, as long as it floated. It couldn't be driven as far as a ball that would sink, but it would respond better to skilful handling in the short game. There would also be an obvious added advantage for golfers, but just as obviously a disadvantage for another group. Macdonald summed it all up quite well in 1927:

> My judgement is we should at once go to a floating ball and give the makers carte blanche to do what they can so long as they conform to the one restriction, the ball must float. Naturally, the manufacturers do not want a floater, but if it fills the bill, certainly the players do, as it will save them many boxes of balls a year, and the approaching and putting will be much more interesting.

The smaller and heavier the ball, the farther it flew and the better it behaved in wind.

Got It

Our present ball, standard worldwide since January 1, 1990, sinks like a rock.

SEND IT FLYING

In the days when golf was played with feather balls, a new ball couldn't be substituted for a damaged one. *(See also the discussion of Article 3 of the original code of 1744 in Part II, Chapter 2, page 16.)* Although the feather balls might, and often did, become damaged, they usually stayed more or less in one piece and play could continue with them.

Fragmentary Evidence

The situation changed with the coming of balls made of gutta percha, first introduced in 1848. They had the unfortunate habit of splitting into fragments. New legislation was called for, and it wasn't long in coming. The 1851 R&A code included a new rule:

> If a ball shall split into two or more pieces, a fresh ball shall be put down in playing for a medal.

That is, a new ball could be substituted in stroke play, but not in match play. Substitution of a new ball in match play followed in the 1858 R&A code, but it brought with it a one-stroke penalty. The same code expressly stated that a new ball could be "put down" (placed?) without penalty in medal play.

Location Is Everything

Notice that the rule neglects to state clearly just where the new ball is to be put down. This was apparently a source of dispute and confusion, resolved in the 1875 R&A code, which specified that "a fresh ball shall be put down where the largest portion of the ball lies." Trying to apply this rule led to obvious difficulties. More than one commentator during the late nineteenth and early twentieth century remarked that it was amazing how often the largest piece was the one found lying on the fairway. An attempt was made to alleviate this difficulty in 1891 by adding the condition that "if two pieces are apparently of equal size, [another ball] may be put down where either piece lies, at the option of the player." This wording still left such obvious uncertainties that in 1908 the R&A rules legislators finally gave up and declared that "another ball may be dropped where any piece lies."

A New Ball Arrives

By then the problem was solving itself, with the coming of the Haskell ball. This forerunner of our modern three-piece (wound) balls, didn't readily split into pieces. By 1933 all mention of balls splitting disappeared from the rule. What remained was a statement that had been added to the rule in 1891:

> If a ball crack or become unplayable, the player may change it, on intimating to his opponent his intention to do so.

This was a step in the direction of our present Rule 5-3 (Ball Unfit for Play). The next step was taken in 1899 with the addition of this sentence:

> Mud adhering to the ball shall not be considered as making it unfit for play.

The modern form of the rule began to take shape in the post–Second World War codes. From 1952 on the player could "replace" rather than "change" the ball, and from 1964 on he could "substitute another ball, placing it on the spot where the original ball lay."

FISSION

The case of balls splitting into pieces, absent from the rule since 1933, reappeared in 1976, reflecting the revival of solid-core balls prone to cracking wide open:

> If a ball breaks into pieces as the result of a stroke, the stroke shall be replayed, without penalty.

The 1980 code specified that the new ball was to be "placed where the original ball lay," but the wide-sweeping reform of the Rules of Golf in 1984 scooped this case under the umbrella of Rule 20-5, which requires that the new ball be dropped.

The changes in this rule during more than one hundred thirty years reflect the constant changes in the nature of the golf ball. Will continuing development of the ball compel further rule changes, or has the golf ball now reached its final form?

A CLUB BY ANY OTHER NAME

The evolution of Rule 5-3 is a good example of the influence of the nature of equipment on the rules of golf. The opposite situation can be found in how a rule the Honourable Company adopted in 1866 influenced golf equipment. That austere body was then playing at Musselburgh. The main road east from Edinburgh ran—and still runs—along the south side of the course. There was a strong tendency for balls to fly onto the road, especially during play of Mrs. Forman's, the famous east-running hole named after the tavern behind the green:

From 1952 on the player could "replace" rather than "change" the ball.

But a ball is not considered to be lost which is seen to fly onto the road or over the fence on the south side of the road at Musselburgh. In that case the ball must be played or the hole lost.

With their wooden soles, the wood clubs of that day were easily damaged if struck against the hard surface of the road. To protect them, a brass plate was fastened to the sole. The "brassie" was born. Eventually the soles of all wood clubs were protected by metal plates, but in many sets even as late as the 1960s and 1970s only the 2-wood had a brass plate, while the other woods were equipped with steel plates. Nowadays, metal clubs made to be played from the fairway and metal drivers with ten, eleven, or even twelve degrees of loft have made the brassie obsolete, but it's still remembered fondly by many older players who used it as a utility club during their youth.

I hae play'd in the frost and the thaw,
I hae play'd since the year thirty-three,
I hae play'd in the rain and the snaw,
And I trust I may play till I dee.

—ANDREW LANG

RULE 6 | The Player

Perhaps better than anyone else ever has, Andrew Lang, the nineteenth-century Scottish folklorist, poet, and enthusiastic golfer, summed up the determination of the golfer to continue playing no matter what the weather (or his age) might be. As a Scot he believed firmly that "Bad weather is not of itself a good reason for discontinuing play," as our present Rule 6-8 puts it in everyday prose.

OF THUNDER HEARD REMOTE

The first rule that banned discontinuing play because of bad weather showed up in the 1891 R&A code, and then only in stroke play. (Discontinuing play in match play is allowed even today, as long as the overall competition isn't delayed.) The penalty in 1891 was disqualification as it is today. No extenuating circumstances, such as danger of being struck by lightning, were recognized. This began to be seen as a problem only after the arrival of steel shafts (which were approved in the USA in 1924 and in Britain in 1929). The problem was discussed by the USGA in 1934. The Executive Committee resolved at that time to leave the decision to postpone or discontinue tournaments because of danger from thunderstorms in the hands of the organizing committee.

A Mantle of Wind and Chill and Rain

Both the USGA and the R&A met the issue head on in their separate codes at the end of the 1940s, the USGA in 1946 in a separate section appended to the rules, the R&A in 1950 by qualifying the rule to allow the player to discontinue play "if he consider that there be danger from lightning." This firmly established the status of the player as sole judge of the danger, and all codes since then have observed this principle. Procedures for discontinuing play were added in 1960:

> When play is discontinued in accordance with the Rules, it should, if feasible, be discontinued after the completion of the play of a hole. If this is not feasible, the player shall lift his ball after marking the spot on which it lay.

THIS PITILESS STORM

These procedures have been somewhat refined since then, but they have remained essentially unchanged. In recent years, following the widely publicized death of spectators caused by lightning at the 1991 US Open and PGA Championships, the USGA has carried on a vigorous campaign to inform players of the dangers of lightning on golf courses. A section entitled "Protection of Persons Against Lightning" has been added to the Appendices in the USGA rules book, and bag tags issued to its members have "Lightning Safety Tips" on their flip sides.

The first rule defining the responsibilities and duties of the player appeared in the R&A's experimental code of 1950. It covered all the most important points of present Rule 6 except for its provisions on keeping score in stroke play (Rule 6-6 in our current code). These were set out in a separate rule.

ANDIAMO!

The important rule (present Rule 6-7) requiring the player to play without undue delay first appeared at this time. There was no specific penalty attached to it, but the Committee was given the power "to disqualify any player or players who in their opinion unduly delays the play of any other player or players." Already in 1952 the penalty for undue delay was changed to loss of hole in match play, two strokes in stroke play, and disqualification for repeated offenses. In 1996 the rule was expanded greatly and power given to the Committee to "lay down pace of play guidelines." The Committee was given the authority in stroke play to modify the penalty for failure to adhere to these guidelines to one stroke for the first offense, two for the second, and disqualification for subsequent offenses.

MARK MY WORDS

The history of the marker himself is interesting. Because most early golf was at match play, it's natural that rules of the time carried little mention of writ-

The USGA has carried on a vigorous campaign to inform players of the dangers of lightning on golf courses.

Details, Details

Making sure he turns in the correct score for each hole is the player's most important responsibility. Failure on the part of the player to do this has led to much personal anguish. Perhaps the best example known of a marking problem occurred at the 1968 Masters. Roberto De Vicenzo scored a birdie three on the seventeenth hole during the final round, but Tommy Aaron, his marker, wrote down a four. When De Vicenzo signed his card with the four on

it, he finished one stroke behind Bob Goalby, rather than tying him and causing a playoff. Although the club player may not have as much to lose by his carelessness as De Vicenzo, it's nevertheless always an excellent idea to check what your marker has put down before you scribble your signature on the card.

ROBERTO DE VICENZO (LEFT) AND BOB GOALBY (RIGHT).

ing down scores. Actually, there were markers (even though they weren't called markers) during the first tournament organized by the Gentlemen Golfers in Leith in 1744. *(See also Rule 2: Match Play.)* The minutes of the Edinburgh Town Council meeting on March 7 of that year, which set the conditions of the competition, stated that each group was to be accompanied by "a Clerk to mark down every Stroke each of them Shall Strike off." The first mention of markers as such appeared in the "Regulations to be observed in playing for the Gold Medal of the Edinburgh Burgess Golfing Society, adopted on 18 May, 1816." These regulations required "That the Competitors shall play in single parties and that each party shall have a marker along with them."

Whyever Not?

This practice didn't catch on. During most of the nineteenth century only the Perth and Blackheath golfers, in 1839 and 1844 respectively, followed the Burgess golfers in sending along attending markers. Neither the Gentlemen Golfers nor their colleagues in St. Andrews required markers in stroke play tournaments. Their stroke play rules concentrated on requiring new holes to be made on medal days and in forbidding practice to those holes. It was 1882 before the R&A mentioned markers in their rules, and then in a rather back-handed way:

> in the absence of a special marker the players will note each other's score.

This assumed a more positive form in 1891:

> The scores shall be kept by a special marker, or by the competitors noting each other's scores.

Gradual changes in phraseology produced our modern definition of a marker. In the first joint R&A–USGA code in 1952 a crucial addition was made to the rule:

> The competitor is solely responsible for the correctness of the score recorded for each hole.

The same code established the responsibilities of the Committee and our present penalties for reporting an incorrect score.

RULE 6-5

The two sentences that make up Rule 6-5, defining the responsibility of the player to be able to identify his ball, first appeared in the rules in 1968 in a note prefacing the rule that governed identifying and cleaning the ball. These two sentences also appear as a prefacing note to our current rule on identifying the ball (Rule 12-2). This note was raised to the status of a rule in 1984 when it was added to the rule setting out the responsibilities of the player, becoming our present Rule 6-5.

Practice

Our present Rule 7 is a composite of several distinct rules affecting practice under differing conditions: before or during a round, or between holes. Some of these rules originated at an early stage in the development of the rules, some not until after the Second World War.

The first of these rules affecting practice appeared in the St. Andrews code of 1829:

> New holes shall always be made on the day the medal is played for, and no competitor shall play at these holes before he starts for the prize.

Fetching sand from the hole to make a tee for the next drive was an early practice.

LITTLE GRAINS OF SAND

This rule reflects the early practice of fetching sand from the hole to make a tee for the next drive, and the necessity of providing a relatively neat hole on stroke play days when all putts had to be holed. *(See Rule 11: The Teeing Ground, page 93, and Rule 16: The Putting Green, page 131).* Because the holes were new and in new places, players couldn't play to them for practice. These two quite different aspects of one situation remained joined in R&A's rules throughout the nineteenth century. By the time of the 1899 code, the rule had assumed the form:

> New holes shall be made for Stroke Competitions, and thereafter no competitor, before starting, shall play any stroke on a putting-green, under penalty of disqualification.

The Honourable Company had added the penalty of disqualification when it adopted the rule in 1839, and the R&A, in turn, had made disqualification a part of its rule in 1842.

PRACTICE, PRACTICE, PRACTICE

Not until after the Second World War were the two questions of the making of new holes and of practice separated. In its 1950 experimental code, the R&A assigned the making of new holes to the rule defining the duties of the Committee (present Rule 33-2b), while the rule forbidding practice before a round moved to the rule defining the duties of the player. These locations were continued in the first joint R&A-USGA code in 1952, but in 1956 the rule forbidding practice before a round was combined with two other rules of related content to form a separate rule. The USGA had introduced a rule in 1946 allowing practice putting after completion of a hole, and in 1950 the R&A had introduced a rule forbidding making a practice stroke during the play of a hole. The rule assumed its present general form with these additions, but in 1984 it was reorganized and a few other details added (no testing of the surface of a putting green, practice after completion of a hole only if it doesn't unduly delay play). A note specifically allowing practice on the course on the day of a match play competition was added to the rule in 1960, before which it was only implied.

That practice is allowed on the course before the play of a match, but not before a stroke play round, is one of the most important of the few remaining differences between the rules governing match and stroke play. Since both competitors in a match play at the same time, they have equal opportunity to practice before starting, which is not the case in stroke play competitions.

The rule forbidding practice strokes during the play of a hole, first introduced in the R&A's 1950 experimental code, quickly collided with the traditions of match play. The USGA took the matter up in a Decision in 1977:

> Q: In match play, on the par-5 first hole, A chips his fourth stroke in for a birdie 4. B lies 4 in a bunker. Therefore, concession of B's next stroke is implied since he cannot tie A.
>
> May B take a "practice" stroke from the bunker? If this is an infraction and B is called for it, does he walk to the third tee two down?
>
> A: B may play the stroke from the bunker without penalty. In match play, strokes played in completing a hole, the result of which has been decided, are not practice strokes within the meaning of that term in Rule 8-2.*

The R&A followed the USGA's lead in 1978 and adopted the identical Decision. When the two Decisions services were consolidated in 1984, this Decision was included in a form with slightly different wording. In 1996 the Decision was elevated to the status of a rule with the addition to Rule 7-2 of the sentence:

> Strokes played in continuing the play of a hole, the result of which has been decided, are not practice strokes.

As is often the case when a Decision becomes a Rule, the situation leading to the Decision has been generalized. Now match players can in good conscience complete the play of a hole already decided with as many strokes as

The USGA introduced a rule in 1946 allowing practice putting after completion of a hole.

---

* Now Rule 7-2.

they might need. Players in Stableford competitions can also play out the hole once they have used up their strokes, although it's usually better if they pick up in order to speed up play.

LAUGHING IT UP ON THE PRACTICE TEE.

Advice; Indicating
Line of Play

Parties are at liberty to ask advice for direction

from their partner, or cadies, in playing, but not

from onlookers, whose observations on the

play are not to be listened to. . .

—MONTROSE GOLF CLUB, 1830

The rule forbidding either giving or asking for advice developed by fits and starts. The Aberdeen golfers were in this, as in so many respects, way ahead of the pack. Already in 1783 they were concerned with what sort of advice could be taken, and from whom. Two separate rules in their first code dealt with different aspects of the problem:

> XIX. The Player shall not be at liberty to draw a Line, or make any Mark as a Direction for holing, nor shall his Partner stand at the Hole, or direct him in aiming . . . .
>
> XXIII. It is understood that Partners may consult with, and give verbal Directions to one another; how to play; but nothing further.

DON'T YOU DARE

It's interesting that their concern united the two separate rules that form our present Rule 8: advice and indicating the line of play. The rules treating these two concerns developed separately during the nineteenth century and weren't joined together until the R&A code of 1908. It's also interesting that the 1783 Aberdonians legislated against other than purely verbal aid when holing out. No other group of eighteenth-century golfers concerned themselves with the question of advice, and even the Aberdonians dropped it when they adopted their next code, in 1815. The problem resurfaced again in Perth, in a footnote appended to the rules adopted by the Perth Golfing Society in 1825. This footnote deserves to be quoted in full:

> N.B.—It may not be improper here to mention certain points of etiquette, which it is of importance should be observed by all who are in the habit of attending matches of Golf. It is understood that no looker-on is entitled to make any observation whatsoever respecting the play—to walk before the players—to remove impediments out of their way—or, in short, to interfere in the most distant manner with the game while playing. The player is at liberty, at all times, to ask advice from his partner or cady, but from no other person.

ROAR OF THE CROWD

Charles Lee's famous painting "The Golfers," showing a match at St. Andrews in 1847, illustrates what seems to have been the problem. The spectators are crowding around the players, almost smothering them. It's perhaps significant that the first code St. Andrews adopted that included a rule concerning giving and taking advice was the code of 1842. By then the influence of observers may have become a problem. Other golfing societies and clubs picked up on the Perth initiative more quickly:

- Burntisland Golf Club in 1828.
- Montrose in 1830 (see the quotation at the head of this chapter).
- The Honourable Company in 1839.

This last took an especially concise form that the St. Andrews golfers adopted verbatim in 1842:

> A Player must not ask advice about the game by word, look, or gesture, from anyone except his own Cady or his Partner.

CHARLES LEE, "THE GOLFERS," 1847.

No looker-on is entitled to make any observation whatsoever respecting the play.

Some version of this rule appeared in all subsequent codes. It clearly forms the basis of our present rule, even though the wording and emphasis may have changed a bit.

SEMAPHORE NO MORE

Rule 8 furthermore prohibits indicating the line of play, both on and off the putting green. This concern appeared in the oldest code, in 1744:

> No man, at Holing his Ball, is to be allowed to mark to the Hole with his Club or anything else.

This rule is probably best associated with our Rule 8-2b governing what we do on the putting green, even though there were no areas that could be clearly distinguished as putting greens in the eighteenth century. *(See Rule 16: The Putting Green.)* All codes of all clubs subsequently included some version of this rule. Toward the end of the nineteenth century, when the putting green began to be distinguished from the rest of the playing area, this rule was usually grouped together with other rules governing play on the putting green. It wasn't consolidated with the rule on advice, where we now find it, until the 1984 reorganization.

With One Exception

The earliest clear direction on how the putting line could be indicated appeared in the 1882 R&A code, which states that, except for the removal of loose impediments,

> the putting line must not be touched by club, hand, nor foot. If the player desires the "line to the hole," it may be pointed out by a club shaft only.

The first rule specifically allowing someone to indicate the line of play other than while "holing out" or on the putting green appeared in the 1908 R&A revision of the rules, which had been undertaken with input from the USGA:

> When playing through the green, or from a hazard, a player may have the line to the hole indicated to him, but no mark shall be placed nor shall any one stand on the proposed line, in order to indicate it, while the stroke is being made.

Our present rule is rephrased slightly but is essentially identical to this 1908 rule. In 1933 the exception was added that allows the flagstick to be held to indicate the location of the hole.

A NATURAL OUTLOOK

A rule must change as the conditions of play change.

The rule on indicating the line of play is an example of how a rule must change as the conditions of play change. Because there were no clearly distinguishable putting areas on the golf courses of the eighteenth and early nineteenth centuries, quite naturally no distinctions were made, such as we find in the two clauses in our present Rule 8-2. The only concern was indicating the line "at Holing the Ball." Only the Aberdeen golfers, progressive as usual, attempted to make a distinction on the basis of whether the player was close enough to see the hole or not. If he could, "no Person shall be allowed to stand at it for a direction." *(See Rule 16: The Putting Green, page 125.)* When distinct putting greens became common, the rule had to be rephrased to accommodate them.

BERNARD LANGER AND CADDIE.

Information as to Strokes Taken

Rule 9 refers primarily to match play, where knowing how many strokes your opponent has taken may affect what strategy you adopt. This rule first appeared in considerably shorter form in 1913, consisting at that time of slightly abbreviated versions of paragraphs 2 and 3 of present Rule 9-2. Starting with the R&A experimental code of 1950, additions were gradually made through the years, until the rule took on its present form in 1992, with the added clause "unless he is obviously proceeding under a Rule involving a penalty and this has been observed by his opponent."

PARADOX

It's not immediately obvious to the modern player why a rule covering such an important aspect of match play as knowing how your opponent lies became part of the rules so relatively late. We assume that strokes have always been counted as they are now—purely numerically: one, two, three, and so on. Even though this is the only way to proceed in stroke play, there are other methods for keeping track of how matters stand in match play. Our present counting of individual strokes is, as a matter of fact, quite a clumsy way of going about it, and of relatively recent date.

A SCORE BY ANY OTHER NAME

In the nineteenth century—and probably also in the eighteenth century and even earlier—the standard method of keeping account of strokes during the play of any given hole in match play was to make use of the terms *the odd, the like, the two more, one off two,* and others equally puzzling to us now. But the system was really very simple; it made counting individual strokes unnecessary.

All those terms refer to the relative standing of the two sides playing the match. If I drove off first, I had played the odd (since we hadn't played the same number of shots). When you drove off, you had played the like. With my second shot I had once more played the odd. If you duffed your second shot (the like) and were still farthest from the hole, you then were playing the odd. If you duffed again and were still farthest from the hole, your next shot was the two more, since I had still only played two shots and you were playing four. If with this shot you finally succeeded in getting your ball closer to the hole than mine, I would then play one off two. Your next shot would then once more be two more, and so on.

CLEAR AS MUD

This approach all seems terribly confusing to us nowadays, but it made the standing of a match extremely easy to follow, especially if the players were evenly matched and were usually playing the odd or the like. If the second ball into the hole was holed on the like, the hole had been halved. It made no difference if that was the second or the tenth shot played, as long as it was the like. You could forget exactly how many shots you had taken (sometimes a blessing!), as long as you knew the relative standing. All that was necessary was to say "like as we lie" when you had played the like. Your opponent then knew that he was playing the odd. The phrase "like as we lie" is still used in matches in Britain, especially in Scotland, by players of all ages.

Casualty of Time

This system of keeping up with a match appeared first in the R&A's 1842 rules, but it had undoubtedly been in use for many years by then. These terms were shifted in 1899 to the definitions section, new in that code. They appeared as part of the Definitions as late as 1933, although they were becoming quite outdated by then. They had fallen victim to the stroke play practice of counting individual strokes.

The sentence that constitutes Rule 9-3, referring to informing your marker about any penalty you incur in stroke play, was added to the rule in 1980.

Order of Play

Since 1984, everything concerning the proper order of play has been covered by a single rule. Before then, the order of play on the teeing ground and the order of play elsewhere had been treated in separate rules in all but a few codes in the middle of the nineteenth century (Perth 1839, Honourable Company 1839, Blackheath 1844). Never in the entire history of the rules has there been any penalty attached to a breach of these rules, even though they have made use of the verb forms "shall" and "must" and other imperative expressions. A ball played out of turn may be recalled by the opponent in match play, but not even this mild form of discipline can be applied in stroke play.

ORDERLY PROGRESSION

The order of play other than on the teeing ground was established already in the original 1744 rules of the Gentlemen Golfers:

> He, whose Ball lyes farthest from the Hole is obliged to play first.

Every code adopted since then has contained some version of this rule, the single exception being the earliest codes of the Edinburgh Burgess Golfers. They joined the rest of the golfing world with the code they adopted in 1814, and since then there has been complete unanimity on this point.

A Toss-up

Longer in coming was a rule establishing the order of play on the teeing ground. In 1839 both the Honourable Company, by then reinstituted and playing at Musselburgh, and the Royal Perth Golfing Society adopted the identical rule:

> At the commencement of the day, if the parties cannot agree which of them is to play first, a toss must take place, and whoever wins it plays first or not, as he or they please. If the party not entitled to it play first at any hole, the ball may be either taken back, and played in its proper order, or it may be held as the regular teed stroke, in the adversary's option.

Despite the somewhat tortured language, this rule is essentially the same as our present rule governing the order of play on the tee in match play.

He, whose Ball lyes farthest from the Hole is obliged to play first.

"Old Captains never die, they just drive off first."

The St. Andrews golfers quickly followed the lead of their fellows in Perth and Musselburgh, adopting a similar rule in their 1842 code:

> The person entitled to play off first shall be named by the parties themselves; and although the courtesy of starting is generally granted to old captains or members, it may be settled by lot or toss of a coin .... The party gaining the hole is to lead, and is entitled to claim his privilege and to recall his adversary's stroke should he play out of order.

Aleatory

Perhaps the St. Andrews golfers adopted the motto "Old Captains never die, they just drive off first," because they continued to defer to those of senior rank through their 1891 code. Chance has ruled since 1899 ("The option of taking the honour at the first teeing-ground shall be decided, if necessary, by lot" in the words of their code of that year.) The term *honor* to describe the privilege of hitting off first didn't appear in any code of rules before the 1882 R&A code, although it certainly had been part of the vocabulary of golfers for some years by then.

Teeing Ground

Teeing Ground

The term *teeing ground* is the precise and official word for what golfers in everyday usage generally call the *tee*. Since the word *tee* is also often used in everyday golf language to refer to the small peg the ball is placed on, as well as to the activity of placing the ball on it, a certain amount of confusion is possible in discussing the teeing ground and teeing the ball.

DISTINCTIVE CURLING LINGO

The term *tee* is, as a matter of fact, one of the most problematic terms in golf. Its meaning is uncertain, but it seems probable that it has the same origin as the identical term in curling, another ancient Scottish game with origins equally obscure as those of golf. Since our first reliable records of golf come from the middle of the eighteenth century and those of curling from the early nineteenth, there's no way of knowing if there's a direct connection. It would seem reasonable, though, to assume a common origin for an identical term in two games that developed roughly at the same time in the same place (the

CURLING ON A NEW ENGLAND POND, 1895.

93

GOLFER TEEING OFF SAND.

Scottish Lowlands) and that were played to a great extent by the same people. Even today many Scottish golfers are also curlers.

In curling, the term *tee* refers to a small hole drilled in the ice that serves as a target for the stones sent sliding toward it. In earlier days, the tee was sometimes marked with a pin or button or other small object to make the target point more visible. Nowadays the tee is surrounded by a set of circles of varying size, color, and number to make it easier to measure the distance of the stones from the tee after they come to rest.

Parts of Speech

In golf, the term *tee* is used as both noun and verb. By analogy with its usage in curling, it would seem most reasonable to assume that it was also first used in golf as a noun, perhaps originally even to refer to the target. As far back as written sources go, however, the term is used as both noun and verb, so any change in usage must have developed very early in the history of golf. Its use in the earliest sources refers to the point from which play was to be initiated for each hole, not to a target, but it may be significant that this point was in the immediate vicinity of the target for the preceding hole, as prescribed in the first of the Thirteen Articles of the Gentlemen Golfers in 1744:

You must Tee your Ball within a Club's length of the Hole.

A number of etymologies have been proposed for the term *tee* by both golf and curling historians, most of them quite fanciful. While there's no way we can be entirely sure of the exact meaning of this term central to these two games, a common origin seems most likely.

TOO CLOSE

It was apparently felt, even in the eighteenth century, that there were disadvantages with driving off so close to the hole as a single club-length. In 1773 the Society of Golfers in and about Edinburgh at Bruntsfield Links (now the Royal Burgess Golfing Society) adopted a rule that "no Ball shall be teed nearer the Hole than two Club lengths, nor farther from it than four." Two years later the Gentlemen Golfers adopted this same limitation in their new code of rules. Yet another two years later, on 20 December 1777, the "Captain and his Council" of the Society of St. Andrews Golfers passed a special resolution that

> none of the Society shall tee their Golf Balls within less than a Play Club length of the hole from which they are to Strick off, nor at a greater distance than Four lengths of said Club from the hole.

This resolution remained in force until 1812, when the St. Andrews golfers adopted a new code of rules that included the two to four club-length rule of their fellows in Edinburgh. Thus, during the final decades of the eighteenth century, the area in the immediate vicinity of the hole was off driving limits for the golfers of the most important rules-making clubs. This sensible development was, however, not followed by all golfing societies. The Society of Golfers at Aberdeen and the Crail Golfing Society continued to tee the ball within, respectively, two and three club-lengths of the hole during the rest of the eighteenth century.

SURELY MORE IS BETTER

In 1851, the St. Andrews golfers, who by then had become the Royal and Ancient Golf Club of St. Andrews, began a gradual extension of the teeing area. In its new code adopted that year, the R&A set the distance between four and six club-lengths and referred to it as "a place called the *tee*." In 1858 the R&A set the teeing area still farther from the hole—to between six and eight club-lengths. The next extension came in the 1875 code, which also provided for the possible use of separate teeing grounds:

> The Ball must be teed not nearer the hole than eight nor further than twelve club lengths, except where special ground has been marked by the Conservator of the Links, which shall be considered the "Teeing Ground," and the Balls shall be teed within and not in advance of such marks.

The R&A codes of 1882 and 1888 refer only to such separate teeing grounds:

> The ball must be teed within the marks laid down by the Conservator of the Links, which shall be considered the "Teeing Ground." The balls shall not be teed in advance of such marks, nor more than two club lengths behind them.

The 1875 code provided for the use of separate teeing grounds.

95

COMING INTO FOCUS

The separate teeing ground was defined still more clearly in the code adopted by the R&A in 1891:

> The teeing ground shall be indicated by two marks placed in a line at right angles to the course, and the player shall not tee in front of, nor on either side of, these marks, nor more than two club lengths behind them. A ball played from outside the limits of the teeing ground, as thus defined, may be recalled by the opposite side.

With very few exceptions, the establishment in 1882 of separate teeing grounds was quickly adopted by other clubs and has remained a permanent part of the rules of golf to this day. Clearly, the wording of the R&A's 1891 provision for recall of a ball played from outside the teeing ground applied to match play. This match play rule is still in effect today, although its wording has varied through the years. The specific provision that the stroke was to be replayed without penalty was added in 1902, it only being implied before then.

No mention of play from outside the teeing ground in stroke play was made in the separate "Special Rules for Medal Play" in the 1891 code. In the code proposed by the Wimbledon Golf Club in 1883, which made the first attempt to combine the rules for match and stroke play, the wording of the pertinent rule was:

> The ball must be teed within the limits of the ground marked out for the purpose, and not more than two club-lengths behind the front line. In match play the penalty for the infringement of this rule shall be the recall of the stroke at the option of the opponent. In medal play the stroke must be recalled, the penalty being the loss of the stroke.

When in 1899 the R&A did make provision for this situation in stroke play, the penalty was severe: disqualification. This harsh penalty remained in effect throughout the entire golfing world until 1908, when it was modified:

> If at any hole a competitor play his first stroke from outside the limits of the teeing-ground, he shall count that stroke, tee a ball, and play his second stroke from within these limits. The penalty for a breach of this Rule shall be disqualification.

There was no substantive change in this rule until the combined R&A-USGA code of 1952. This code required that the player

> count that stroke and any subsequent stroke so played and then play from within the teeing ground with the privilege of teeing his ball.

This rule in turn remained in effect until 1980, when the present rule was adopted, which assigns two penalty strokes but nullifies any strokes made from outside the teeing ground.

St. Andrews golfers adopted a rule that required new holes to be cut on medal days, when all putts had to be holed.

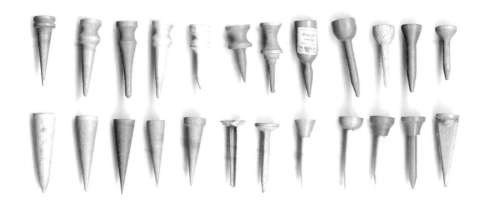

RARE MIXED TEES,
CIRCA 1920–1930.

The specific provision that the player may stand outside the teeing ground to play a ball within its limits was added to the rule in 1933.

Teeing the Ball

The act of teeing the ball has varied greatly at different stages of the game. In the eighteenth century, a golfer teed his ball on a small mound of sand, which was the traditional method as far back as any mention is made of such things. Schoolmaster David Wedderburn's Latin vocabulary of golf terms from 1636 contains the gloss "*Statumina pilam arena*—teaz your ball on the sand." The boxes that can still be found on the teeing grounds of many Scottish golf courses (nowadays generally used as refuse baskets) held sand to be used for this purpose well into this century. Such boxes also were found on the links in the early days of golf in the United States. Sand-filled tee boxes figured prominently in the great golf-playing sequences in Charlie Chaplin's 1921 comedy *The Idle Class*.

SUCH QUANTITIES OF SAND

In the early days of the game, before such boxes of sand were provided, golfers fetched sand or soil for their tees from any nearby source, often from the very hole to which they had just played. As a result the hole grew in size, since there were no hole-liners and new holes were cut only infrequently. As early as 1829 the St. Andrews golfers adopted a rule that required new holes to be cut on medal days, when all putts had to be holed. This rule is still in force today as present Rule 33-2b. The Company of Edinburgh Golfers (later The Royal Burgess Golfing Society) had adopted a rule in 1773 forbidding tees made from anything within ten yards of the hole. A number of other clubs followed suit. Musselburgh Golf Club adopted this rule in 1829, then went a step further in 1834 and banned any "Cady . . . who does not carry a bag with moist sand or clay for the tees."

MOTHER EARTH WINCES

The eighteenth-century golfer might also have made a welt in the turf with an iron club or the heel of his boot, as some players still do. We have no direct proof of this, but there's good negative evidence in the fact that in 1786 The Crail Golfing Society adopted a rule that required the player not "to break the ground on the teeing of his ball." Other golf clubs, such as Perth, Blackheath, and Musselburgh adopted similar rules against breaking or raising the turf to tee the ball during the early nineteenth century. This seems perfectly reasonable because the ball was teed only a short distance from the hole in those days. *(See the preceding section: Teeing Ground.)* It's actually surprising that more clubs didn't follow suit, but neither the Society of St. Andrews Golfers nor the Honourable Company nor any of the other Edinburgh clubs seemed concerned about this type of damage to the area near the hole. At least they never adopted any rule to discourage it. Perhaps the explanation is that the golfers of Edinburgh and St. Andrews were a more civilized lot than their fellows elsewhere and didn't engage in such barbaric practices as welting the ground in the immediate vicinity of the hole.

UPLIFTING CHATTER

An interesting definition of the term *tee* is provided by H. B. Farnie in his well-known work *The Golfer's Manual,* published in 1857:

A pat of soil on which the ball is elevated for the first stroke.

Horace G. Hutchinson gave a slightly different definition in his *Golf*, published in The Badminton Library in 1890:

The pat of sand on which the ball is placed for the first stroke each hole.

The somewhat cryptic Article 2 ("Your Tee must be upon the Ground") in the first written code of rules from 1744 was apparently not entirely clear to all players even in the eighteenth century. In 1776 The Company of Edinburgh Golfers amended it to read:

Your Tee must be on the ground and unconnected with any Conductor or leader to the Ball.

This edict would seem to have banned once and for all the use of any artificial connection between the ball and the ground, but toward the end of the nineteenth century various ball-elevating devices became common, and are now almost universally used.

Actually, there was nothing in the 1924 rules that legislated against such an extraordinary teeing device as that used by Harold Gillies. The R&A could do no more than administer a mild slap on the wrist to Dr. Gillies, but since 1960 all such things have been kept under control by some variant of Rule 14-3: "Artificial Devices and Unusual Equipment." Any equipment contrary to the tradition and spirit of the game can now be banned outright after review by the equipment watchdogs of the USGA and R&A.

Now We're in Business

The first official definition of teeing the ball appeared in the code adopted in 1908:

> In "teeing" the ball may be placed on the ground, or on sand or other substance in order to raise it off the ground.

This would seem to incorporate both Farnie's and Hutchinson's definitions above, as well as any sort of artificial device. This definition appeared, unchanged, in all subsequent codes through 1976. It was modified slightly in 1980:

> In "teeing," the ball may be placed on the ground, on an irregularity of surface created by the player on the ground or on sand or other substance in order to raise it off the ground.

Higher, Higher

Some players have gone to great extremes in exploring teeing devices. The best known such player was Harold Gillies (later Sir Harold Gillies, knighted for his pioneering contributions to plastic surgery). In 1924 he apparently decided to see how far things could be carried. During the British Amateur Championship at St. Andrews he teed his ball up on a piece of rubber tubing attached to the neck of a beer bottle, then struck the ball great distances with a sweeping blow of a large-headed driver. The Royal and Ancient Golf Club, in front of whose dignified clubhouse this sacrilege was carried out, was definitely not amused. A notice was posted requesting that golfers not make use of "abnormal methods of play, or abnormal implements" and deploring that players "should endeavour to overcome the difficulties of the game by using implements which have never been associated with it." It can be seriously questioned whether beer bottles should be described as "implements which have never been associated with" golf, but at any rate they've not traditionally been used in connection with teeing the ball.

The objections of those early nineteenth-century clubs that had adopted rules forbidding welting the ground in the vicinity of the hole thus were finally overcome, but by 1980 all teeing had long been done far from the green of the preceding hole.

At Long Last

In 1984 the definition of teeing was taken out of the Definitions section of the rules and established as the first paragraph of Rule 11-1. One slight addition was made in 1984: the noun form *tee*, referring to the small peg nowadays used by almost all golfers, was finally given official recognition, so that now the ball can officially be placed "on the ground, on an irregularity of surface created by the player on the ground or on a tee, sand or other substance." This definition still allows quite a bit of latitude in the selection of a teeing device, so there should be no reason to stray outside the limits of golfing propriety and tradition.

Searching for and Identifying the Ball

Rule 12 is a rare thing in the world of golf rules: it requires us modern golfers to perform under more difficult conditions than our golf-playing forefathers had to put up with. We have to abide by the regulation: "A player is not necessarily entitled to see his ball when playing a stroke." If your ball is buried in deep grass you're allowed to part the grass enough to see and identify your ball, but if the grass then falls back and covers your ball, as it often does, you have to swing blindly.

WHYEVER WOULD YOU NEED TO SEE IT?

Eighteenth-century codes of rules had nothing to say on the subject, but the first nineteenth-century code drawn up by the Honourable Company, in 1809, allowed the player "a view of his ball before he plays." The St. Andrews golfers followed suit in 1812 and this right to see the ball became a permanent fixture in all the important codes of the nineteenth century. The Honourable Company adopted a new code in 1839 that placed this rule under the heading "Entitled to see the Ball." This heading was incorporated into the codes of many other clubs, including all R&A codes between 1842 and 1888.

If the grass falls back and covers your ball, you have to swing blindly.

**GOLFERS SEARCHING THE ROUGH AT THE
1991 U.S. AMATEUR, THE HONORS COURSE.**

In the first code of rules drawn up by the newly appointed Rules of Golf Committee, the R&A code of 1899, the rule began to change. The new 1899 rule allowed the player to touch only so much of the offending grass "as will enable the player to find his ball." He was no longer expressly allowed to have a view of the ball when he played, but he wasn't denied a view of it, either. There was no change in the rule until the USGA and the R&A issued codes independently of each other in, respectively, 1946 and 1950. The USGA legislated that the player "is not of necessity entitled to a sight of the ball when playing his stroke but must play the ball as it lies." The R&A was more modest in its demands but rephrased the old rule somewhat to allow only so much grass to be touched "as will enable the player to find and identify his ball; nothing shall be done which can in any way improve its lie." The USGA and the R&A harmonized the slight differences in their rules on this point and arrived at a formulation in their first joint code in 1952 that is essentially identical to our present rule.

EVERY GROWING THING

Another significant modernizing change was made in the rule in 1952. The original 1809 Honourable Company version referred to the ball being "completely covered with fog or grass" while the 1812 St. Andrews referred to "fog, bent, whins, etc." This doesn't make much sense to us nowadays unless we know that both "fog" and "bent" denote varieties of heavy grass common in the dank climate of Britain. Local conditions could make a difference, however: "nettles" is substituted for "fog" in all the codes of rules adopted by the golfers playing at Blackheath in London from 1844 on. The revision seems to indicate that the grassy variety of fog was rare at Blackheath (at least rarer than nettles), although the meteorological variety certainly isn't, not now and probably not then. The 1946 USGA rule mentions only "bushes, long grass, or the like" while the 1950 R&A rule was extremely garrulous: "in fog, bent, long grass, rushes, or the like or in bushes, whins, heather, or the like." In the 1952 compromise version the more important British obstacles were retained: "long grass, rushes, bushes, whins, heather, or the like." This list of nasties has been retained to this day.

Our present rule on finding and playing a ball in a hazard developed from similar rules in both the 1946 USGA code and the 1950 R&A code. The 1952 version allowed the player to uncover as much of the ball as needed to enable him to see it. Not until 1988 was the condition added that any excess removed had to be replaced. From 1972 on, the player has been allowed to probe for a ball in a water hazard "with a club or otherwise." These rules on searching for a ball in a hazard were part of the rule on hazards until the 1984 reorganization, when they were moved to their present location.

IS IT MINE?

The first rule specifically allowing a player to lift his ball for identification appeared in 1908. It was a short, concise rule at that time:

> A ball in play may, with the opponent's consent, be lifted for the purpose of identification, but it must be carefully replaced.

The rule gradually grew longer, as conditions were added ("except in a hazard"), but through 1980 it was still reasonably concise. Our present extremely detailed wording (Rule 12-2) was adopted in 1984. Little essential was added, but just about every possible contingency is specifically mentioned now, for better or for worse.

| RULE 13 | # Ball Played as It Lies |

Acceptance of the conditions which the player finds on the course is a vital part of the game.

Many golfers lament the length and complexity of the rules of golf, and it has often been claimed that the game could be played perfectly well with many fewer rules. It has even been suggested that stating the two principles contained in the traditional golfing wisdom quoted above would suffice. Our present Rule 13 combines these two basic principles. Richard S. Tufts emphasized their importance in 1960 in his excellent collection of essays *The Principles Behind the Rules of Golf:*

> One of the great features of golf is that it tests the player's ability to execute a great assortment of strokes under a perplexing variety of conditions. Golf would cease to be a game of skill if the player were permitted to get the best of the conditions which confront him through their elimination rather than to overcome them by the expert execution of his stroke. . . . The acceptance of the conditions which the player finds on the course is therefore a vital part of the game.

SHORT AND SWEET

The simple, short sentence making up our present Rule 13-1 is of the utmost importance in both the rules themselves and their history:

> The ball shall be played as it lies, except as otherwise provided in the Rules.

The history of the development of the rules of golf has to a great extent occupied itself with defining the exceptions allowed for in this statement. This is in itself no small matter, as Richard S. Francis pointed out in 1937 in his book *Golf, Its Rules and Decisions:* "Of course, the Rule has to be as it is, but 'except as otherwise provided' is a big phrase."

Some commentators have found it odd that the basic requirement that the ball be played as it lies wasn't mentioned in the original thirteen articles

104

of the Gentlemen Golfers in 1744. They assume that this was because it was a generally accepted rule that needed no mentioning, but there's actually nothing in any of the early codes that allows us to make this assumption. To the contrary, just the opposite may have been a basic principle of the game from earliest times, allowing the player to lift and drop at any time on loss of a stroke—just as we may nowadays.

PROBING MORE DEEPLY

The confusion that reigns on this point may be caused by a difference in interpretation. What we mean by "playing the ball as it lies" and what the golfers of the eighteenth century meant may be two different things. When we say that we play the ball as it lies, we're fully aware that we have the option of declaring it unplayable anywhere on the course and lifting and dropping it elsewhere on loss of a stroke. We then play the ball as it may happen to be lying—unless we decide it's still unplayable and lift and drop it again, in which case we have to pay another stroke penalty. If we decide not to exercise the unplayable ball option at all, we play the ball as it happens to be lying. That's what we mean when we say that we play the ball as it lies. When the late-eighteenth-century golfer used the same phrase, he meant that he had no other option but to play the ball as it was lying, unless he was specifically granted an exception. All the written codes adopted between 1744 and the end of the eighteenth century included such specific exceptions, usually involving water or "made" hazards.

ONE PERSPECTIVE

C. B. Clapcott, the most thorough commentator on early rules, was of the opinion that before 1744 the player had the right to declare the ball "unplayable" (to use a modern term) and lift it upon loss of a stroke at any time.

In 1945 Clapcott wrote the article "Some Comments on the Articles and Laws in Playing the Golf" in which he commented in detail on the 1744 code of the Gentlemen Golfers of Leith and wrote up a code of rules as he thought they might have been a hundred years earlier. He proposed that golfers in the middle of the seventeenth century might have played by such a rule as

> You may lift your Ball anywhere and allow your Adversary a stroke for so doing.

It was his opinion that the drafters of late eighteenth-century codes were experimenting with limiting this right to lift the ball anywhere. They were, in any event, struggling with the problem of when the ball was to be played as it lay and when it could be lifted.

FIRST RULES HISTORIAN

C. B. Clapcott was the first to become interested in the early development of the rules of golf. Born in 1867 and trained in law at Cambridge, he spent many years serving on the bench in Egypt. After his retirement in 1923 he moved to the London borough of Chelsea (where he was mayor in 1929), joined Royal Wimbledon Golf Club, and started investigating early codes of rules. His major contribution was a small volume, now a collector's item, entitled *The Rules of Golf of the Ten Oldest Golf Clubs*, published in Edinburgh in 1935. He also wrote several articles on the history of the Honourable Company and the rules of golf, which Alastair J. Johnston has published in his excellent collection *The Clapcott Papers*.

EXCEPTIONS PROVE THE RULE

According to Article 5 of the rules drawn up for the inaugural tournament in 1744, the ball could be lifted when it lay "among Watter, or any Wattery Filth" (upon loss of a stroke), but according to Article 10 had to be played "where it lyes" after interference by an outside agency ("by any person, horse, dog, or anything else" in the phraseology of that day). In 1775 The Gentlemen Golfers, now calling themselves The Golfing Company, adopted a new code that stated clearly that the ball "must be played where it lyes" except when it was in "a made Hazard, or in any of the Water-tracts for draining the Links." The following year the golfers at Bruntsfield Links allowed a ball in water to be dropped behind the hazard at the cost of a stroke, but they required that "if it be in the Meadow Ditch it must be played where it lies."

It comes as quite a surprise, then, that a completely different approach was taken to the problem in most of the new codes adopted in the first decades of the nineteenth century. The Edinburgh Burgess Golfers, the Honourable Company, and the newly reconstituted Aberdeen Golf Club all adopted new codes between 1807 and 1815 that included rules allowing the ball to be lifted "at any time," "in every case," or "at all times" upon loss of a stroke. The Aberdonians had, as usual, the most modern way of looking at the matter. They allowed the player "at all times" to lift and "drop the ball over the back of his head, which must then be played however it lies." That is, they played the ball "as it lies" in exactly the same sense that we do now (but dropped it very differently). *(See Rule 20.)* Only the new 1812 code of the St. Andrews golfers continued to permit lifting only in specific cases. There's no way for us to know whether or not the practice of the majority of these clubs was a return to an earlier rule, as Clapcott suggests, but the problem continued to be a major concern of rules-makers during the remainder of the nineteenth century. *(See also Rule 28: Ball Unplayable.)*

A HAZARD BY ANY OTHER NAME

Most of the Definitions section of our present Rule 13 is taken up with definitions of "hazards." Although the term was employed frequently in the many codes of rules during the eighteenth and nineteenth centuries, no definition of it was given before the 1891 R&A code. This first definition was extremely broad and included many items no longer classified as hazards:

> A "hazard" shall be any bunker of whatever nature:—water, sand, loose earth, mole-hills, paths, roads or railways, whins, bushes, rushes, rabbit-scrapes, fences, ditches, or anything which is not the ordinary green of the course, except sand blown on to the grass by wind, or sprinkled on grass for the preservation of the links, or snow or ice, or bare patches on the course.

THE BRIAR PATCH

The 1891 definition of hazards quickly reveals its Scottish roots, including items of special significance in the history of the game in Scotland: railways, rabbit-scrapes, whins, rushes, and sand and more sand. Among the items in this list of hazards whins deserve special mention. Also known as gorse or furze and going under the Latin name of *Ulex europaeus*, this particularly fierce member of the pea family (Leguminosae) is a monstrous hazard by any name, although it no longer technically is one. Its long, sharp spines guarantee that a ball sunk six feet deep in its bosom is just as irretrievably unplayable as one sunk six feet deep in water.

This broad definition of hazards remained in force for several decades. As new codes were adopted in the first decades of our century, elements of the definition gradually dropped out, but as recently as in the code of 1933 it still had the form:

> A "Hazard" is any bunker, water (except "casual water,") ditch, sand or road. Sand blown on to the grass, or sprinkled on the Course for its preservation, bare patches, scrapes, tracks and paths, snow, ice and casual water are not hazards.

The codes issued separately by the USGA in 1946 and the R&A in 1950 both contained definitions essentially identical to this 1933 definition. The breakthrough in modernizing the definition of hazards came with the first joint USGA-R&A code in 1952:

> A "hazard" is any bunker, or water hazard. Bare patches, scrapes, roads, tracks and paths are not "hazards."

This definition is identical to our present definition, with the second sentence omitted, since the modern golfer is used to accepting such items as integral parts of the course unless declared otherwise by Local Rule.

WHIN OR LOSE

The definition of hazards is of primary importance, because it determines where loose impediments may be touched and moved and where the club may be grounded. *(See Rule 23: Loose Impediments.)* Both these actions are specifically forbidden in Rule 13-4. The purpose of the injunction against grounding the club in a hazard is not to forbid touching the ground of the hazard per se but to ensure that the condition of the hazard isn't changed in any way whatsoever. This intent is made clear even in the earliest reference to this principle in the rules, in the 1773 code of the "Society of Golfers, in and about Edinburgh, at Bruntsfield Links" (now The Royal Burgess Golfing Society):

> Every Golfer addressing himself to his Ball shall not have liberty to put down Earth, sand or anything else, nor in drawing his stroke take anything away from behind his Ball except a Stone or a Bone.

The next statement of this principle in the rules, referring more specifically to play in hazards, appeared in the 1815 code of the Aberdeen golfers.

> In playing out of sand or loose ground, the player shall neither beat down nor draw away the sand or soil from the ball, nor shall the player through the green beat down or alter the ground about the ball before playing, under the penalty of one stroke.

Every Golfer addressing himself to his Ball shall not have liberty to put down Earth, sand or anything else.

Throwing in the Towel

Present-day golfers happen to know the rule against building a stance better than many others because of the well-publicized incident in the third round of the 1987 San Diego Open when Craig Stadler was penalized under the rule because he spread a towel to kneel on while playing a shot from under a tree. It occurred to no one present at the scene of this crime that this constituted an

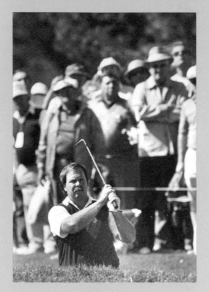

infringement of a rule, although a Decision (present Decision 13-3/2) had recently been issued on a similar case. It wasn't until the next day, after a television viewer saw a replay and called in, that Stadler was disqualified for having turned in a scorecard that failed to include two penalty strokes. The irony of the situation was that the television viewer thought he was watching a live event and was only trying to warn the Walrus that he had to include the penalty on his scorecard.

This surprisingly comprehensive early rule includes the essence of both our present Rules 13-2 and 13-4. It remained for the 1839 code of the Honourable Company to express the principle clearly in reference to hazards:

> When the Ball is in sand, or in a hazard, the player must take care, in aiming at the Ball, that he does not alter or improve its position.

The St. Andrews golfers followed in 1842 with a rule that clarified the issue further:

> When a ball lies in a bunker or sand, there shall be no impression made or sand removed by the club before or in playing.

TAKING A STAND

In the R&A code of 1858 the phrase "before or in playing" was changed to "before striking at the ball," and the rule remained in this form until the R&A adopted its greatly revised code of 1891. At that time the rule took on a more modern form and included the first mention in the nineteenth century of problems connected with taking a stance:

> When a ball lies in or touches a hazard, the club shall not touch the ground, nor shall anything be touched or moved before the player strikes at the ball, except that the player may place his feet firmly on the ground for the purpose of addressing the ball, under the penalty of the loss of the hole.

The widespread adoption of our modern principle of not "building a stance" was late in coming about. The Aberdeen golfers were also in this respect ahead of their time when they took up the problem in 1783:

> No person shall be at liberty to vary or better his Stance in playing, by breaking the Surface of the Green, by placing or removing Stones, Sand, or any other Substance ....

This early initiative, however, was not followed up by other clubs.

The wording permitting the placing of the feet firmly on the ground "for the purpose of addressing the ball" in the 1891 code quoted above remained in force until 1920, when it was changed to entitle the player "to place his feet firmly on the ground when taking his stance." In 1933 a final phrase was added to this formulation: "but he is not allowed to build a stance." From this point on, only the slightest linguistic changes have been necessary to produce our present Rule 13-3.

A Pure and Simple Accident

A recent important change in Rule 13 came in 1992, when relief was provided for the situation in which a player accidentally touches the ground in a hazard as the result of falling or in trying to keep from falling. This rule change was based on a Decision adopted as long ago as 1954. This time lapse exemplifies the basically cautious approach to changes in the rules taken by the rules-makers. The mills of the Rules Committees do indeed grind slowly, but they also grind exceeding small.

Striking the Ball

The most crucial element in the game of golf is the act of striking the ball. The ball may be moved by means of contact with the club in many ways, but not all of these are necessarily acts of striking. Accidental contact between club and ball is not considered to be a stroke. In order for a stroke to be performed, the player must intend to strike the ball. This is the kernel of our modern definition of the stroke.

FAIRLY STRUCK

Defining the stroke in terms of intention to strike goes back to the 1883 code of rules of the Wimbledon Golf Club. This code contains a number of original features, but none more original than the definition of the stroke found in it:

> The ball must be fairly struck, and not "pushed," "scraped," or "spooned," and any movement of the club, made with the intention of striking at the ball, must be considered a stroke."

This definition was adopted with slightly different wording of its second clause in the next revision of the rules adopted by the R&A, in 1891:

> Any movement of the club which is intended to strike the ball is a stroke.

Nowadays we specify that the movement must be a forward movement, but the definition of the stroke has remained in all important respects unchanged from 1883 until today.

JUST WHAT IS IT, PRAY?

Although our modern definition of the stroke first appeared in 1883, the problem of what constitutes a stroke occupied the writers of the rules long before that. Their primary concern was not to define the stroke as such, however, but to make allowance for the unfortunate contingency of a club breaking during a stroke. In the early days of the game, before metal shafts were taken into use, this was an ever-present danger and was recognized as such in Article 11 of the original code of 1744:

> If you draw your Club, in order to Strike & proceed so far in the Stroke, as to be bringing down your Club; If then, your Club shall break, in, any way, it is to be Accounted a Stroke.

For a stroke to be performed, the player must intend to strike the ball.

Some version of this rule appeared in all the important codes through the 1888 R&A code. The version in the Honourable Company's 1775 code served as model for all later versions:

> If, in striking, your club breaks, it is nevertheless to be accounted a stroke, if you strike the ground, or pass the Ball with the club.

Even the version in the 1888 R&A code differs only in the final clause:

> If, in striking, the club breaks, it is nevertheless to be counted a stroke, if the part of the club remaining in the player's hand either strike the ground, or pass the ball.

Something More Precise, Please

This formulation actually implies a definition of the stroke, but such an excessively vague and roundabout one that not all golfers in the eighteenth and early nineteenth century were satisfied by it. The Aberdeen golfers made an attempt in 1783 to develop a more rigorous definition:

> If a Stroke is made, and the Club pass the Ball and strike the Ground, it shall be reckoned against the Player; though the Ball be mist, or the Club happen to be broke.

In 1815 the Aberdonians made another attempt, and came closer to a true definition:

> All strokes aimed at the ball must count, whether the ball be hit or not, even if in striking the club should break.

It Needs Defining

It remained for the drafters of the code of rules adopted by the Montrose Golf Club in 1830 to reach an actual definition of the stroke. They based their 1830 code on the 1809 Honourable Company code, but were also influenced by the 1815 Aberdeen code. Their version of the Aberdeen rule reads:

> Every attempt to strike shall be considered a stroke, whether or not the Club break, touch the ground or pass the Ball.

In this formulation they came close to the modern concept of intention in the stroke, but their club wasn't influential in matters dealing with the rules and their initiative wasn't followed. It remained for the Wimbledon golfers to originate our modern definition of the stroke 53 years later.

PALL-MALL

The problem of clubs breaking plagued the players of games other than golf in earlier centuries. A good example of this is given in a set of rules drawn up in 1717 by one Joseph Lauthier for the French game *Jeu de mail*, known in

A GENTLEMAN PLAYING *JEU DE MAIL* **OR PALL-MALL, 1717.**

Britain as pall-mall. (The street in London named Pall Mall was a court for playing the game during the middle decades of the seventeenth century.) The implement used to strike the ball was mallet-headed, but with a shaft as long and whippy as that of eighteenth-century golf "playclubs." The game resembled croquet more than golf, the goal being a hoop or suspended metal ring, but was considerably more athletic than croquet. The ball was hit with a swing similar to the golf swing of that day, so there was more than enough force generated to break the mallet.

Links to Yet Another Game

Lauthier's rule book was translated into English and published in St. Andrews in 1910. Because golfers were involved in its publication, it's not surprising that the terminology employed is quite similar, as we can see from the wording of the translation of the rule concerning the stroke:

> Any player who misses the globe, or as it is commonly expressed, makes a twirl *(pirouette)*, loses a stroke. When the mallet breaks or when the head flies off in a downward stroke, the stroke is counted, if the head passes the ball: but if the head remains behind the ball, the stroke is cancelled, and the player begins again without losing anything.

The term *globe,* meaning a golf ball, was common at the turn of the century and is found in various glossaries of golf terminology from that time.

Sometimes You Wonder

It's tempting to speculate about possible influences of the rules of the French game of *Jeu de mail* on the early rules of golf. We know that the game of pall-mall was played in Scotland as well as in England, although the evidence is scant. (Mary Queen of Scots was criticized for playing pall-mall, as well as golf, at Seton shortly after the death of her husband, in 1567.) The similarities between a number of the rules could possibly be explained by a knowledge of the rules of pall-mall on the part of the Gentlemen Golfers in Leith in 1744, but it would seem to be just as likely that those similarities were due to the partial similarities in the two games: all ball and club games resemble each other to some degree. The greatest similarity between the two sets of rules is found in the rule governing clubs breaking quoted above, and that similarity is perhaps best explained by similarity of equipment and circumstances in the two games rather than by direct influence, for which there is no reliable evidence.

Nice and Clear, Finally

All talk about clubs breaking dropped out of the rules of golf in 1891. There's no longer any necessity to provide for this contingency since the modern definition of the stroke is broad enough to cover the case where a club breaks, rare as it may be nowadays. It does still happen, though, and several Decisions have been handed down dealing with such accidents (present Decisions 14/2, 3, 4, 5). These provide clear guidelines: if the club breaks during the backswing, no stroke is considered to have been made with what remains in the player's hands (since it's no longer a club). However, once the downswing has begun with a whole club, which then breaks, a stroke must be reckoned unless the player is able to check the forward movement of the club.

A MISS IS AS GOOD AS A MILE

An especially tricky situation arises in golf if the player for some reason or other intentionally misses the ball. It's clear from the definition of the stroke that no stroke has been made in such a case, and therefore a problem of interpretation arises. An early Decision, made in 1911 by the Rules of Golf Committee on the basis of an inquiry submitted by the Brisbane Golf Club, covered this situation:

> **In a mixed foursome competition, at the 17th tee, from which a creek has to be carried, A drove out of bounds. B thought she was unable to carry the creek, so her partner openly, and in the hearing of their opponents, told her to miss the ball—B did so. Later A mentioned the incident to other players, stating the miss was intentional.**

The Decision handed down was unequivocal:

> **B's action was not a "Stroke" and therefore her partner played out of turn. A and B are disqualified.**

This Decision has stood the test of time, and its current form is found in Decision 29-1/7.

THEY'RE NOT PLAYING HOCKEY

Intention seems also to have played a role in the evolution of another rule now included under Rule 14: striking the ball more than once (14-4). This contingency was first taken into account in two codes of rules adopted in 1839, one by the Royal Perth Golfing Society and the other by the Honourable Company (then playing at Musselburgh). They both penalized with loss of hole the player who "strikes twice at the ball." This penalty may have been directed at players who in this way tried to redirect errant putts. The R&A was quick to pick up on this in their new code in 1842, but included the case where the second strike is unintentional. The player lost the hole "if he strikes the ball or strikes at it twice, before it stops motion." During the 1850s the

An especially tricky situation arises if the player intentionally misses the ball.

113

R&A decided it was all the same whether the second strike was intentional or unintentional, and by 1858 their rule was formulated:

> or if he strikes the ball a second time while in the act of playing, the player loses the hole . . . .

Varied Locutions

Since 1858, striking the ball more than once during the same stroke has been penalized in every important code of rules, but the exact formulation of the rule has shown considerable variation. Striking the ball "a second time" yielded to "twice" in the R&A code of 1875 and finally to "more than once" in 1984, to make allowance for those rare occasions when a ball is struck three or more times with one stroke (a neat trick if you can pull it off). The phrase "in the act of playing" gave way to "in the act of striking," then to "when making a stroke," and finally (also in 1984) to "in the course of a stroke." Perhaps no other rule illustrates so well the linguistic tinkering and fiddling that has gone on during the development of the rules of golf.

Before 1882 no mention was made of striking the ball more than once in the rules for stroke play, but at that time a one-stroke penalty was applied. This one-stroke penalty replaced loss of hole in match play in 1899, and since then the penalty has been the same in both forms of play.

Shuffled About from Here to There

This injunction against hitting the ball more than once was initially included, in all the codes in which it was adopted, in the rule covering "rubs of the green." It remained in close contact with this rule throughout the nineteenth century, but at the beginning of the twentieth century it set out on a lonely wandering existence that lasted until 1952, when it was united with the rule requiring the ball to be fairly struck at (present Rule 14-1). In 1984, these two rules were combined with a number of others to form present Rule 14. The separate rules governing playing a moving ball (14-5) and a ball moving in water (14-6) had both entered the R&A-USGA codes in 1908, but had for years been relegated to locations far distant from each other.

EXPOSED TO THE STORM

Our present Rule 14-2, which prohibits receiving any physical assistance or protection from the elements, first appeared in 1968. It was at that time attached to the rule prohibiting giving or asking for advice and indicating the line of play (present Rule 8), but also was moved to its present position in 1984.

No other rule illustrates so well the linguistic tinkering and fiddling that has gone on during the development of the rules of golf.

NO GADGETS ALLOWED

The USGA-R&A code of 1968 was the first to prohibit the use of artificial devices which might assist the player "in making a stroke or in his play," now the first clause of Rule 14-3. Devices for measuring or gauging distance had already been barred in 1960. Regulations affecting the grip came in 1976 (before then they had been included in the rule governing the form and make of clubs). All these clauses were for many years part of the rule defining the responsibilities of the player (present Rule 6), but were also moved in 1984 to their present position.

The composition of Rule 14 is among the best examples of the principles behind the 1984 reorganization of the rules. It illustrates how rules covering related aspects of one area of the game were collected into one place. All its six clauses deal in one way or another with the act of making a stroke and therefore belong together, according to the theory behind that reorganization.

**ARCHIE GRAHAM
(DATE UNKNOWN).**

RULE 15 Playing a Wrong Ball

Our present Rule 15 stems from the first joint USGA-R&A code of 1952. It has been slightly rephrased and recast several times since then, but has remained essentially unchanged. Before 1952, however, the wrong ball rule had undergone a long and at times confused development.

Present Rule 15-1 is a modern version of Rule 3 of the original 1744 code of the Gentlemen Golfers:

> You are not to change the Ball which you Strike off the Tee.

In various codes during the late eighteenth and early nineteenth centuries even greater restrictions than changing the ball were in force. The player was also not allowed variously to lift, touch, or handle the ball in any way. These rules were in conflict with a number of other rules, the most obvious being rules concerning lost balls that didn't legislate loss of hole. (*See Rule 27: Ball Lost or Out of Bounds.*) They were also in conflict with rules allowing the ball to be lifted under various circumstances. In its 1851 code, the R&A arrived at a formulation that served as the basis for future development:

> The balls struck off from the tee must not be changed, touched, or moved, before the hole is played out (except in striking, and the cases provided for by Rules . . .

A list of rules governed such cases as water hazards, balls splitting, and certain obstructions, which made it necessary to touch and lift or replace the ball. Present Rule 15-1 covers all such cases with the blanket condition

> unless a Rule permits [the player] to substitute another ball.

MISTAKEN IDENTITY

It was in connection with this rule that the first concern about playing a wrong ball arose early in the nineteenth century. A good deal of confusion could arise about whose ball was whose. The balls were handmade feather balls, without brand name or number. Although they might vary considerably in size and color, they could be difficult to tell apart, especially when they became wet or dirty. The concern about playing the right ball was certainly

116

justified. In 1809 The Gentlemen Golfers amended their rule to take this into account:

> You are not to change the ball struck from the tee before the hole is played out, and if at a loss to know the one ball from the other, neither of them to be uplifted till both parties agree.

In making this addition, the Honourable Company was actually taking a cue from the Edinburgh Burgess golfers, who had introduced a similar rule in the code they had adopted seven years earlier, in 1802:

> That if any golfer shall be at a loss to know his own ball from his opponents [sic] he shall not lift any of the balls till they both agree.

The St. Andrews golfers in turn adopted a form of the rule close to that of the Honourable Company's when they adopted a new code in 1812:

> The Ball struck from the tee must not be changed before the hole is played out, and if the parties are at a loss to know the one Ball from the other, neither shall be lifted till both parties agree.

Not content with this, they went the Honourable Company one better by adding a final clause to their rule on "Rubs of the green":

> If the Player strike his adversarys' [sic] Ball with his Club, the Player loses the hole.

At this point the rule was close to the essence of our present match play rule, but that still wasn't the end of the story. Other golfers than those in Leith and St. Andrews were beginning to worry about playing a wrong ball. The Aberdeen golfers, as usual, had an original approach:

> A ball cannot be changed between holes without consent of both parties, and if either party play the wrong ball, it shall be optional for the other either to hold the stroke for himself, or take the ball and play it as he pleases within a yard of the place it was struck from, and play it again.

Here was a strong incentive to make sure you weren't playing your opponent's ball: if you played it and hit a good shot, he could continue with it if he so chose. No penalty is mentioned in this Aberdeen rule, but it was probably penalty enough if your cracker of a shot benefited your opponent.

In 1828 the Blackheath golfers followed the lead of the Aberdonians, but eliminated the option:

> If the Player by mistake strikes his Opponent's Ball in playing through the Green, the Stroke shall not be reckoned against either, and the Ball must be played as it may chance to lie.

It was probably penalty enough if your cracker of a shot benefited your opponent.

117

Under this rule you at least might have stuck your opponent with a bad shot. Once more, no penalty is mentioned. It would be interesting to know what they did if this wrong ball was lost, but the rule is silent about such an eventuality.

Follow the Leader

Most golfing societies and clubs, however, followed the lead of the St. Andrews golfers and attached a penalty of loss of hole to playing the opponent's ball. The Honourable Company expanded the rule considerably in 1839:

> If one Party strikes his adversary's Ball with his Club, his foot or otherwise, that party loses the hole; but if he play it inadvertently, thinking it his own, and the adversary also play the wrong ball, it is then too late to claim the penalty, and the hole must be played out with the Balls thus changed. Or if the mistake occurs from information given to one party by the other, the penalty cannot be claimed, and the mistake, if discovered before the other party shall have played, must be rectified by replacing the Ball as nearly in the place in which it lay as possible.

This form of the rule was adopted verbatim by the St. Andrews golfers in their next code of rules in 1842 and formed the basis not only of their rule during the rest of the century but of our modern rule as well.

Do Be More Careful

In 1891 the St. Andreans substituted a one-stroke penalty for loss of hole, but this was short-lived; it was rescinded in 1899. An important permanent addition was made to the rule in 1891, however: the possibility of mistakenly playing not only the opponent's ball, but also a wrong ball outside the match. The penalty for this was loss of hole. No mention of this contingency in stroke play was made until 1908; from 1899, however, the general penalty of two strokes was to be applied in cases where the penalty in match play was loss of hole. In 1908 a specific rule was added:

> If a competitor play a stroke with a ball other than his own he shall incur no penalty provided he then play his own ball; but if he play two consecutive strokes with a wrong ball, he shall be disqualified.

In 1933 this approach was abandoned, and the penalty changed to two strokes for striking a wrong ball in stroke play.

Eventual Resolution

The match play rule was changed in 1902 to allow the player to escape the loss-of-hole penalty for playing his opponent's ball by allowing him to correct his mistake before his opponent played his next shot. This remained part of the rule until after the Second World War. Both the USGA and the R&A experimented with changes in this rule in their separate codes of, respectively, 1946 and 1950. The USGA wanted to return to the stroke play rule in force between 1908 and 1933 (one free strike on a wrong ball, but disqualification for the second). The R&A drafted a monstrously long rule on playing a wrong ball, the most important point of which was a return to the penalty in force during most of the 1890s: one stroke. These different approaches to the problem were resolved by the R&A and the USGA in their 1951 conference, when they agreed on a rule in all important respects identical with our present rule.

The Putting Green and the Flagstick

When Is a Green Not a Green?

Nowadays we take for granted that a putting green is a putting green, and we have few doubts about where it begins and ends. It wasn't, however, always so.

In the early days of golf there was no talk of putting greens for the simple reason that there was no area immediately around the hole that could be clearly distinguished from the rest of the playing area. The entire playing area was quite simply referred to as "the green." This usage developed from how open grassy public areas were referred to in those days (the village green) and can be found in other sports (e.g., a bowling green). This meaning of the word is reflected in several golfing terms still in use: *through the green, rub of the green, green fee* (the paying of which gives you the right to play on the entire course), as well as *greenkeeper* and *green committee* (which oversees the care of more than just the putting greens).

Guy B. Farrar sums up the whole process of early golf course construction in his history of the Royal Liverpool Golf Club:

> Course construction in those days was a very simple affair—the flattest piece of land free from rabbit holes was selected, a hole cut with a penknife, and there was a green, ready for play!

THROUGH THE GREEN

In the earliest codes of rules the term *Green* was frequently used to describe the entire playing area exclusive of hazards, that is, what we refer to nowadays as "through the green." It also often appeared in the term *the fair Green*, corresponding to our modern term *fairway*. The rather quaint expression *through the green* made its first appearance in the 1783 Aberdeen code and has somehow miraculously survived to this day in spite of all the changes in playing conditions and terminology that have taken place since then.

WATCH YOUR STEP

Even in the absence of any clearly distinguished area around the hole, attempts were made in the earliest rules to impose special conditions on play

The flattest piece of land was selected, a hole cut with a penknife, and there was a green, ready for play!

120

near the hole. Both the 1744 Leith and 1754 St. Andrews codes contained the rule:

> No man, at Holing his Ball, is to be allowed, to mark to the Hole with his Club or, anything else.

Most of the codes adopted by various clubs during the rest of the eighteenth century and the first quarter of the nineteenth century contained such a rule, which is clearly the forerunner of our present Rule 8-2 (Indicating Line of Play). Such a vague definition of the putting, or holing, area didn't satisfy all golfers even at that time. In 1776 the predecessors of the Royal Burgess Golfing Society (at that time calling themselves "The Company of Golfers which meet at Thomas Combs, Bruntsfield Links") adopted a rule defining the putting area in terms of club-lengths from the hole (as also the teeing ground was defined at that time):

> When your Ball comes within four or five Club lengths from the hole to which you are playing, you must not mark, or cause to be marked, the direction to the hole, nor must any person whatever stand at the hole to point it out or to do any other thing to assist you in putting.

The teeing area at Bruntsfield Links at that time was between two and four club-lengths from the hole, so the teeing and putting areas overlapped to a large extent.

BIT BY BIT

A note in the minute book of the Society of St. Andrews Golfers in 1779 makes a reference to "the hole green," which seems to imply that by that time they were somehow able to distinguish the putting area from the rest of the playing area. The new code that they adopted in 1812 twice refers to "the putting green," without, however, defining it precisely. The precise definition of the putting area came about in connection with the problem of the removal of loose impediments in the vicinity of the hole. In 1815 the Aberdeen golfers were the first to define the putting area precisely:

> all loose impediments may be removed on the putting green, which is declared to be 15 yards from the hole all round . . . .

The St. Andrews golfers followed suit in 1829, but increased the distance to twenty yards, a definition of the putting green that lasted all of 123 years. It wasn't until 1952, when the first joint R&A-USGA code of rules opened the modern era of golf, that our present definition came into force:

> all ground of the hole being played which is specially prepared for putting or otherwise defined as such by the Committee.

Most codes of rules adopted after 1829 included the twenty-yard rule, although some clubs continued for a while to play with different definitions (e.g., in 1838 the Edinburgh Burgess Golfing Society legislated three club-lengths).

In all their codes adopted between 1842 and 1875, the St. Andrews golfers referred to "the Putting Green or Table Land," a rather good description of at least some of the putting areas on the Old Course, as well as on any number of other Scottish links courses. In 1882 the new R&A code refined the definition of the putting green by excluding hazards within the twenty-yard distance from the hole, and at this point another consideration entered into the picture: what to do about the flagstick.

The Flagstick: To Strike or Not to Strike

The flagstick had been mentioned for the first time in the R&A code of 1875, and then only in connection with the problem of the ball resting against it:

> If, in holing out, the ball rests upon the flag-stick in the hole, the player shall be entitled to have the stick removed, and if the ball falls in, it shall be considered as holed out; but either party is entitled to have the flag-stick removed when approaching the hole.

This rule remained unchanged in match play for the rest of the nineteenth century, but already in 1882 it was modified in stroke play ("when on the Putting-Green, the flag must be removed"), although no penalty was assigned for breach of the rule.

GETTING PICKY

It was 1899 before a penalty was assigned in connection with the flagstick (and then only in stroke play):

> When a competitor's ball is within 20 yards of the hole, the competitor shall not play until the flag has been removed, under penalty of one stroke.

It should be noted that this penalty applied also when the ball was played from a hazard within twenty yards of the hole, not just from the "putting green" as then defined ("all ground within 20 yards of the hole, except hazards").

During the early decades of the twentieth century the rules concerning striking the flagstick had begun to change slowly but surely. In 1902 a penalty of loss of hole in match play was assigned if a player's ball struck a flagstick that had been removed by himself, his partner, or their caddies. In 1908 the

rule affecting stroke play was changed so that a one-stroke penalty was no longer assigned for playing from within twenty yards of the hole before the flagstick had been removed, but rather a two-stroke penalty for striking "either the flagstick or the person standing at the hole."

BIG CHANGE

No further changes were made in either the match or stroke play rules until 1933, when a critical change was made in the match play rule: striking a flagstick held as well as removed was now penalized by loss of hole. The penalty was to be assigned to the player's side if a member of his side was involved in removing or holding the flagstick, but to the opponent's side if a member of his side had been involved.

WE HAD FINALLY GOTTEN USED TO IT, AND THEN

Postwar golf saw continuing change in these rules. Changes in both the conditions and the penalties were made in the experimental rules of the USGA in 1946 and the R&A in 1950, though not the same changes in both codes, resulting in quite a confusing situation for those few years. The joint 1952 rules stabilized the situation, but not entirely satisfactorily. In match play a rule was adopted that expressly allowed striking an unattended flagstick without penalty (up until then it had only been implied). Striking an attended or removed flagstick carried a penalty of loss of hole to the attending side, as earlier. An added condition was that the opponent could require the flag to be removed if he considered that the player could be aided by having it in the hole. In stroke play the old twenty-yard rule (including hazards) remained in force, even though the 1952 code defined the putting green as all ground especially prepared for putting.

SPELLING IT OUT

The penalties for striking the flagstick in match and stroke play were finally unified and simplified in the new joint code in 1956. Striking an attended or removed flagstick was penalized in both forms of play: by loss of hole in match play, by two strokes in stroke play. Most remarkable of all, there was no penalty for striking an unattended flagstick, no matter from what place on the course the ball was played. This eminently sensible rule was both simple and practical. Not everyone agreed that striking the flagstick should be allowed in both forms of play, but there was widespread acceptance. Richard S. Tufts wrote in 1960, in reference to the 1956 rule:

> The differences in procedure between match and stroke play, the rights of the player and the opponent to have the flagstick attended or not, the application of the penalty sometimes to one side and sometimes to the other, were all done away with and the play of the game without caddies greatly expedited. Traditionalists still take offense at the use of the flagstick as a backstop but experience indicates that when it is so used, the breaks in the player's favor are closely matched by the breaks against him.

This happy situation lasted until 1968, when the traditionalists won the day. Since then the rules have called for a general penalty for striking the flagstick when a shot is played from the putting green.

Two other rules affecting play on the green were adopted in the same code. Neither of them was fated to be of long life: cleaning the ball was permitted only before the first putt, and in stroke play continuous putting was made mandatory, after having been authorized by local rule in the United States since 1966.

LET'S GO

The purpose of these new rules was to counteract slow play on the putting green, which even then was beginning to be a problem. Both rules quickly proved to be both impractical and unpopular. Varying conditions during stroke-play competitions gave unfair advantage to players lucky with the weather, and continuous putting was in direct conflict with the traditional order of play. *(See Rule 10.)* As a result, these rules were dropped in midstream, in a specially amended code in 1970. This is the only instance of any substantive change being made in the rules of play between the regular four-year revisions since 1952. Unfortunately, there was no return at the same time to the sensible rules in force between 1956 and 1968 permitting striking an unattended flagstick, and present-day golfers consequently have to waste much time running back and forth to attend or remove it.

A CLEAR VIEW

A final note on the flagstick may be in order. In the Aberdeen code of 1783 there was an interesting rule concerning standing at the hole:

> When the hole is distinctly in view of the Player, no Person shall be allowed to stand at it for a direction.

This rule implies that it was otherwise permitted for someone to stand at the hole to indicate its location (perhaps one of the fore-caddies that in those days often were sent ahead to keep track of the ball). Very likely there was nothing else to indicate the location of the hole.

In 1828 the golfers at Blackheath in London adopted this Aberdeen rule, and even in the 1870s no flags seem to have been in use there. In Robert Clark's *Golf: A Royal and Ancient Game* we find a report from the *Daily News* for June 1874, of a match at Blackheath that includes this description:

> (The players) are preceded by a scout, who carries a red flag.

An accompanying illustration shows a man in the distance holding up a flag to indicate the line of play, but no other flags can be seen.

AN ELEGANT MARKER

The rules of play adopted by the Liverpool Golf Club at its inception in 1869 included the condition that during competitions it was the duty of "the first couple to place a feather, or some other object, in the hole to mark its position for those following." (How the first two were to find the holes was not explained.) In 1875 the Liverpool golfers adopted a new code of rules that was an adaptation of the 1875 R&A code. Although several of the Liverpool rules

When the Voices of the Children Are Heard on the Green

Even today the flagsticks usually are absent from the holes at Bruntsfield Links, in Edinburgh, one traditional location where golf is still played under near eighteenth-century conditions. It's now a city park, its sloping natural golfing terrain crisscrossed by asphalted paths and constantly frequented by a large number of people of all ages and activities: boys cycling along the paths or playing soccer or throwing frisbees, dogs galore, grandmothers tending children, plus a scattering of golfers. The golf societies and clubs that played there in the eighteenth and nineteenth centuries have moved away or ceased to exist, but a new club has risen from the ashes: the Bruntsfield Links Short Hole Golf Club, which plays over a 36-hole pitch-and-putt course. It holds regular tournaments and club championships. During competitions, but not otherwise, there are small flags in the holes. You can find golfers at Bruntsfield Links just about every day of the year, practicing and enjoying its classic golfing terrain.

were quite freely rewritten, the rule governing "Holing Out the Ball" was an almost verbatim copy of the R&A rule, except for the phrase: "If, in holing out, the ball rests upon *the stick marking the hole*," where the words italicized here are substituted for the words "the flag-stick in the hole" in the R&A rule. It would seem that by this time the Liverpudlians had some sort of permanent marker for the hole, though not yet one that could be dignified by the term *flagstick*.

CROWDED LINKS

A careful study of paintings of golf matches from the middle and last half of the nineteenth century reveals considerable variety in both the use of flagsticks and the size and nature of those that were in use at some courses. The famous painting, "The Golfers," by Charles Lee, depicting a match at St. Andrews in 1847, shows that flagsticks were in use there at that time, but it isn't known just when they first appeared. Most golf in the early days of the game was played on public land that was used for multiple activities, and, as a consequence, there was always heavy traffic on the links. It probably wasn't practical to leave flagsticks in the holes when there was no competition: they might have just disappeared.

Golf Isn't Croquet—Or Is It?

The code of 1968 saw another change affecting putting. As early as 1909 the Rules of Golf Committee of the R&A had issued Decisions banning the use of croquet mallets ("A croquet mallet is not a golf club and is not admissible") and of "the vertical croquet stroke as a method of putting." This Decision led to a major disagreement between the R&A and the USGA (and especially Charles Blair Macdonald) over the use of so-called center-shafted putters (such as are probably used by most present-day players). Macdonald was adamant in his insistence that such putters were not mallets, and the R&A was just as adamant in banning "all clubs of the mallet-headed type or such clubs as have the neck bent as to produce a similar effect." The R&A ban lasted until 1952, when it was lifted in the spirit of harmony that pervaded the 1951 joint R&A-USGA rules conferences in London and St. Andrews. *(See Part II, Chapter 5, for more detail.)*

SAM SNEAD'S PUTTING TECHNIQUE.

Putting with a croquet stroke has never been common in golf, nor did it attract much attention on the rare occasions when it was used, until the late 1960s when Sam Snead adopted it with great success. This led in 1968 to the insertion of a clause banning putting from "a stance astride, or with either foot touching" the line of the putt. Sam has continued using a croquet stroke, but with both feet to the left of the line of the putt, and some golfers have followed his example.

Snead isn't the only golfer in the history of the game who has adopted the techniques of croquet. In the eighteenth and early nineteenth centuries there was considerable dispute about croquetlike practices. One of the rules in the earliest codes of the golfers at Leith and St. Andrews banned them:

> At Holing, you are to play your Ball honestly for the Hole and not play on your Adversary's Ball not lying in your way to the Hole.

This sounds reasonable enough to modern golfers, since we accept the principle that each player must be allowed to play his or her own game unhindered by any sort of interference from other players, but our golf-playing forefathers were made of sterner—more aggressive—stuff. The temptation to pot the opponent's ball into the nearest deep bunker seems to have been irresistible to some of them.

LET'S BE CIVILIZED

There is general agreement among commentators on the early rules that to "play on your Adversary's Ball" was a standard part of the game in the eighteenth century, when first the Honourable Company and then the St. Andrews golfers tried to outlaw the practice. Not everyone, however, was inclined to go along with this. In 1790 the Edinburgh Burgess Golfers insisted on a golfer's right ". . . to play his Ball in any direction he chuses, either upon his Adversary's Ball or otherwise." They elaborated on the exact technique involved in their code of 1814:

> It shall be deemed fair to play a ball against the adversary's ball, provided the player does not touch the adversary's ball with his club.

They persisted in these violent tactics until 1838, when they decided to join the rest of the civilized golfing world. In that year they adopted a rule that effectively banned the practice and put an end to croquet tactics in golf:

> In putting, when within three club-lengths of the hole, if a ball lie directly between the adversary's ball and the hole, such ball either to be played first, or lifted until the other is played.

From this it can be seen that this matter of playing "on the Adversary's Ball" is closely tied up with another fascinating aspect of the rules dealing with the putting green: the stymie.

BOBBY JONES AT HIS LAW OFFICE IN 1959.

The only place where I think a real mistake was made came with the elimination of the stymie.

—BOBBY JONES, 1959

The Stymie—Hail and Farewell!

Many golfers agreed with Bobby Jones that the banning of the stymie in 1952 meant that an essential feature of match play had been lost. Jones felt so strongly about the matter that he devoted an entire chapter to it ("The Stymie—Let's Have It Back!") in his 1959 book *Golf Is My Game.* At that time he wrote:

> It has been appalling to me to find that there are golfers of today who do not even know the meaning of "stymie."

SAY WHAT?

What would he have said if he could experience the ignorance of golfers of the 1990s on this point! He would also have to resign himself to the fact that the stymie will never be back. Attitudes toward the playing of the game have changed so vastly during the past forty or fifty years that the modern golfer would be quite unable to accept the interference with his own game that the stymie makes possible. He just isn't prepared to submit himself to what one of the correspondents in the debate about the rules of golf in the pages of *The Field* at the end of the 1880s described as "one of the most glorious uncertainties of the game of golf—viz., the stimy."

The best way to understand the stymie is to look at its history. It developed out of Article 6 of the first code of rules of the Leith golfers in 1744:

> If your Balls be found anywhere touching one another, you are to lift the first Ball till you play the last.

Lifting the ball is perfectly reasonable because it's hardly possible to play one such ball without disturbing the other. However, two balls don't actually have to be touching in order for one to interfere with the playing of the other. This situation was acknowledged by the Leith golfers in their 1775 code of rules, in which the range of touching was extended: ". . . touching or within six inches of one another." Also pertinent is the ban imposed by the Leith and St. Andrews golfers on playing ". . . on your Adversary's Ball *not lying in your way to the Hole,*" and in this connection the last phrase (italicized here) is of crucial importance. You would have no choice but to risk hitting your adversary's ball if it lay on your path to the hole at a distance of more than six inches from your own ball. Under these circumstances you were "stymied," and you were allowed to do anything necessary to hole your putt, even if it meant striking the ball in your path. Many present-day golfers are puzzled by the fact that even today there's no penalty for striking another ball when putting in match play, but it's simply a relic of the days when we played stymies. *(See Rule 19-5.)*

SKILLFUL HAS BEEN THE HAND

Golfers who began playing after 1952 wonder how it was possible to putt out under such conditions. The rules in force before 1952 allowed a player to concede an opponent's next putt only after he himself had holed out, so there was no way to avoid facing up to the situation brought about by a stymie. It often meant either going over the intervening ball, with a deft flick of your trusty niblick, or cutting the putting stroke so that the ball traveled a curved path. Negotiating a stymie was a great art that required much practice. Bobby Jones, in his 1959 defense of the stymie, pointed out:

A stymie often meant going over the intervening ball, with a deft flick of your trusty niblick, or cutting the putting stroke so that the ball traveled a curved path.

129

Also, within a radius of two feet, a competent player can make, almost every time, any stymie that can be laid him.

Needless to say, he was a consummate negotiator of stymies, a fact confirmed by his superb record as a match player.

Naturally, a player who has been laid a stymie and failed to negotiate it may be unhappy about the very existence of such a contingency. Even in the early days of golf there were those who campaigned against it. The first successful effort to ban the stymie was recorded on 27 September 1833 in the minute book of the Society of St. Andrews Golfers:

> The meeting resolve that in future "Stymie" shall, in playing the Game of Golf, be abolished, and that all Balls on the putting green which is defined to be twenty yards from the Hole be lifted at the option of the Player.

TRADITION RESTORED

The defenders of tradition rose to the challenge, however, and gave battle so successfully that this ban on the stymie failed by one day to become even a year old. At the next fall meeting, on 26 September 1834, it was rescinded, and the stymie restored to its proper place of honor. Perhaps the dignity of having been granted royal patronage and becoming the Royal and Ancient Golf Club had brought the St. Andrews golfers to their senses and given them a proper perspective on the value of tradition.

It was nearly a hundred years before the next serious attack was made on the stymie (although a muffled muttering about it could be heard throughout the golfing world almost without pause during the rest of the nineteenth and early twentieth century). The question of abolishing or modifying the stymie was taken up by the Executive Committee of the USGA several times between 1931 and 1934, responding to appeals for change made by several regional golf associations in the United States. These appeals were all denied; the USGA requested that the regional associations maintain uniformity with the R&A code. During the autumn of 1934 the USGA appealed to the R&A to consider abolishing the stymie, but to no avail.

DOWN FOR THE COUNT

In 1938 the USGA unilaterally adopted a modification of the rule that permitted the lifting of a ball creating a stymie within six inches of the hole. This form of the rule became a permanent part of USGA rules in 1941. During the 1951 rules conference both bodies decided to abolish the stymie once and for all, since opinion in Great Britain was also seriously divided over its merits. *(The background details of this radical move are described in the section "The*

Stymie" in the Preface to the 1952 joint R&A-USGA code; the complete text appears in Appendix 5.)

Although the stymie had been abolished, a player could still use his opponent's ball in match play, usually as a backstop, when he putted. This practice lasted until 1984, when it was banned, to the dismay of many traditionalists. *(See Rule 22: Ball Interfering With or Assisting Play.)* It had been outlawed in stroke play as early as 1891, even before there had been any penalty for striking another ball on the putting green (which came in 1902). Playing stymies was never practiced in stroke play, but had not been expressly banned until 1851, in the code adopted that year by the R&A:

> All balls must be holed out on medal days, and no stimys allowed.

There have been many imaginative spellings of the name of this reminder of past golfing glories, and just as many imaginative attempts to explain its etymology, none of them convincing. The stymie has faded, unexplained and for the most part unmourned, into our golfing past.

The Hole Truth

Present-day golfers tend to take not only the putting green itself, but also the hole, for granted. We expect to find a nice neat hole, lined by a firm cup, to receive the results of our brilliant putting efforts. Once again, it wasn't always so. It's quite possible that a modern golfer would be more shocked at the condition of the hole in the early days of golf than at anything else about the primitive conditions of that time. A popular theory has it that the first golf holes were those dug by rabbits. This isn't at all unreasonable, if you keep in mind the huge number of holes dug by rabbits—usually called rabbit scrapes in the early rules—found on the Scottish links lands where golf developed.

WHAT A HEADACHE

We know for sure that there was contention about the condition of the hole in early times. *(See Rule 11: Teeing Ground, page 97.)* The practice of taking sand from the hole to mold the tee for the next drive caused the condition of the hole to deteriorate rapidly. The size and condition of the hole in early golfing days obviously varied greatly from place to place and from day to day. By the end of the 1880s, well into the first golf boom, golfers agitated for a standard hole size. The cry for uniformity even showed up in the debate about the rules of golf in the pages of *The Field*. In 1888 one of the correspondents wrote very sensibly:

> My desire is to see a rule determining the size of the golf hole on all links. On Luffness the holes are so large and the putting green so good that a fair player

will generally hole out from any distance short of three yards, while at Sandwich they are so small that they add at least five strokes to the round.

EASY ENOUGH TO SETTLE

The R&A standardized the size of the hole in its new code in 1891. The size adopted at that time has remained unchanged to this day: 4¼ inches in diameter and at least 4 inches deep. We don't know why the R&A prescribed just that diameter, but the decision possibly was related to the size of the first known hole-cutter, which appeared in 1829 at Musselburgh. This tool is still in the possession of the Royal Musselburgh Golf Club and happens to be 4¼ inches in diameter, once again for unknown reasons. The possibility of the hole's being lined was first mentioned in the 1908 code ("If a metal lining be used, it shall be sunk below the lip of the hole and its outer diameter shall not exceed 4¼ inches"), but there is disagreement among golf historians as to just where and when such liners were first taken into use.

To Fall or Not to Fall—That Is the Question

An especially pesky situation arises in golf when the ball decides to park itself right on the edge of the hole and not fall in as it should. Our present rule covering this situation is admirably clear, and also admirably fair. You're allowed to wait ten seconds at the hole for the ball to drop—but only ten seconds. If you wait longer than that, and the ball then drops into the hole, the result is the same as if you had tapped the ball in: the addition of one stroke. When this ten-second limit was first adopted, during the major overhaul of the rules in 1984, the general penalty of loss of hole in match play and two strokes in stroke play applied. This penalty seemed too harsh, however, and our present rule was formulated and adopted in 1988.

STOPWATCH

The ten-second limit imposed in 1984 was the first specific time limit mentioned in the history of the rules in connection with a malingering ball. Imposing such a limit is actually a quite recent concern. The 1899 code of the R&A mentions for the first time the situation in which a ball resting on the lip of the hole falls in:

> If, after the player's ball is in the hole, the player neglect to knock away the opponent's ball and it fall in also, the opponent shall be deemed to have holed out at his last stroke.

DO BE GRACIOUS

No time limit was set, so it was obviously advantageous to be quick to concede a putt under such conditions. This approach applied, of course, to match play. No mention of this situation in stroke play was made in any code of rules during the nineteenth century. *(For more detailed information on concessions, see also the discussion of present Rule 2-4 in Rule 2: Match Play.)*

A sentence was added to the match-play rule in 1933:

> If the opponent's ball has not been knocked away, the opponent shall play any subsequent stroke without delay.

There was still no mention of this situation in stroke play. The matter rested there until 1956, when an attempt was made to settle it in a general manner:

> Whether a ball has come to rest is a question of fact. If there be reasonable doubt, the owner of the ball is not allowed more than a momentary delay to settle the matter.

This was revised in 1964:

> When any part of the ball overhangs the edge of the hole, the owner of the ball is not allowed more than a few seconds to determine whether it is at rest.

TEETERING

It was the vagueness of such phrases as "without delay," "momentary delay," "a few seconds" that led those who revised the rules in 1984 to legislate a specific ten-second waiting period.

There is still some vagueness even in our present exemplary rule. The player "is allowed enough time to reach the hole without undue delay" before the ten seconds start to tick away. However, one man's "without undue delay" may be another man's dawdling. Most golfers would probably agree that a player detouring via his bag to pick up his putter (if he had chipped to the hole) would not constitute undue delay, but that dropping into the clubhouse for a beer en route very definitely would.

One man's "without undue delay" may be another man's dawdling.

Ball at Rest Moved

Despite the fact that Rule 18 is an extremely complex rule—since there are many ways in which a ball at rest can be moved—it's very easy for the player to proceed on the basis of its present form: the ball that has been moved shall be replaced. If it was the player himself who caused the ball to move (except under certain circumstances listed in Rule 18-2a), he is assessed a stroke penalty. This extreme simplicity is, however, of very recent origin.

OOPS

The contrast between old rule and new becomes immediately clear if we look at the rule as it was stated as recently as 1972. When a ball at rest moved during a search, it was to be replaced without penalty if it had been moved by an outside agency or by an opponent in match play or fellow-competitor in stroke play. On the other hand, it was to be played as it lay if it had been moved

1. by the player accidentally,
2. by the player touching a loose impediment, or
3. if it moved after address.

In all these cases the player was assessed a stroke penalty.

If a player's ball had been moved by his opponent's ball, the player could in match play choose either to replace his ball or play it as it lay, but in stroke play he always had to replace it.

Changes in the rule during the following sixteen years gradually removed these inconsistencies. In 1976 cases 1 and 2 above were changed so that the ball was now to be replaced, but the ball was still to be played as it lay in case 3. In 1984 the rules removed the match-play option either to replace the ball or to play it as it lay when it had been moved by the opponent's ball. Since then even in match play the player must always replace the ball. *(Yet another reduction of the differences between match and stroke play: see Rules 2 and 3.)* Eventually, in 1988 the rule was changed to require also that a ball that moves after address must always be replaced.

The resultant rule is very simple to remember (always replace the ball), but sometimes fraught with practical difficulties. A ball that moves after the player has addressed it often does so precisely because it's precariously balanced, on loose grass or soft leaves or other delicate objects. In such cases the player sometimes has to resort to Rule 20-3d: Ball Fails to Remain on Spot. That rule, and several Decisions referring to it, explain how to proceed in this situation: by placing the ball at the nearest spot where it will remain at rest. Even this can sometimes be difficult, but the present form of the rule is probably the fairest possible, and certainly easy to learn for new players.

On the other hand, older players accustomed to playing the ball as it lies in some cases, may instinctively do so, thereby calling down upon themselves a general penalty (loss of hole in match play, two strokes in stroke play).

SO BUSY WRITING OTHER RULES

Actually, a ball at rest being moved is a fairly recent concern in the history of the rules of golf. The contingency is not even mentioned in any code of rules before the 1899 code of the R&A, the first code drawn up by the Rules of Golf Committee. In that code this concern was brought up in connection with the removal of loose impediments:

> If the player's ball move after any such loose impediment has been touched by the player, his partner, or either of their caddies, the penalty shall be one stroke.

The rule applied no matter if the loose impediment was on the putting green, in contrast to our present rule, or anywhere else. The rule didn't mention whether the ball was then to be replaced or played as it lay. On the other

Even such a seasoned trooper as Tom Kite made the mistake of improperly playing the ball as it lay on the last hole of the third round of the Centennial US Open at Shinnecock Hills in 1995. He had a one-foot putt for a bogey five, but after he had addressed the ball he stepped away momentarily before tapping it in. He later reported to the referee that he thought his ball had moved slightly after he had addressed it. Since he had not replaced the ball before holing out, he finished the round with a triple-bogey seven.

hand, a new rule in the 1899 code decreed that the ball was to be replaced without penalty if it moved when an obstruction was removed. No mention was ever made before 1899 of the problem of the ball's moving when an obstruction was moved—not even when clothes left to bleach on the links had to be pulled out from under it. *(See Rule 24: Obstructions.)*

A FINE POINT

Not until 1956 did the rules mention where the ball was to be played from if it moved after the player had touched a loose impediment; the decree then was that the ball was to be played as it lay. This approach was in use for twenty years (see above). The problem of the ball's moving after address was first taken up in the 1908 code. The condition that it be played as it lay was first mentioned in the 1950 R&A experimental code and remained in force for nearly forty years until 1988. In 1960 the penalty was canceled for a ball's moving on the putting green after loose impediments were touched.

THE AIR IS WILD WITH LEAVES

The problem of the ball's being moved by natural forces (specifically, wind and water) was never addressed before the 1899 R&A code, and that mentioned only wind:

> If a ball at rest be displaced by any agency outside the match, excepting wind, the player shall drop a ball as near as possible to the place where it lay, without penalty. On the putting-green the ball shall be replaced by hand without penalty.

It was 1960 before the rule was changed to require replacing the ball rather than dropping it through the green. Water didn't appear on the scene in this respect until 1976, when a telling note was added to the rule governing a ball at rest moved by an outside agency:

> Neither wind nor water is an outside agency.

In 1984 this sentence was moved out of the rule itself (present Rule 18-1) to become part of the definition of an outside agency.

Rule 18 has experienced a truly checkered career, but it seems to have arrived safely in harbor now. It's among the clearest and most consistent of all rules and is easy to apply. Little more can be asked of a rule of golf.

The problem of the ball's moving after address was first taken up in the 1908 code.

Ay, there's the rub.

—HAMLET, ACT III, SCENE I

Ball in Motion Deflected or Stopped

RULE
19

Rule 19 is the dwelling place of one of the most peculiar terminological carryovers from our golfing past: the expression *a rub of the green,* referring to the accidental collision of a ball with something outside the match. Perhaps it has survived all changes in the English language and in playing conditions through the centuries precisely because of its extreme peculiarity. Many golfers seem to have a special fondness for quaint relics from past times. For golfers with an interest in literature, the phrase may even conjure up visions of Prince Hamlet stepping down from the parapets of Elsinore Castle and, on seeing his ball ricocheting over the green off the helmet of a passing watchman, intoning: "Ay, there's the rub."

THE TIE TO LAWN BOWLING

However that may be, the quaint expression *a rub of the green* has deep roots in the history of the rules of golf. The term seems, however, to have originated in another game played on a green. Sixteenth century records document the use of the term *rub* in lawn bowling, where it refers to the deflection of the ball by some unevenness of the surface of the bowling green, a deflection from which no dispensation was given. In golf, the term *rub of the green* appeared first in the 1812 St. Andrews code:

> Whatever happens to a Ball by accident, must be reckoned a Rub of the green.

This includes, but goes far beyond, mere deflection by unevenness of surface.

EVERY DOG HAS HIS DAY

Although the term didn't appear in any code of golf rules before 1812, rubs of the green had always been present. In the eighteenth century the emphasis

The quaint expression "a rub of the green" has deep roots in the history of the rules of golf.

137

was on interference with the flight of the ball by living beings on the course (what we nowadays call outside agencies). We meet them already in the first written code of rules from 1744:

> If a Ball be stopp'd by any person, Horse, Dog, or anything else, The Ball so stop'd must be play'd where it lyes.

A HORSE IS A HORSE—OF COURSE, OF COURSE

Although conditions of play have changed greatly since 1744, there has been little change in this respect. Extraneous persons, as well as dogs and horses and a host of other animals, still wander around golf courses, interfering with play in all parts of the world. Nowadays armies of spectators at professional tournaments create a special problem by occasionally—sometimes even deliberately—getting in the way of the ball. This has made it necessary to issue a number of Decisions under Rule 19-1 taking account of such situations.

All important codes adopted since 1744 have included some version of the rule of the Gentlemen Golfers quoted above. The exact identity of the stopping or deflecting agency was first mentioned in the Gentlemen Golfers' code of 1775. Since this was the first code adopted by them after 1744, the change in the wording is worth studying:

> If a Ball be stopped by accident, it must be played where it lyes; and if stopped by the adversary, his cadie, or servant, the party who stops the Ball to lose one.

INTENTIONAL INTERFERENCE

When an opponent stopped a ball in motion, a penalty (generally a loss of hole in match play or two strokes in stroke play) was imposed on him. This penalty prevailed for over two hundred years until 1980, when our present rule, which treats only the case of accidental involvement by the opponent, was adopted. Intentional involvement on the part of any participant in the game is covered by Rule 1-2: Exerting Influence on Ball.

The first provision for a penalty when a player's ball strikes a member of his own side came in the 1812 St. Andrews code:

> If it strike his own Cady, the Player loses the hole.

This penalty was extended to the player's clubs in the St. Andrews code of 1829, and to the player himself and his partner in 1842. The rule's exact form in the R&A code of 1842 is of special interest. By that time the gentlemen of the R&A had begun to take the expression "whatever happens to a ball by accident" overly literally and added all sorts of incidents of a more or less accidental nature, making the rule a complete hodgepodge:

Extraneous persons, as well as dogs and horses and a host of other animals, still wander around golf courses, interfering with play in all parts of the world.

138

**INDIGENOUS OUTSIDE AGENCIES
AT JASPER PARK LODGE GOLF
COURSE, ALBERTA, CANADA.**

X.—RUBS OF THE GREEN. Whatever happens to a ball by accident, or is done to it by third parties, or by the forecady, must be reckoned a rub of the green, and submitted to. If, however, the player's ball strike his adversary, or his adversary's cady or clubs, the adversary loses the hole; or if it strikes himself or his partner, or their cadies or clubs, or if he strikes the ball, or strikes at it twice, before it stops motion, the player loses the hole. If the player touch the ball with his foot, or any part of his body, or anything except his club, or with his club moves the ball preparing to strike, he loses the hole; and if one party strikes his adversary's ball with his club, foot, or otherwise, that party loses the hole. But if he plays it inadvertently, thinking it his own, and the adversary also plays the wrong ball, it is then too late to claim the penalty, and the hole must be played out with the balls thus changed. If, however, the mistake occurs from wrong information given by one party to the other, the penalty cannot be claimed; and the mistake, if discovered before the other party has played, must be rectified by replacing the ball as nearly as possible where it lay.

QUITE INCLUSIVE INDEED

It can be seen rather quickly that this covers almost all the sections of our present Rule 19, plus a good many more rules located in different places in the current rule book. It wasn't until 1882 that this overblown rule began to be disassembled. Many of the rules had been expanded by then to include so many different situations that the nineteen rules of the R&A's code of 1875 were detonated into forty-five rules in the code of 1882. The various clauses

139

under the elephantine rub-of-the-green rule under consideration were still grouped near one another in 1882, but they gradually found their way to different locations through many subsequent reorganizations.

A THIRD PARTY

Most of the many codes adopted by various clubs during the middle of the nineteenth century referred to "third parties," "a third party," "any person not engaged in the match," and other such terms to describe an agent causing a problem. The 1891 R&A code used the variation "any agency outside the match," which begins to have a modern ring to it, and all R&A codes from 1891 through 1933 used this phrase. After the Second World War both the USGA, in 1946, and the R&A, in 1950, introduced our modern expression "any outside agency" into their unilateral codes. The first definition of this expression (identical with our present definition) appeared in the first USGA-R&A joint code in 1952.

GREATER DESCRIPTIVE POWER

The expression "Whatever happens to a ball by accident" in the 1812 R&A code remained in all R&A codes through the 1891 code. In the new code of that year the rule took the form:

> Whatever happens by accident to a ball *in motion,* such as its being deflected or stopped by any agency outside the match, or by the fore-caddie, is a "rub of the green," and the ball shall be played from where it lies.

Use of the words *in motion* (italicized in the 1891 rule) removed the temptation to include many of the different types of "accidents" listed in earlier rules, but it left the definition broad enough to cover all sorts of chance bounces.

GREATER PRECISION

When the newly founded Rules of Golf Committee issued its first code in 1899, it revised the formulation of this rule, limiting its scope appreciably:

> If a ball in motion be stopped or deflected by any agency outside the match, or by the fore caddie, the ball must be played from where it lies, and the occurrence submitted to as a "rub of the green."

The wording of this rule, and also of our present definition, would seem to exclude chance bounces off inanimate objects from being rubs of the green, but this certainly isn't in keeping with everyday usage. Decision 19-1/1 makes this clear:

BALL DEFLECTED BY DIRECTION POST.
Q. A ball is deflected by a direction post. What is the ruling?
A. It is a rub of the green and the ball must be played as it lies, without penalty.

LOST IN THE TRANSLATION

We have no information about why the members of the first Rules of Golf Committee decided to restrict the definition of rubs of the green in 1899. They were obviously trying to avoid using the phrase "whatever happens by accident" that had misled earlier drafters of the rules to include too much under the rule, but it would seem unlikely that they intended to exclude chance bounces off inanimate objects. They may have assumed that they were implied in the term itself, although their use of the word *agency* seems to imply that they had in mind something animate capable of performing an action.

The drafters of the rules have been struggling with this problem ever since, especially in connection with another important provision of Rule 19 that covers the case of a ball that, in the words of present Rule 19-1a, "comes to rest in or on any moving or animate outside agency." In 1899 this contingency was expressed by the phrase "If a ball lodge in anything moving . . . ," a formulation used in all codes through the Second World War. The R&A expanded it in its experimental code of 1950 to "If a ball lodge in anything moving or any mobile object which is at rest . . . ." This wording also appeared in the first R&A-USGA joint code in 1952. When it became obvious, however, that any mobile object at rest is no different from any movable obstruction, this addition was dropped from the rule in 1956, leaving once more only "anything moving" for the ball to lodge in.

AGREED

The rule remained like this until 1976, when it was rephrased once again: "If a ball lodge in any moving outside agency . . . ." A further clarification in 1980 produced our present formulation: "any moving or animate outside agency." It should be noticed that this reference to an animate outside agency carries with it the implication that inanimate objects can be outside agencies, too. Since 1984 the ball no longer lodges in, but "comes to rest in or on" the offending agency, moving or at least animate. The rule now seems to work well enough, as long as you don't worry too much about the precise meaning of its terms. What seems to be something of a terminological mixup on this point may merely be due to the strange mixture of ancient and modern expressions.

This mixture may deprive the rule of some degree of clarity and precision, but it definitely imparts to it a special atmosphere and flavor.

THE SHEEP'S IN THE MEADOW

Although Rule 19-1a is clear and unambiguous in its present form, golfers often make errors when applying it. This surfaced in some amusing contributions published in *The Daily Telegraph* in June 1995:

Golfer Wins by a Sheep at 17th Hole

A golfer had a stroke of luck after his drive from the 17th tee wedged beneath the tail of a grazing sheep.

Peter Croke chased the ewe as it ran off before conveniently depositing the ball 30 yards closer to the green, while his playing partner John Maher watched in disbelief.

Mr. Croke, a deputy head-teacher, lined up to take his next shot as the animal wandered off apparently unharmed. He went on to finish the 416-yard par-four hole in five shots to win the match.

Officials at the Southerndown Golf Club, near Porthcawl, South Wales, later found the rules had been observed because a footpath where the sheep finally dropped the ball was in bounds.

Mr. Croke, 47, of Cowbridge, South Glam, said: "The sheep looked mildly surprised by the whole thing, but we were in hysterics. It walked off toward the 17th hole and then seemed to shake the ball free like laying an egg.

Although R&A officials usually don't have the time to comment on all such curious things that happen on golf courses and are reported in newspapers, this incident proved to be irresistible:

One in Hole

SIR—I cannot help wondering if the officials of the club where the golf ball became wedged beneath a sheep's tail are trying to pull the wool over our eyes.

Under Rule 19-1a of the game, if a ball in motion after a stroke comes to rest in an animate outside agency (the sheep), the player shall drop the ball as near as possible to the spot where the sheep was when the ball came to rest in it. The ball may be cleaned.

Contrary to the report, the player did not proceed properly and his opponent could have claimed the hole. I feel a little sheepish about bringing this to your attention, but felt matters should be put right.

—JOHN GLOVER, Rules Secretary
Royal and Ancient Golf Club, St. Andrews, Fife

FAIR IS FOUL, AND FOUL IS FAIR

It may also be worth pointing out that a rub of the green is anything that happens to a ball in motion, not just something that works to the disadvantage of the player, as many golfers tend to think. A rub of the green can just as well be a good bounce as a bad bounce. The Aberdeen golfers had already realized this by 1783. They ended their pertinent rule with the observation: "the Parties being obliged to submit to the Accident, whether for or against the Player."

Golf is a game of chance. In the long run the bad bounces even out with the good. It has frequently been observed that while most games are an imitation of war, golf is an imitation of life itself, in which one has to learn to take "the bitter with the better." The principle of "the rub of the green" is the expression in golf of this basic fact of life.

In the long run the bad bounces even out with the good.

RULE
20

Lifting, Dropping, and Placing

Ｔhe requirement that the position of the ball "shall be marked before it is lifted under a Rule which requires it to be replaced," under penalty of one stroke, ranks among the most important aspects of our present rule governing lifting a ball in play. Although nowadays we take this procedure for granted, it actually is of very recent date. As applied to a ball lifted anywhere on the course, mandatory marking was introduced in the code of 1984. Before then a ball to be lifted and replaced through the green could be lifted without first marking it. Starting in 1976 a ball lifted on the putting green had to be marked. This requirement had developed from a note amended in 1956 to the rule governing activities on the putting green to the effect that the position of a ball lifted from the putting green "should be marked," but not requiring it to be. In 1956 the same note recommended that "a small coin or similar object" be used as a marker.

DROP A DIME

It was twenty years before that present-day popular object, the ball-marker, gained recognition. From 1976 until 1988 the use of "a ball-marker or other small object" was recommended. Coins may have fallen out of official favor, but anyone who played golf in those years knows they were still in widespread use. Recognition was taken of this in 1988, and since then the note in question (which was moved to Rule 20 in 1984) recommends that the position of any lifted ball be marked with "a ball-marker, a small coin or other similar object." There's no indication of what "small" might mean in this context. It can be questioned whether some of the coins seen on putting greens around the world can really be considered to be small. Decision 20-1/12, which sanctions the practice of marking the position of a ball with the toe of a club (usually a putter on the putting green), suggests that "small" can actually be quite large.

JUST DROP IT, OK?

The practice of dropping the ball has a checkered history. The first mention of any activity resembling dropping came in the 1754 code of the Society of St. Andrews Golfers. That code was identical to the original code of the

Honourable Company, except for Article V, governing lifting a ball from water. The Honourable Company teed the ball behind the water, but the St. Andreans had to "throw it behind the hazard, six yards at least." They failed to specify exactly how it was to be thrown. The Edinburgh Burgess golfers were the first to do that. In 1776 they specified that a ball lifted from water was to be thrown "over your head, behind the water."

STEP BY STEP

In 1809 the Honourable Company took a more systematic approach to the problem. In that year they adopted a new code that mentioned four situations in which a ball could be lifted and dropped, and also included a separate rule on the method of dropping:

> In all cases where a ball is to be dropped, the party dropping shall front the hole to which he is playing, and drop the ball behind him over his head.

Many clubs proceeded to adopt this rule, including the St. Andreans in their new code in 1812. The Aberdeen golfers went everyone a bit better in 1815 and specified that the player had to "drop the ball over the back of his head." In 1816, however, the Edinburgh Burgess golfers, who had originated all this over-the-head business, apparently began to realize how awkward it was. They then allowed the player to drop the ball "over his shoulder."

BIT OF A TUSSLE

Now followed a rather confused period during which some clubs followed the over-the-head practice of the Honourable Company and St. Andrews (Montrose 1830, Perth 1839), while others adopted the new over-the-shoulder method (Perth 1825, Burntisland 1828, Blackheath 1844). In 1838 the Edinburgh Burgess golfers specified the right shoulder, but nobody followed their lead. In 1842 the St. Andreans (now a royal club) changed their mode of expression to one of the most peculiar phrases that has ever graced the rules of golf: the player was thenceforth to drop the ball "behind him from his head." The change from "over his head" to "from his head" is anatomically puzzling, but it probably meant that the ball was to be dropped over the shoulder at head height. The process must have been clear enough to our great-grandfathers, at any rate, since it remained defined in that way until 1908. The new code of that year allowed the player to drop the ball "behind him over his shoulder." This method of dropping the ball, impractical as it still was in many respects, remained in force until the major rewriting and reorganization of the rules in 1984.

ROLL WITH THE PUNCHES

Dropping the ball over the shoulder involved one major problem—unless you were a contortionist you couldn't see where it landed. Of course, that was the original purpose; the ball was dropped blindly to make it difficult for the player to pick out an advantageous spot. The exact location of the spot it landed on was left to chance, in keeping with the philosophy of the game in earlier days. Actually, where the ball landed made little difference as long you didn't have to place it on a specific spot if it refused to stay put. No mention of this problem was ever made in the early rules: you just dropped the ball and played it from where it ended up. No mention of redropping the ball ever was made before 1899, when you were allowed to redrop if the dropped ball rolled into a hazard. The first step toward our present situation was taken in 1933:

> If the ball when dropped come to rest nearer to the hole it shall be re-dropped without penalty, and in cases where it is impossible owing to the configuration of the ground to prevent a dropped ball from rolling nearer to the hole the ball shall be placed.

You just dropped the ball and played it from where it ended up.

TURNING POINT

When the USGA unilaterally adopted a new code in 1946, it made no change in this rule, but when the R&A drew up its experimental code of 1950 it added three more situations in which the ball needed to be placed:

> to prevent a dropped ball from rolling nearer to the hole, or into a hazard or out of bounds or into casual water . . . .

Our present rule was beginning to take shape. The joint R&A-USGA code of 1952 specified for the first time that the ball should first be redropped before placing it to prevent it from rolling to where it shouldn't be (in that code only nearer the hole, into a hazard, or out of bounds). A separate rule required that a ball dropped in a hazard must remain in the hazard or be redropped.

ON A ROLL

In 1960 the problem of the ball's rolling "more than two club-lengths from the point of dropping" was first mentioned, and in 1964 it was specified that the ball "shall be placed at the point where the ball was last dropped." In 1980 the condition was added that the ball was to be re-dropped if it rolled onto a putting green. In 1984 the entire matter was greatly simplified with the introduction of our present method of dropping: at arm's length at shoulder height. It's now possible to see the point (since 1984 called a "spot") at which the ball strikes the ground when re-dropped.

AN UNAVOIDABLE DEVELOPMENT

A neat list of conditions requiring re-dropping was drawn up in the 1984 code: if the ball rolls

- into or out of a hazard,
- onto a putting green,
- out of bounds,
- back into a condition permitting dropping under Rule 24-2 (Immovable Obstructions) or Rule 25 (Abnormal Ground Conditions),
- more than two club-lengths, or
- nearer the hole.

The 1996 code transferred to this list the condition formerly in Rule 26-1 (Water Hazards), that the ball must be re-dropped if it rolls nearer the hole than the point where it last crossed the margin of the hazard, and at the same time extended it to cover situations in which relief is taken for a ball lost in an abnormal ground condition. These precise instructions for dropping and re-dropping and placing are such an important part of our present rules that it's difficult to imagine how players went about the business in days of yore. The development of such detailed re-dropping requirements is a good example of the extreme precision required of the rules of golf under present high-pressure playing conditions.

RIVER, LAKE, AND GLIMMERING POOL

The early rules that allowed for lifting from water specified only that the ball be dropped (or teed) behind the hazard. In the 1858 R&A code a ball in the Swilcan Burn on the first hole could be taken out and teed "on the line where it entered the burn, on the opposite side from the hole to which he is playing." This wording is a bit unclear, but it was improved in a code adopted by the Royal Liverpool Golf Club in 1875. In reference to a ball in water, the Liverpool code allowed the player to "drop it over the shoulder behind the hazard as nearly as possible in a direct line to the hole he is playing to." The R&A adopted a similar dropping rule in 1891 that applied to hazards in general (hazards being at that time rather broadly defined). (*See Rule 13.*):

> [The player] shall front the hole, stand erect behind the hazard, keep the spot from which the ball was lifted (or in the case of running water, the spot at which it entered) in a line between him and the hole, and drop the ball behind him from his head, standing as far behind the hazard as he may please.

A RUDE STREAM

Clearly, this 1891 R&A approach served as the basis for correct procedure with respect to water hazards and unplayable balls right up until 1984. The dropping procedure that we use now was adopted then, but it quickly ran into difficulties. It called for the player (in Rules 26-1b and 28c) to keep the spot where the ball last crossed the margin of a water hazard or where an unplayable ball was lifted "between himself and the hole." This wording meant that if the player faced the hole while he dropped the ball, as older players had been doing, it could land an arm's length to the side of the line to the hole. A quick change in 1988 corrected this giveaway, and now the ball has to land on a spot in line with the hole and the point where the ball crossed the margin of the hazard or the spot where it was lifted. This rule's development shows the difficulties inherent in writing unambiguous golf rules. Those brave souls who have taken this task upon themselves need all the support and sympathy we can give them.

WHERE, OH WHERE

For many years a special problem could arise when it wasn't possible to determine the exact spot at which a ball was to be dropped, especially in stroke-and-distance situations. As late as 1988, Rule 20-2b, which governs such situations, decreed that a ball was to be dropped "as near as possible to the spot where the ball lay, but not nearer the hole." Because the exact spot where the original ball lay often couldn't be determined, there might be no way to know whether the new ball rolled closer to the hole than the position of the original ball. A conscientious player, seeing his ball roll toward the hole after he dropped it, might instinctively re-drop, and be penalized a stroke for lifting the ball when he shouldn't have.

MANY A SLIP

Even if the exact spot where the original ball lay was known (from, let's say, a divot mark), a player could be penalized for re-dropping in this situation. Bernhard Langer encountered such a penalty in 1987 at the European Open at Walton Heath, as reported in *The Guardian* on 14 September of that year:

> Langer, the overnight leader, had started with three straight pars when he drove into the rough at the fourth. He had a swing, but not much of one, and in attempting to hit the ball too far, struck it into the trees, never to be seen again.
>
> Now, of course, he had to retreat to the spot from which he had played his second shot and drop another ball, which he did. But the ball jumped forward, ahead of the divot mark that Langer had located as being the spot from which he had previously played.
>
> The West German, seeking to be fair and thinking that he could not play his ball from a spot that was clearly nearer the hole, picked it up and re-dropped.
>
> But Mike Stewart, a PGA official who was watching, was aghast. He raced over in his buggy, told Langer that not only was he in error and the ball he picked up was in play, he would also incur yet another penalty shot if he played the ball from where it now lay.
>
> Langer had to replace the ball in the position it had occupied after the original drop and play out the hole. With the penalty for the lost ball and the penalty for picking up a ball in play, it cost him a triple bogey seven and, effectively, his chances of winning.

Fredrik Lindgren fell into exactly the same trap in the PLM Open in Sweden in 1990. These cases led to the making of a small, but important, change in Rule 20-2b in 1992. Now the ball is to be dropped "not nearer the hole than the specific spot which, if it is not precisely known, shall be estimated." Once the specific spot has been estimated, the ball must be re-dropped if it rolls closer to the hole than that spot. This alteration may seem to be extreme hair-splitting, but now the conscientious player will always be able to proceed correctly.

YOU CAN'T GET THERE FROM HERE

Tom Watson and Frank Hannigan, in *The Rules of Golf, Illustrated and Explained,* refer to the wording of Rule 20-7 (Playing from Wrong Place) as being "on the heavy side." Being perfect gentlemen, they make use of polite understatement, where others might tend to be harsher. Undeniably, the rule

The Merest Oversight

The most famous incident of playing from the wrong place in the history of competitive golf occurred on the 72nd hole of the 1957 British Open at St. Andrews.

Bobby Locke held such a big lead that when he hit his approach shot a yard to the left of the hole, he could take four putts and still beat the runner-up Peter Thomson, who was going for his fourth straight British Open win. Locke's ball lay on his fellow competitor's line, so he marked it a putter-head to the side, as the rules of the time allowed if the fellow competitor wanted it marked. He replaced the ball at the marker, however, instead of at its original location, and putted out. His error wasn't noticed at the time, but even if it had been, there was no rule then covering such a situation. When someone pointed out that Locke had proceeded incorrectly, the Committee ruled that he had gained no advantage from his error, so his score was allowed to stand. Nowadays (since 1972), he would have been penalized two strokes, but he still would have won by one stroke. All's well that ends well, even in golf.

Undeniably, the rule is a bit difficult to understand.

is a bit difficult to understand, but the rules-makers were obviously trying to cover all possible situations in which a ball can be played from a wrong place. Playing a ball from a wrong place actually is a very recent concern in the rules of golf. It was first dealt with specifically in the 1972 code, and then the general penalty was applied (loss of hole in match play, two strokes in stroke play). A note added to that rule specified that a serious breach was to be dealt with by the Committee. A serious breach was provided for in the rule itself in 1980; it was to be punished by disqualification unless rectified, as at present. Through the 1980 code, the rule on playing from the wrong place was grouped together with the rule on playing a wrong ball. It was moved to Rule 20 in 1984 and given its present weighty form.

Rule 20-7 isn't applied often, not because playing from the wrong place isn't quite common, but rather because it's not always noticed.

It's one if you lift

And you clean

Your ball when it's not

On the green.

Unless it could never

Be played

And the requisite

Penalty's paid.

—DORIS RUMJAHN, *GOLF RULES IN RHYME*

Cleaning the Ball

RULE
21

Our present rules governing lifting and cleaning the ball are so lenient and liberal that if our golf-playing forefathers could see how we behave on the course—and especially on the putting green—they would be justified in wondering what strange variety of handball we're playing. Actually, it wouldn't be necessary to go farther back in the family line than the parents of most present-day adult golfers to find someone who would be amazed by our behavior. The act of cleaning the ball is not even mentioned in any code of rules before the 1946 USGA unilateral code. Back in the days when men were men and golfers were true golfers, it was forbidden to manhandle the ball in the way that we do nowadays.

A thought-provoking picture of what problems might arise if indiscriminate cleaning of the ball were permitted can be found in a book by the American golfer Richard S. Francis: *Golf, Its Rules and Decisions,* first published in 1937. Even in those far-off days some golfers argued that cleaning the ball in play should be permitted, but Francis pointed out that if it were permitted always to clean balls, players would lift them so constantly that it would be a perfect nuisance; there would always be the question of exact replacement and the delays would be great and tiresome.

One only wonders what he would say if he could witness or take part in one of our five-hour-plus rounds nowadays, complete with all the incessant pawing at the ball that goes on.

A WATERSHED

Richard Francis was, as a matter of fact, addressing an issue that was coming to the fore in American golf at that time. As early as 1935, the Rules of Golf Committee of the USGA had proposed to the R&A that a note be added "at an appropriate place in the Rule Book" listing certain specific situations in which a lifted ball could be cleaned. The R&A failed to adopt this proposal, and the USGA took unilateral action in its 1946 code. In that code, in which cleaning the ball is mentioned for the first time in the rules of golf, we find these stern words:

> Cleaning a ball when in play entails a penalty of two strokes in stroke play and the loss of the hole in match play, except under special rulings by the committee in charge.

However, the definition of "in play" in this code includes certain conditions under which a ball may be cleaned:

> A ball lifted from a water hazard or casual water or from ground under repair may be cleaned; otherwise a player may not clean a ball except to the extent necessary for identification.

These conditions served as the basis for later development, although this radical USGA lead wasn't followed by the R&A in its experimental code in 1950. The possibility of cleaning the ball is mentioned in this code, but only under very limited conditions:

> Unless permitted by Local Rule a ball "in play" may not be cleaned.

INCH BY INCH

The joint R&A-USGA code of 1952, however, included four conditions under which the ball could be cleaned: the three from the 1946 USGA code (when the ball is lifted for identification, from abnormal ground conditions, and from a water hazard), plus the local rule condition from the R&A 1950 code. Another condition was added in 1956: when the ball is lifted from an unplayable lie. Yet a new condition came in 1960: the ball could be lifted and cleaned on the putting green.

If it were permitted always to clean balls, it would be a perfect nuisance.

152

BACKING OFF

The 1968 rules made two changes in regard to cleaning the ball. Henceforth the ball could also be cleaned when it was lifted for relief from an obstruction, but unrestricted cleaning of the ball on the putting green was no longer allowed: the ball could now be cleaned before the first putt only. This restriction was made in an attempt to speed up play, which had slowed down considerably because of indiscriminate cleaning of the ball on the putting green. Well-intentioned though it was, this restriction proved to be quite impractical and was rescinded in midstream in 1970. It had originally been permitted by local rule in the United States since 1966, along with the continuous-putting rule. *(See Rule 16: The Putting Green, page 124.)*

THE GRAIL IS FOUND

Two more additions were still to be made to the conditions for cleaning a ball. Since 1980 cleaning has been permitted in the case of an embedded ball, and since 1984 when play has been suspended. By this time the list of conditions for cleaning the ball had become so long that in 1988 it was seen to be more practical to list those few instances in which the ball may not be cleaned. As a result, our present Rule 21 is short and sweet and easy to remember.

The harsh general penalty (loss of hole in match play, two strokes in stroke play) imposed in the 1946 USGA code in cases where a ball is illegally cleaned was carried over into the 1952 joint R&A-USGA code and remained in force until 1980, when it was alleviated to one stroke in both forms of play, and has remained so ever since.

Ball Interfering with or Assisting Play

Rule 22 developed out of the same rule in the 1744 code of rules of the Honourable Company that produced the stymie. (*See Rule 16: The Putting Green, page 128*) In that very first code, interference took place only when two balls were actually touching, and the one nearer the hole was to be lifted while the other was played. In 1775 interference was redefined to take place when the balls were touching or within six inches of each other. This definition remained in force throughout the rest of the eighteenth and the entire nineteenth century.

During the nineteenth century, interference was treated by various means in various codes. In match play the interfering ball within the six-inch limit was always to be lifted, but frequently in stroke play the interfering ball was to be played first. No provision was made throughout most of the nineteenth century for the possibility that the original lie of the lifted ball might be altered.

By 1891, improved conditions of the playing surface probably began to make such things as altered lies more noticeable and discomforting than they had been in the past. The 1891 R&A code provided for placing the ball in a nearby lie "as nearly as possible similar to" the original lie. This is the basic rule we still play by. It was moved in 1964 to the rule covering lifting and placing the ball (Rule 20-3b) and improved in detail.

LEND A HELPING HAND

Those same 1891 R&A rules considered for the first time that the position of one ball might assist the play of another ball. In stroke play the player whose ball was in such a position nearer the hole was given the option of lifting or holing out first if his ball might "give an advantage to the other competitor." In the code of 1899 the player was given the same option if his ball "might either interfere with the competitor's stroke, or in any way assist the competitor," wording that has remained essentially unchanged to this day. It should be noted, however, that these regulations applied only to stroke play.

Before 1984, the right of a player to gain assistance from his opponent's ball was an integral part of match play. Many players felt it was an advantage to have a ball close to the line of putt left in that position, either to serve as a visual guide or as a ricocheting post in case of an offline putt. Since there never has been any penalty in match play for striking another ball on the putting green whether the player is putting or not (and still is none), there was no compelling reason not to have the opponent's ball left in place. *(See Rule 19-5.)* The right to require the opponent to leave his ball in place in match play was removed in 1984, further reducing the differences between the two main methods of playing the game. *(See Rules 2 and 3: Match Play and Stroke Play.)*

A loose impediment is not
What's firmly rooted to the spot.
All leaves or loose grass-cuttings spread
Around, or worms, alive or dead,
All these you are at liberty
To scatter with impunity.
Move fallen branches, large or small,
AS LONG AS YOU DON'T MOVE THE BALL!

—DORIS RUMJAHN, *GOLF RULES IN RHYME*

 RULE 23 # Loose Impediments

The rule governing the removal of what we nowadays call loose impediments in the first code of the Gentlemen Golfers in 1744 was basically the same as our present rule. The players at Leith Links in 1744 proceeded for all practical purposes and intents just as we do now, although they looked at the matter a bit differently. They were allowed to remove such objects only "upon the fair Green" (that is, on what we now call the fairway), and then only within a club-length of the ball.

We're allowed to remove loose impediments anywhere, except when both the offending object and the ball lie in or touch the same hazard. We approach the matter from this point of view because we want to be sure that we can remove such things from both the putting green and from the teeing ground, which would be excluded if we adopted the Gentlemen Golfers' rule in modern form. They didn't have to worry about this because their putting and teeing areas (which were one and the same thing) were in no way distinguished from the rest of the "fair Green." *(See Rule 11: Teeing Ground and Rule 16: The Putting Green.)*

156

IRRITANTS

As the area within which teeing the ball was allowed was gradually moved farther away from the hole, however, the question of clearing the putting area began to assume greater importance. The term *loose impediments* first appeared in 1809 when the Honourable Company added a clause to its rule governing holing the ball: "all loose impediments may be removed within six club-lengths of the hole."

Most codes of rules adopted by various clubs throughout the remainder of the nineteenth century included some such distance limit, expressed either in club-lengths or yards. Gradually the distance of twenty yards (the distance set in the St. Andrews 1829 code for the putting area) became the accepted norm. Not all players in the eighteenth century looked favorably upon removing objects interfering with the stroke. Sternest of all were the Aberdeen golfers in 1783, who categorically forbade removing anything: neither "in a Hazard, nor on the fair Green." By 1815, however, they decided to join the rest of the golfing world and allowed themselves the luxury of clearing the land "within 12 feet of the player."

DEM BONES, DEM DRY BONES

The definition of what constitutes the sort of items that may be removed has to be of considerably greater interest than these number games. Compared to the list of mostly innocuous sounding objects named in our modern definition (some stones and twigs and a little dung), eighteenth and early nineteenth century golfers had to contend with an imposing list: "Stones, Bones and Break-clubs." Actually, the term "Break Clubs" (sometimes with, and sometimes, without a hyphen) was never precisely defined, but it's safe to say they were anything that could cause a club to break during a stroke, although it appears that it had to be a pretty solid item.

The only outright attempt to define the term (in the 1830 Montrose Golf Club code: "Break-clubs, such as stones, bones, &c.") is really of very little help. When the Aberdonians finally allowed such things to be removed in 1815, they appended a telling sentence to the rule: "Turf is no break club." Despite this, the rather fragile wooden clubs of those days might very well have broken as the result of a resounding whack at a firm piece of links sod. There's no doubt that a stone or a bone would have wrought more than a little damage.

Not all players in the eighteenth century looked favorably upon removing objects interfering with the stroke.

DOGGEDNESS

The presence of bones on the golf courses of those days gives one pause. You would think that all the dogs that seem to have populated the eighteenth-century links, if we're to judge from how frequently they're mentioned in old rules, would have been able to keep things tidy, but this was apparently a problem of considerable proportions. (*For example, see the 1783 Aberdeen code, Rules VI and XIII, in Appendix 4, Example 3.*)

The dung situation also seems to have assumed quite considerable proportions at times, at least if we're to judge from any number of rules in early codes. In the 1776 code of the "Company of Golfers which meet at Thomas Combs, Bruntsfield Links" (now The Royal Burgess Golfing Society) we find the rule:

> If your Ball lies amongst Human Ordure, Cow Dung or any such nuisance on the fair green, you may, upon losing one, lift it, throw it over your head, behind the nuisance and play it with any club you please.

This sentence has to be read carefully. It was the ball, not the "nuisance" that the player threw over his head. If the player chose not to lose a stroke, it would seem he had to take his chances at removing or playing from the midst of "nuisances" of this sort.

SACRED COWS

The Hawick Golf Club, a few miles south of Edinburgh, adopted a local rule in 1889:

> A ball lodging in cow droppings may be lifted out, cleaned or changed, and dropped behind without a penalty.

THE FINEST MERINO

The presence of sheep as "greenkeepers" on golf courses, especially during the nineteenth century, led to many local rules being adopted to deal with possible offensive situations. Having contracted with nearby sheep farmers for services in 1900, the Royal Adelaide Golf Club, in Australia, adopted the rule that

> a ball (not in a hazard) lying in or touching any objectionable animal matter may be lifted and dropped behind same (no penalty).

Certainly another good reason for trying to stay out of hazards! In general, "animal matter" (whether objectionable or not) has usually been treated as a loose impediment to be removed, as it is in our present rule.

"Animal matter" (whether objectionable or not) has usually been treated as a loose impediment to be removed.

BEDROCK

The rules governing loose impediments adopted by the R&A during the middle of the nineteenth century are of special importance, since they formed the basis for our present rules. A great deal of experimentation and change took place at this time. The St. Andrews golfers, having previously allowed the removal of break-clubs and such when the ball lay "on grass," decreed in 1842: "There shall be no lifting or removing of any impediment or obstruction whatever on or off the course" except on the putting green (which by that time had been defined). This 1842 code contained several rather stern rules changes. *(See Rule 27: Ball Lost or Out of Bounds, for the three strokes-and-distance rule imposed in stroke play in the same code.)* Fortunately, the St. Andreans soon reversed themselves, and in the new code adopted in 1851 they returned to allowing "loose impediments" to be lifted when the ball lay on grass.

In the R&A codes of 1858 and 1875 loose impediments could also be removed only when "on grass," but the new code adopted in 1882 took a more modern approach:

> All loose impediments within a club length of the ball may be removed, unless the ball lies within a bunker, on sand, on a molehill, on a road, or other hazard, or touching a growing whin.

PRETTY SMART

An even more modern definition followed in 1891 when this long list of environments was replaced by the phrase "not lying in or touching a hazard." This simplification was made possible by the definition of the term *hazard* for the first time in that 1891 code. *(See Rule 13.)*

THE SHAKEOUT

Strangely, the 1891 code provided for no penalty in case the ball moved on removal of a loose impediment. This oversight was corrected in 1899, in the first code produced by the newly formed Rules of Golf Committee. A penalty of one stroke was assessed if the ball moved after the removal of a loose impediment lying within a club-length of it through the green and within six inches of it on the putting green. To this day we continue to penalize the case in which the ball moves through the green. *(See Rule 18-2c.)* However, there has been no penalty since 1960 if the ball moves on the putting green. In 1960, the rule permitting free lifting and cleaning of the ball on the putting green was adopted. *(See Rule 21: Cleaning the Ball.)*

Little of substance has changed in the rule concerning loose impediments since 1899, although it has been arbitarily rephrased several times, and the rules-makers have struggled a bit to provide us with an adequate definition of the central term. The first attempt was made in 1908:

> The term "loose impediments" denotes any obstructions not fixed or growing, and includes dung, worm-casts, mole-hills, snow and ice.

This definition is interesting because it illustrates the confusion between the terms *obstructions* and *loose impediments* that we meet frequently in codes throughout the nineteenth century. Otherwise, the definition is quite modern. Our present definition is more precise (even making a fine distinction between natural and manufactured ice), but is essentially the same as that of 1908. *(See also Rule 24: Obstructions.)*

A Resonance of Emerald

A word about the history of the rather peculiar term *through the green* may be in order here. It was 1891 before it was used in any code adopted by the golfers in St. Andrews, but it certainly had been used by golfers for many years by then. It made its first appearance in any rule in the code drawn up by the Aberdeen golfers in 1783. (*See Rule XVI in that code reprinted in Appendix 4, Example 3.*) It was also used in the codes of the Edinburgh Burgess Golfers and the Musselburgh Golf Club during the early nineteenth century.

In all these early codes, it always appeared in the form "in playing thro' (through) the Green" as introduction to some contingency or restriction (lost ball, no removal of break-clubs, and others). The phrase also appeared in this form in the 1891 R&A code, but it's difficult to say what it meant precisely because it was never defined. In its earliest occurrences it may have been used to mean the entire playing area (the "green"), even including hazards. When it was finally defined for the first time in 1899, these were excluded:

> The term "through the green" shall mean all parts of the course except "hazards" and the putting-green which is being played to.

It was 1933 before the teeing ground of the hole being played was added, and 1950 before the definition assumed its current form in the R&A experimental code.

Obstructions

Various codes of the first half of the nineteenth century used the terms *loose impediments*, *impediments*, and *obstructions* quite casually, resulting in considerable confusion. All these terms seemed to refer to what we nowadays call loose impediments.

CLEAN AND BRIGHT AND SHINING, O!

The first mention of what we would now call an obstruction was written into the 1838 code of the Edinburgh Burgess Golfing Society in their rule governing the removal of loose impediments:

> All loose impediments may be taken away provided the ball be not thereby moved; but should a ball lie upon clothes, they may be drawn from under it.

No mention is made of what sleight-of-hand trick could remove the clothes from under the ball, assuming that the ball was not to be moved. Bruntsfield Links wasn't the only golfing area where the local ladies took up the practice of spreading their clothes to bleach. We find the St. Andrews golfers also providing for this contingency starting in 1842, once again in a sentence added to their rule governing the removal of loose impediments:

> There is to be no lifting or removing of any impediment or obstruction whatever on or off the course.

Two exceptions were made: on the putting green and

> When a ball lies on clothes or within a club-length of a washing-tub, the clothes may be drawn from under the ball, and the tub may be removed.

That is, in modern terms both tub and clothes were to be treated as movable obstructions. No mention was made of how to proceed if the ball moved when the clothes were snatched out from under it: replace it or play it as it lay? Perhaps golfers of that period were so dexterous they could flick the clothes away without moving the ball.

ALL COME OUT IN THE WASH

Although the right to remove loose impediments when the ball lay on grass was restored in 1851, the gentlemen players of St. Andrews had to continue sleight-of-hand tricks when they came up against their wives' laundry.

Historical records are silent on the matter, so we can only imagine the scenes of domestic discord that were occasioned by sparkling-clean laundry being smudged by errant balls and attempts to flick the clothes from under them. Fortunately, the good men of the R&A came to their senses in 1858 and adopted a new rule:

> and when on clothes the ball may be lifted and dropped behind them.

A washing-tub was still to be treated as a movable obstruction, but the clothes had now been transformed into immovable obstructions. Domestic tranquility was restored to St. Andrews.

WHAT A MESS!

The evolution of our present rule on obstructions was gradual. In 1882 "implements used in the upkeep of the links" joined washing-tubs as movable obstructions. The first attempt to define obstructions was made in 1891, including specifying some of the "implements" first mentioned in 1882: wheelbarrows, rollers, grass-cutters (which were quite new implements then), and others. Included in the same rule was ground under repair. This constellation, rather peculiar from our modern point of view, continued until 1952. (*See Rule 25: Abnormal Ground Conditions.*)

The list of objects defined as obstructions started growing in 1908. By 1933 it included vehicles, bridge planking, huts, hydrant covers, and more. This practice of attempting to define obstructions in specific terms reached absurd heights in the 1946 USGA unilateral code:

> An "obstruction" is any flagstick, sand box, ball-washer, implement, stake, guidepost, vehicle, seat, shelter or similar obstruction; clothes; ground under repair; drain covers; a hole made by the greenkeeper; material piled for removal, including a pile of leaves or cut grass; guy wires and other material used to support trees, poles and other objects; artificial poles for electric wires; artificial steps not made entirely of earth, but not steps of building which are not classified as obstructions under this Rule; parts of bridges and abutments not in confines of hazards; protective screens, rope and railings; stakes defining hazards and boundaries, but not fences or fence posts; parts of water systems and their covers, containers, bases and supports, including fountains, pumps, pumphouses, tanks, valves, hose and sprinklers; traps for insects and animals; boards for scores and notices; tents; refreshment stands; paper, bottles and similar artificial objects.

Fortunately the R&A took a totally different tack in their 1950 experimental code:

> An "obstruction" is anything artificial erected or placed on the course and anything temporarily left on the course. Boundaries are not obstructions.

162

This eminently sensible approach to the problem of defining obstructions became part of the joint USGA-R&A code in 1952 (with minor changes in phrasing). It was reworded in 1960 and expanded slightly, and given its current form in 1984.

The point at which the ball must be dropped to obtain relief from interference by an obstruction was specified for the first time in the 1891 R&A code as "at the nearest point of the course." The 1899 code changed this to "as near as possible to the place where it lay, but not nearer the hole." These requirements remained in force until the R&A 1950 experimental code specified that the ball be dropped at a distance of not more than two club-lengths. Our current precise instructions for determining the nearest point that avoids interference were adopted in 1976, and in 1980 the dropping distance from that point was reduced from two club-lengths to one. A recent change in Rule 24 was the addition, in 1992, of Rule 24-2c providing for a ball lost in an immovable obstruction.

Abnormal Ground Conditions

The main body of this rule treats problems that arise with certain types of abnormal conditions, specifically, casual water, areas of ground under repair or damage wrought by various burrowing and digging creatures. The equivalent nature of these three types of situation is obvious to the modern golfer, and for this reason they're grouped together in one rule in our current code. The recognition of this equivalence was, however, a long time coming. If these situations have been treated at all, they've been treated under different rules during most of the history of the written rules of golf.

EARTH AND WATER SEEM TO STRIVE AGAIN

Before 1883, no code recognized what we nowadays call casual water.

Before the Wimbledon golfers adopted their innovative rules of 1883, no code recognized what we nowadays call casual water. Earlier on, water was quite simply water; it cost a stroke to lift out of it. (*See also Rule 26: Water Hazards.*)

The first code of the Gentlemen Golfers in 1744 mentioned abnormal ground conditions of a sort:

> Neither Trench, Ditch, nor Dyke made for the preservation of the Links . . . shall be counted a Hazard.

The St. Andrews golfers adopted the same rule in 1754. Such works as those described probably could be considered what we nowadays call ground under repair. Such a condition is clearly described in the next code adopted by the Gentlemen Golfers in 1775, when a free drop was granted when the ball was

> in any of the Water-tracts for draining the Links, when the cut of the Spade appears at the place where the Ball lyes.

This sort of difficulty seems to have been fairly common in the early days of golf, but free drops weren't always granted. In 1776 golfers at Bruntsfield links in Edinburgh had to play the ball as it lay in both the "Meadow Ditch" and the "Quarries' Pipe Track."

The actual term *ground under repair* first appeared in the 1882 R&A code, and has remained an important part of the rules ever since. It was described very specifically: "ground under repair by the conservator of the Links." The significance of the exact wording of this rule for the history of the rules, and for the history of golf in general, lies in the fact that the "conservator" mentioned was Tom Morris. He had returned to St. Andrews from Prestwick in 1864 to take over combined duties as both professional and what we nowadays call *greenkeeper*. If a ball lay on ground that Old Tom was repairing, it could be "lifted, dropped behind the hazard, and played without losing a stroke."

JUST EXACTLY WHERE?

In the R&A code of 1891 the dropping point was "at the nearest point of the course." The 1899 code put the dropping point "as near as possible to the place where it lay, but not nearer the hole." These requirements remained in force until 1972, when they were changed to "within two club-lengths of the point on the margin of such area nearest to which the ball originally lay, but not nearer the hole." The instructions for determining the dropping point were rewritten in 1976 and took on a form close to our present rule, but they still specified two club-lengths. Two club-lengths gave way in 1980 to a single club-length; the rule has remained essentially unchanged since then. This specification is in keeping with the rulings in the earliest USGA codes, which consistently interpreted "as near as possible" as "within a club length."

The rule governing ground under repair was combined with the rule on obstructions in 1891 and remained part of that rule until 1952. The first joint R&A-USGA code, in 1952, separated it from the rule on obstructions and joined it with the rules governing casual water and damage caused by burrowing animals. This produced a rule that was basically the same as our present rule, with relief from all these conditions as described in the foregoing paragraph.

THE VOICE OF NATURE LOUDLY CRIES

The third main concern of present Rule 25 is that of damage caused to the course by the activity of various types of burrowing and digging animals. This concern turned up in the early St. Andrews codes, where it referred to damage caused by rabbits. The St. Andrews golfers didn't join other clubs that adopted rules allowing the ball to be lifted and dropped anywhere (with one stroke penalty). They continued to allow lifting only under certain circumstances. (*See Rule 13: Ball Played as It Lies*.) Their 1812 code contained this rule:

> If the Ball lie in a Rabbit-scrape the Player shall not be at liberty to take it out, but must play it as from any common hazard, if however it be in one of the burrows, he may lift it, drop it behind the hazard, and play with an Iron without losing a stroke.

This rule remained in all St. Andrews codes through 1857, but it was discarded in 1858 when a more general unplayable ball rule was adopted.

165

This new rule required the ball always to be played as it lay in match play or the hole given up, but allowed lifting and teeing the ball upon loss of two strokes in stroke play. *(See Rule 27: Unplayable Ball.)* Some clubs that had followed the St. Andrews golfers by adopting their rabbit-scrape rule continued to abide by it. The Honourable Company had adopted it in 1839, and it was still a part of their last independent code in 1866. When the Liverpool Golf Club adopted the 1875 R&A code, they added to it a rule that gave them a free drop from a rabbit scrape on the putting green within ten yards of the hole.

MOUNTAINS AND MOLEHILLS

All mention of rabbits disappeared from the rules of the R&A until 1891, when they suddenly popped into view again. Rabbit scrapes were included in the first list of hazards, which appeared in the 1891 code. *(See Rule 13 for the complete list.)* The same list named molehills, moles being another candidate for the title of most damaging burrowing animal. Although mention of moles disappeared from R&A codes in 1899, the animals continued to be a problem, especially on inland courses, which were being founded with increasing frequency at just that time. This led to the Midland Golf Association's addressing the issue when it adopted a set of local rules on 10 June 1908:

> A ball lying on or touching a mole hill, or dung which cannot well be removed with a club, may be lifted and dropped behind without penalty.

These local rules were subsequently approved by the Rules of Golf Committee and were widely applied. They remained essentially unchanged until the rule combining the three main concerns of present Rule 25 came in 1952. Its development from that point on has already been described.

HAPPY WANDERER

Our present rule also includes the contingency of a ball finding its way onto a green other than that of the hole being played—a wrong putting green. This contingency has been part of this rule only since 1984. Between 1952 and 1984 it was part of the rule covering play on the putting green, which was a bit illogical since a ball on the wrong putting green can't be played there. Before 1952, such a rule was found only in the 1946 unilateral USGA code. A somewhat similar concern goes much farther back than that, however—one hundred seventy years farther back, to be precise.

In 1776, the forerunners of the Royal Burgess Golfing Society, playing then at Bruntsfield Links, adopted a rule granting a free drop "If your Ball falls into any of the Short Holes made for the practice of putting." Some similar rule can be found in most of the codes adopted by most golf clubs during the nineteenth century. The St. Andrews golfers were initially concerned in

1812 with "the supernumerary hole on the hole-across green" (that is, the huge expanse that now serves as putting green for holes 5 and 13 on the Old Course), but after 1832 all their greens except the two end greens had two holes. As this rule developed during the nineteenth century and early twentieth century, the definition gradually changed to a variety of terms such as *a made hole*, *a hole made for golfing*, and others. In the 1920s and 1930s the general description "a hole made by a greenkeeper" was in use.

AND TRAVELED FAR

Originally the primary concern was a ball going into a wrong hole, since there was no clearly defined putting green, but eventually, when putting greens became distinct, it was enough for a ball to be on a wrong putting green rather than in a wrong hole. *(See Rule 16: The Putting Green.)* A surprisingly long time passed before this distinction was made. The situation was first taken into account in the same set of local rules adopted in 1908 by the Midland Golf Association that covered the case of molehills. The rule became part of the USGA unilateral code of 1946, and finally became a permanent part of the rules in 1952.

GOING NOWHERE

The contingency of the embedded ball covered by paragraph 25-2 has caused quite a few problems through the years. Our present rule took form as recently as 1984, when the term *closely-mown area* was defined to include "paths through the rough, cut to fairway height or less." It's a rather surprising fact that this was the first time that the term *fairway* appeared in the rules of golf, even though it has been in use in the speech of golfers during most of this century. The rules have studiously avoided employing this everyday term. Between 1908 and 1933, for example, the teeing ground was to be "indicated by two marks placed in a line as nearly as possible at right angles to the line of play," where the phrase "the line of play" was a substitution for "the course," used in this definition in all codes of the R&A between 1891 and 1907.

GREEN TURF BENEATH MY FEET

The course was in wide use in the sense of *fairway* during the entire nineteenth century and the first decade of the twentieth, sometimes giving way to the expressions "the driving course" and "the fair course." These terms had in turn gradually replaced the eighteenth-century term *the fair Green*. The situation wasn't made any less complicated by a good deal of terminological overlapping. Horace Hutchinson supplied a glossary of golf terms in his book *Golf* in The Badminton Library, published in 1890, in which he gave the definition:

167

Course.—That portion of the Links on which the game ought to be played, generally bounded on either side by rough ground or other hazard.

Certainly every golfer will agree that's where the game ought to be played! In the 1899 R&A code we find *course* used in the modern sense in the definition:

> The term "out of bounds" shall mean any place outside the defined or recognised boundaries of the course.

In this same code, *course* was also used in the sense of *fairway* in the definition of the teeing ground ("indicated by two marks placed in a line, as nearly as possible at right angles to the course").

We find perhaps the most peculiar term for what we now call the fairway used in a rule adopted in 1857 by the (Old) Manchester Golf Club: "the highway." Perhaps it's not really so peculiar after all. *Fairway* was originally a nautical term meaning a clear channel, in other words, a highway at sea. The idea is clearly the same, but it was the term *fairway* that caught on in the speech of golfers.

ROUGHING IT

The rules also used the term *rough* for the first time in the definition of "closely mown area" in 1984. The drafters of the rules have always been careful not to use or try to define these terms so familiar to all golfers, simply because they defy definition. The meaning of the phrase "cut to fairway height" is highly relative. "Fairway height" on one course can be the height of the rough on another, or even on the same course at a different time and under different

"Fairway height" on one course can be the height of the rough on another.

AN EARLY WALKER CUP TRIAL AT ST. ANDREWS.

conditions. Both *fairway* and *rough* are used frequently in Decisions, however, reflecting everyday usage. Decision 24-2b/8 points out their equivalent status in the rules:

> **Q. A player whose ball lies in the rough close to the fairway is entitled to relief from an immovable obstruction. In obtaining relief under Rule 24-2b(i), may the player drop the ball on the fairway?**
>
> **A. Yes. There is no distinction in the Rules between fairway and rough, both are covered by the term "through the green."**

The use of the terms *rough* and *fairway* in Rule 25-2 is not intended as a general definition, but rather serves another purpose. Here these terms refer only to conditions on a given course at a given time, making possible direct comparison between what is rough and what is fairway at that place and time.

JUST PLAIN STUCK

To return to the embedded ball, the forerunners of the Royal Burgess Golfing Society mentioned it first in their 1773 code:

> If a Ball shall be so played as to stick fast to the ground, the said Ball shall be loosened by the opposite party to the owner of the Ball so fastened.

This rule appeared only in Burgess rules until the Society of St. Andrews Golfers adopted it in 1829, but without the restriction that the opponent had to loosen the ball:

> A ball which is stuck fast in the ground may be loosened.

From this code it was adopted into those of other clubs (Perth 1839, Honourable Company 1839, and Blackheath 1844).

THE WATERY SOD

The Royal and Ancient Golf Club rephrased its embedded ball rule a bit more precisely in 1842:

> A ball stuck fast in *wet* ground or sand, may be taken out and replaced loosely in the hole it has made.

This rule remained unchanged through the R&A code of 1891. Willie Park, Jr., in his commentary on that code, had this to say about it:

> This only applies to *wet* ground or sand, and the ball must be replaced in the hole; the hole cannot be closed and the ball placed on the top.

When the newly formed Rules of Golf Committee drew up its first code of rules in 1899, there was no mention of the embedded ball. From then on, a player who found his ball embedded either had to play it or treat it as unplayable. Relief finally came in 1980, when our current rule was adopted.

169

When I first played the game in 1872 at
St. Andrews . . . There was no difference between
water and casual water, it was just water.
Lift your ball and lose a stroke.

—CHARLES B. MACDONALD, 1927

RULE 26 Water Hazards

The first distinction between permanent and casual water was made in the 1883 Wimbledon code.

The contingency of a ball finding its way into water on a golf course has been recognized throughout the entire history of the rules in written form. The eighteenth-century golfers of Edinburgh and St. Andrews were free to lift from "Watter, or any Wattery Filth," but it cost them a stroke. They made no distinction between water permanently present on the course and water temporarily present (what we now call casual water). *(See also Rule 25: Abnormal Ground Conditions.)* It was a very long time before this distinction—so obvious to the modern golfer—was made at all.

As late as 1896, Willie Park, Jr., in his commentary on the 1891 R&A code, was able to say:

> Water means any water on the course, either streams or ponds or pools formed by rain. It is optional to the player either to lift or to play, and he may sometimes prefer to do the latter when the ball lies in a small shallow rain-formed pool.

Park was referring to the 1891 rule:

> If the ball lie or be lost in water, the player may drop a ball under the penalty of one stroke.

So much for free drops from soggy conditions so dear to modern golfers!

THE BRIMMING WATER AMONG THE STONES

The first distinction between permanent and casual water was made in the 1883 Wimbledon code. Despite the distinction, the player was still penalized a stroke for lifting, but making the distinction was in itself significant:

170

If the ball lie in casual water on the course, the player may take it out, change the ball if he please, tee it, and play from behind the hazard, losing a stroke.

If the ball be in a hazard, or the water itself be a recognised hazard, it may be lifted and dropped behind the hazard, under the same penalty.

WAVE THEORY

This code applied a slightly more lenient penalty in the case of a ball in casual water, since the player was then allowed to tee a ball. This lesser penalty can be seen as the first step in the direction of the free drop. The first code of rules issued in 1899 by the Rules of Golf Committee of the R&A made a clear distinction between "casual water through the green" and "water in a hazard," allowing a free drop in the first case, and one stroke penalty in the latter, and so it has remained to this day. The USGA had stolen a slight lead by recognizing casual water on the putting surface in a ruling on the 1891 R&A rule quoted above. This ruling in the first USGA code, issued in 1897, was worded:

> When the ball lies in casual water on the putting green, it may be lifted without penalty and replaced by hand to one side but not nearer the hole.

The USGA was also quicker than the R&A to pick up on the Wimbledon term of a recognized water hazard. It did so in a ruling when it adopted the 1899 R&A code. The R&A followed suit in the code it adopted in 1908, in part because of suggestions from the USGA. *Recognized water hazard* was an unavoidably imprecise term because the definition of hazards in gen-

CASUAL WATER AT ST. ANDREWS DURING THE BRITISH OPEN IN 1927.

171

eral was then so broad and imprecise. *(See Rule 13 for discussion of this problem.)* The joint R&A-USGA conference in 1951 resolved these problems of definition.

AN EVER-ROLLING STREAM

The problems that arise when it isn't physically possible to drop behind a hazard were also resolved by the 1951 conference, through the creation of the concept of the "lateral water hazard." These problems had been recognized as early as 1809, in the Honourable Company's code of that year, and the solution adopted at that time served as the basis for later procedure:

> but where [the player] cannot get behind the hazard without going off the green, he shall be entitled to drop his ball on the green, on a line with the place where it lay.

This principle lies behind our modern lateral water hazard rule, which has remained essentially unchanged from 1952 to this day.

GREEN GROW THE RASHES, O

The reason the precise definition of the lateral water hazard was so long in coming is quite simply because the problem so rarely arose at St. Andrews; the club's early rules made no allowance for this contingency. The main water hazard there was, and still is, the Swilcan Burn in front of the first green. It was actually possible to hit a ball into the North Sea on the first hole through much of the nineteenth century, since construction on the embankment that now holds it at bay wasn't begun until well into the 1860s. This contingency was taken into account starting with the R&A code of 1851, which allowed the player to place a ball a club length "in front of" the sea upon loss of a stroke. It was probably a fairly rare occurrence even in those days.

ON THE BONNIE, BONNIE BANKS OF THE TAY

What we now call lateral water hazards were more of a problem at other golfing venues than they were at St. Andrews, and they led to some quite original solutions. The rules of the Royal Perth Golfing Society and The King James VI Golf Club, formed in 1858 by a group of players splitting off from Royal Perth, are of special interest. These two clubs played over the North Inch on the outskirts of Perth. This lush parkland area is bounded by the River Tay along its western side. Some of the holes were (and still are) laid out right up to the edge of the river, making it very easy to hit a ball into the water. The problems that arose were solved somewhat differently at different times by the two clubs.

The Green Mantle of the Standing Pool

An interesting pre-1952 handling of a lateral water hazard took place during the final round of the 1930 US Open Championship at Interlachen in Minneapolis. Bobby Jones had started the day with a five-stroke lead but was having problems, including three double bogeys on par-three holes. One of them came on the seventeenth hole, which Jones himself described: "at 262 yards it was about as long as a par three could get."

He hit a wood shot into a marsh to the right of the hole, a position that didn't allow him to drop behind the hazard. The referee, USGA official Prescott Bush (father of a later Presidential golfer), told him the marsh was a "parallel water hazard" and he should drop beside it, adding a penalty stroke. Jones balanced the resulting double bogey five with a birdie three on the last hole and, as the whole world knows, won the tournament as the third leg in his Grand Slam in 1930.

BOBBY JONES AT THE 1930 U.S. OPEN.

When the King James VI club adopted its first code of rules in 1860, it copied very closely the 1858 R&A rules—probably because the club's first captain, the Rev. Charles Robertson (better known in Scottish golfing history as "Gowfin' Charlie") was also a member of the Royal and Ancient. The R&A code, however, made no provision for a broad river flowing closely alongside several holes. The King James VI golfers made an interesting addition to the R&A water hazard rule, permitting the player to tee a ball beside the river with loss of a stroke:

> Should a ball be driven into the Tay and seen by both parties, it is considered not lost; if not seen by both parties, it is lost, and must be played according to Rule X [Ball Lost]. When not lost, the ball must be placed a club-length in front of the river, the player or party losing a stroke.

In other words, there had to be what we nowadays call reasonable evidence that the ball had gone into the river if the player was to be allowed to treat it as a lateral water hazard. Otherwise, he had to play stroke-and-distance.

A FISH STORY

Difficulties apparently arose in applying this rule, perhaps because of the reluctance on the part of some players to admit they had seen their opponent's ball go into the river. In any event, this special rule lasted only six years, and in April 1866 those two sentences were changed to

> Should a ball be driven into water and lost, or, if seen, not recovered, another ball will be substituted, and played according to the preceding portion of this rule as if the ball had not been lost.

That is, the penalty was now always stroke-only.

BY THY MURMURING STREAM

The Royal Perth Golfing Society had always played by a code of rules adapted quite freely from R&A rules, but in April 1870 they amended their water hazard rule:

> with reference to a ball driven into the Tay the Rule in future shall be, that a ball driven from any part of the Course and *lofting* into the Tay shall, whether seen or recovered or not, be held as a lost ball and another must be played from the spot at which the first ball was struck the player or party losing the distance besides a stroke; but that in the case of a ball lofting on any part of the course and afterwards rolling or otherwise getting into the Tay whether seen or recovered or not and not being playable, another ball shall be played opposite the spot at which the first ball went in & within a club length of the water's edge the player or party losing a stroke only.

This ingenious distinction between a ball entering a water hazard on the fly or on the bounce is unique in the history of the rules. It's not known exactly how long this Royal Perth rule was in force, but their club's minute books suggest that R&A rules were adopted in toto in 1878.

DOWN IN THE REEDS BY THE RIVER

The stroke-and-distance option of proceeding in the case of a ball in a water hazard that is part of present Rule 26 first appeared in the 1933 code, when it was allowed only if the ball had been played from the teeing ground. The distance-only penalty adopted by the 1950 R&A experimental code in the case of a ball lost, out of bounds, or unplayable was also applied to a ball in a water hazard. This experimental distance-only penalty was abandoned in 1952. *(See Rule 27: Ball Lost or Out of Bounds.)* The earlier stroke-and-distance penalty was restored and retained in the case of a ball in a water hazard.

The joint USGA-R&A code of 1952 permitted the playing of a provisional ball for a ball that might be lost in a water hazard. We look on this now as being rather strange, since the use of a provisional ball is specifically limitcd by our present provisional ball rule (Rule 27-2: "If a ball may be lost outside a water hazard"). Use of a provisional ball in connection with a water hazard was first allowed by local rule in the 1946 USGA unilateral code, and then adopted as part of both the water hazard and provisional ball rules in 1952. It remained part of the USGA code until 1960 and the R&A code until 1964. *(See Rule 27: Ball Lost or Out of Bounds, page 183, for details.)*

An important part of the rule specified that if the original ball was found in the water hazard and the player elected to play it, he had to play it as it lay and could not drop free of the hazard with loss of a stroke. After this rule had been removed from the main body of the rules, it was reintroduced by both the R&A and the USGA as a suggested local rule in 1968. It continues to be allowed by local rule under special circumstances. *(See also Local Rules.)*

FROGS IN THE MARSH MUD

This all leads into a mention of one of the most problematic situations that a golfer can find himself in: if he has elected to play a ball in a water hazard and, after playing it, the ball is still in the hazard or unplayable either in or outside the hazard. Fans all over the world felt a great sense of sympathy for Payne Stewart when he found himself in just such a pickle on the eighteenth hole of the Belfry during the final round of the 1989 Ryder Cup Match there. No recognition was made in the rules of this often nightmarish situation before 1956. The code adopted that year included a note attached to the water hazard rule that allowed the player to drop the ball outside the hazard if he had not succeeded in hitting it out, naturally on payment of the usual stroke penalty. The only reasonable way to proceed was thus given legal status. This note remained a part of the rule through 1980.

This situation was completely rethought for 1984, and the rule dealing with it rewritten in connection with the reorganization of the rules at that time. The main elements of present Rule 26-2 appeared then, but further additions and adjustments were made in both 1988 and 1992 to produce our current compendious rule. The complexities of this rule are so great, however, that they can easily confuse a player trying to figure them out—especially if he happens to be standing ankle-deep in water at the time. The rules authorities have kindly come to the aid of the golfer beset by this very special golfer's sea of troubles by providing a detailed analysis, with helpful chart, in Decision 26-2/1. The wise golfer will study it carefully beforehand.

Ball Lost or Out of Bounds

Lost Ball

The problem of how to handle a lost ball has caused the longest and most complex dispute in the history of the rules of golf. Strangely enough, the very same rule was observed during both the first few decades and the most recent decades of the more than two hundred fifty years of written rules. From 1775 to 1968, however, chaos reigned.

GOOD BEGINNING

Initially, clarity and harmony prevailed in the approach to a lost ball. The Gentlemen Golfers in 1744 and the St. Andrews Society of Golfers in 1754 adopted the identical rule:

> If you should lose your Ball by its being taken up, or in any other way, you are to go back to the spot where you struck last, and drop another ball, and allow your adversary a stroke for the misfortune.

This rule is in all essential respects the one we play by at the end of the twentieth century, although the mode of expression has changed considerably. When the "Society of Golfers in and about Edinburgh at Bruntsfield Links" (now the Royal Burgess Golfing Society) adopted a code of rules on 8 April 1773, they held to the same principle:

> Any Golfer losing his Ball either by accident or in a hazard, shall go to the place from whence he last struck and lose one.

So it was that three of the most important golf clubs in existence in the early 1770s (and the only ones whose rules we know about) treated a lost ball according to the same principle: what we know today as stroke-and-distance.

THEIR OWN APPROACH

This unanimity was, however, short-lived. In 1775 the Gentlemen Golfers adopted a rule of essentially different character:

The problem of how to handle a lost ball has caused the longest and most complex dispute in the history of the rules of golf.

> If you lose your Ball, you are to drop another as near as can be judged to the
> place where your Ball was lost, and allow your Adversary a stroke for the mis-
> fortune.

They had reduced the penalty for lost ball to stroke only; the player no
longer had to return to where the lost ball had been struck.

YET ANOTHER VIEW

In 1776 the Burgess Golfers at Bruntsfield Links also adopted a new code of
rules, a rather close adaptation of the 1775 code of their colleagues in Leith,
but it didn't include their new penalty for a lost ball. Instead they treated this
contingency in yet a third way:

> If you lose your Ball, you lose the Hole.

They were trying in this way to resolve the conflict between the stroke-
and-distance penalty, which required putting a new ball in play, and the rule
that legislated against changing the ball during the play of a hole ("You are
not to change the Ball which you Strike off the Tee"). This meant that in 1776
the St. Andrews golfers and the two most important clubs in Edinburgh all
played under different rules for a lost ball. This situation set the stage for a
dispute that wasn't finally resolved for nearly two hundred years.

A fourth treatment of this contingency made its appearance in 1790,
when the Burgess golfers gave up their stern lost ball-lost hole rule and adopted yet a new and different rule:

> That when any person having played his ball, loses the same he shall go back
> to the place from which he played and shall thereby *lose only one stroke*,
> namely, that stroke by which his Ball was lost.

This distance-only rule was in effect at Bruntsfield Links until 1802,
when the Edinburgh Burgess Golfing Society, as they were by then called,
went back to playing lost ball-lost hole.

NEVER REALLY KNOW WHAT TO DO

Penalties for a lost ball varied greatly during the nineteenth century. St.
Andrews introduced a new variety in 1812 when they specified that the new
ball should be teed:

> If a Ball is lost, the stroke goes for nothing, the player returns to the spot
> whence the Ball was struck, tees it, and loses a stroke.

Until then both the St. Andrews and Leith golfers had always specified
that the new ball was to be dropped. The stroke-and-distance penalty was in
this way somewhat ameliorated by allowing the ball to be teed. It's worth
pointing out that it also involved a clear-cut exception to the principle of play-

177

ing the ball as it lies. *(See Rule 13 for a detailed discussion of this important question.)* The development of the penalty for lost ball in the codes of these clubs during the eighteenth and nineteenth centuries can be summed up schematically:

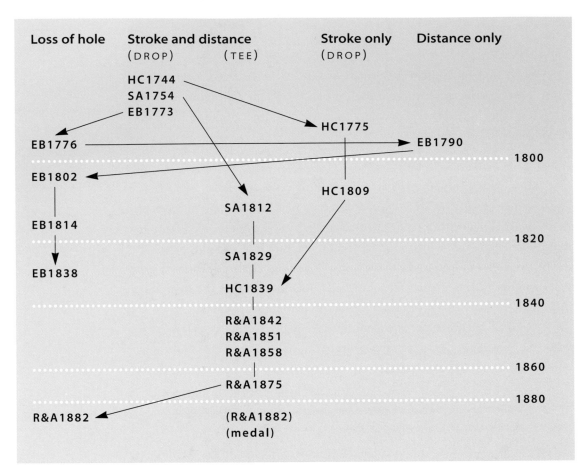

For the sake of simplicity and clarity, only the rules of the three clubs that had adopted codes of rules before 1780* are included on this chart. Other golf clubs that adopted codes of rules during the nineteenth century copied or made adaptations of the lost ball rule of one or the other of these three clubs. They usually followed the Honourable Company in the first three decades of the century before its temporary suspension of activity and the R&A after 1840. *(See Appendix 4.)*

Also for the sake of both simplicity and clarity, no indication of the rules used in stroke play appears on the chart before 1882. During the period 1800-1840 the Edinburgh Burgess Golfers played stroke-and-distance (drop). No

* HC = Honourable Company, EB = Edinburgh Burgess, SA (R&A after 1834) = St. Andrews.

separate mention of the rule in stroke play appears in the St. Andrews rules before 1842, since the same penalty was applied in stroke as in match play (stroke-and-distance [tee]). The R&A adopted a separate stroke play rule in 1842:

> The party losing a ball on a medal day shall, after five minutes search, go back and lose three strokes and the distance as penalty.

This astonishingly stern penalty actually remained in force for four years. On 6 May 1846, the powers-that-were in St. Andrews relented and ordained that "the penalty for a Ball lost on a Medal Day should be the same as on ordinary occasions vizt. the loss of the distance and one stroke."

The R&A had also clarified the language in its lost ball rule by 1842. The ambiguous phrase introduced in the 1812 rule (and continued in the code of 1829), "the stroke goes for nothing," was removed and the penalty made clear:

> If a ball is lost, the player (or his partner, if a double match) returns to the spot where the ball was struck, tees another ball, and loses both the distance and a stroke.

ABOUT FACE

The R&A made a major change in its lost-ball rule in 1882. It retained the penalty of stroke-and-distance (tee) in stroke play, but adopted the penalty of lost ball-lost hole in match play. The R&A had steadfastly refused to adopt this penalty during the 106 years since it had been adopted at Bruntsfield Links. The reason for the change was explained in the recommendations of the committee appointed to draw up the new code: they considered "that in the crowded state of the green it will save time." A very modern consideration!

This change didn't meet with universal approval. Many golf clubs that played by their own rules or adaptations of R&A rules continued to play stroke-and-distance in both match and stroke play. The Royal Wimbledon Golf Club adopted stroke-and-distance in its innovative 1883 code. The 1882 lost ball-lost hole rule was one of the changes in the 1882 R&A code that had inspired the Wimbledoners, led by William Laidlaw Purves, to produce their own code.

TRIVIAL PURSUIT

In their 1882 code the St. Andreans for the first time imposed a general time limit on a search for a lost ball. The only time limit that the R&A had ever imposed was a five-minute limit in the short-lived three-strokes-and-distance rule in the 1842 code. The first time limit on search for a lost ball had appeared in the code adopted by the Aberdeen golfers in 1783, a code that was

179

quite innovative in many ways. This five-minute time limit was later adopted by several clubs (Blackheath, 1828; Musselburgh, 1829; Edinburgh Burgess, 1838), but neither the Honourable Company nor the St. Andrews golfers had ever shown any interest in imposing a general time limit.

SEARCH PARTY

When the R&A adopted the lost ball-lost hole rule in 1882, however, it adopted a ten-minute time limit on search. This excessively long search period was itself short-lived. It was abandoned in 1891, when it was reduced to the more traditional five minutes. In the first universally valid code of 1899, the statement of this time limit was shifted out of the lost ball rule itself and into the new Definitions section, where it has ever since remained safely ensconced.

Even those clubs that had objected to the lost ball-lost hole rule in match play were finally forced to accept it when they recognized the R&A as the pre-eminent authority in rules matters, following the establishment of the Rules of Golf Committee in 1897. Differing penalties for a lost ball in match and stroke play remained in effect throughout the golf-playing world until 1920. The development of the penalty for a lost ball after 1920 is closely tied to the penalty for a ball out of bounds.

Ball Out of Bounds

The ball-out-of-bounds contingency wasn't provided for in the early rules, simply because no clear-cut limits to the playing area were recognized then. If a ball disappeared (or was absconded with) on the public grounds that served as golf courses, it had to be treated as lost. Only one attempt to soften this harsh reality was made in the early period of the game. In 1816 the Aberdeen Golf Club, which at that time followed the lead of the Edinburgh Burgess Golfers and played lost ball-lost hole in match play, adopted the following stroke play rule:

> In case of a lost ball, another may be submitted if in the fair course, without penalty, but if driven off the ordinary ground another may be dropped in its place, as near as possible to the place where the ball was lost, and the player to lose one stroke.

The phrase "off the ordinary ground" was the only attempt in the early codes to define what we now call out of bounds.

Golf, and the conditions under which it was played, had changed sufficiently by the end of the nineteenth century to require a precise definition. The first such appeared in 1899 in the first code of rules prepared by the R&A's new Rules of Golf Committee:

The term "out of bounds" shall mean any place outside the defined or recognised boundaries of the course.

The penalty:

> If a ball be driven out of bounds, a ball shall be dropped at the spot from which the stroke was played, under penalty of loss of distance.

This penalty applied to both match play and stroke play. The definition was changed somewhat in the R&A code of 1908:

> "Out of bounds" is all ground on which play is prohibited.

The penalty remained the same, but provision was made for teeing the ball if the new ball was to be played from the teeing-ground.

BY LOCAL RULE

In some quarters it was felt that distance only was too lenient a penalty, and that the contingency of ball out of bounds should be treated the same way as a lost ball. To make allowance for this point of view, the Rules of Golf Committee agreed in September of 1909 to allow clubs to make this adjustment by local rule, and it adopted the following Note to the rule prescribing the penalty of distance only:

> (a) In match and stroke play, a ball may be played as provided in paragraph (1) with the addition of a penalty stroke. (b) In match play, a ball which lies out of bounds may be treated as a lost ball.

This Note provided a wide range of options: in the case of a ball hit out of bounds, the penalty of stroke-and-distance was now possible in both stroke and match play. The provision remained in force until 1920.

INTRANSIGENCE

It was indicative of the debate that later developed around this matter that the USGA chose not to follow the lead of the R&A on this point. The USGA failed to adopt the Note that allowed the addition of a penalty stroke by local rule. Thus, a ball hit out of bounds in the United States was always penalized by distance only.

In the code of rules adopted by the R&A on 29 September 1920, the penalties for both lost ball and ball out of bounds were extensively revised. In both match and stroke play the penalty for lost ball was once again established as stroke-and-distance, returning to the situation in the codes of the R&A before 1882. Now, however, the ball could be teed only if played from the teeing-ground, as in the case of ball out of bounds. A ball out of bounds was to be treated the same, but in this case the rule provided that "the penalty stroke

Breathing a Sigh of Relief

The rule concerning a ball hit out of bounds played a dramatic part in the famous playoff in the 1913 US Open at The Country Club in Brookline, Massachusetts, between the great British professionals Harry Vardon and Ted Ray and the local amateur Francis Ouimet. On the long par-4 fifth hole Ouimet hit a brassie shot to the green out of bounds. The distance-only penalty allowed him to salvage a bogey five that kept him even with Vardon and Ray. He refused to crack under pressure and eventually won the championship.

FRANCIS OUIMET AND CADDIE.

may be remitted by Local Rule." Thus the situation was now reversed in the case of ball out of bounds. Between 1909 and 1920, the basic penalty for a ball out of bounds had been distance only, but a penalty stroke could be added by local rule. After 1920 the basic penalty was stroke-and-distance, but the penalty could be remitted by local rule. These penalties remained in force in Britain until 1 January 1950.

BEATING ABOUT THE BUSH

Once again, the USGA took a more lenient position than the R&A. In the United States the penalty stroke in the case of both lost ball and ball out of bounds could be remitted by local rule. This situation remained until the USGA unilaterally adopted its radical code of rules in 1946. At that time local option was abandoned and the penalties for lost ball and ball out of bounds were separated: stroke-and-distance for lost ball and distance only for ball out of bounds.

When the R&A issued its 1950 experimental code of rules, it went in the opposite direction: the penalties in the two cases were unified and became distance only in each case. Having arrived at this point, the rules-making bodies on the two sides of the Atlantic Ocean had reached an impasse. There was no way to reconcile the differing penalties for lost ball and ball out of bounds, and there was a real danger that golf would be played according to different rules in different parts of the world. Fortunately, the 1951 conference on the rules resolved this problem, along with others, and the R&A and USGA adopted identical stroke-and-distance penalties in both situations.

SHILLY-SHALLYING

This resolution was, however, not the end of the matter. The USGA experimented further and reduced the penalty for both lost ball and ball out of bounds to distance only as of 1 January 1960. This change lasted only one year, however, and the stroke-and-distance penalty was restored for 1961. At the same time, though, an alternate penalty was allowed by local rule for a ball out of bounds, permitting a ball to be dropped within two club-lengths of the place where it last crossed the boundary line, with a penalty of one stroke. This stroke-only penalty had not been in effect anywhere since the Honourable Company dropped it in 1839. Nor was it fated to outlive the 1960s. It was dropped by the USGA on 1 January 1962, then reinstated on 1 January 1964, and finally abandoned on 1 January 1968. Since then the penalty for both a lost ball and a ball out of bounds in both match and stroke play has remained stroke-and-distance, with no exceptions. A rules controversy that originated in 1775 was finally settled.

Provisional Ball

The provisional ball is relatively new to the rules of golf; it was first used only for a ball possibly out of bounds. In 1902 this sentence was added to the rule, introduced in 1899, governing a ball "driven out of bounds":

> If it be doubtful whether a ball has been played out of bounds, another may be dropped and played, but if it be discovered that the first ball is not out of bounds, it shall continue in play without penalty.

This restricted use of the provisional ball continued until 1920. It was referred to then as a provisional ball, and its use was extended to include balls that might be either lost or unplayable. This revision also added that the provisional ball must be played before the player went forward to search for the original ball. A further condition was added in 1933: that the provisional ball could be played until the player reached "the place where the previous ball is likely to be."

The use of a provisional ball for a ball that might be lost in a water hazard first appeared in the 1946 USGA code and was incorporated into the joint R&A-USGA code of 1952. When the USGA experimented with the penalty for ball lost or out of bounds in 1960, it also unilaterally eliminated the use of a provisional ball in connection with a ball that might be unplayable or lost in a water hazard. The R&A followed suit in 1964 for a ball that might be lost in a water hazard, and in 1968 for a ball that might be unplayable. Since 1968 a provisional ball has been allowed only for a ball that may be lost outside a water hazard or out of bounds in all the codes adopted by both the USGA and the R&A. In 1956 the condition had been added that the player must state his intention to play a provisional ball, and in 1972 the further condition was added that if he failed to do so, the new ball played was to be considered the ball in play.

During its short seventy-year history the provisional ball rule has become one of the best known and most frequently used of all golf rules, saving players enormous amounts of time.

Ball Unplayable

The evolution of the rule governing an unplayable ball is closely tied up with the rule governing a ball that is lost or out of bounds. Indeed, from 1952 through 1980 these three contingencies were covered in the same rule. In many respects, however, there's such an essential difference between an unplayable ball and a ball lost or out of bounds that these cases are best handled separately, as they are in our present code of rules. Because a ball may be unplayable in so many different situations, the question arises as to what penalty should be assigned if a player really considers he can't play a shot. Is the ball unplayable in the sense that a lost ball or a ball out of bounds is unplayable, or is it unplayable in the sense that a ball in a water hazard is (usually) unplayable? An answer has to be found, since different penalties are assigned in each of these cases. The evolution of the rule governing an unplayable ball is tied to this problem of an appropriate penalty.

ALTOGETHER UPLIFTING

The question of an unplayable ball is also closely tied to the rule governing playing the ball as it lies. It's generally assumed that this is one of the basic principles of the game, but as far back as written rules go, it never has been strictly adhered to. It's even quite possible that before 1744 the player could lift and drop his ball, with loss of a stroke, anywhere on the course. Most codes of the second half of the eighteenth century restricted such free lifting and dropping in some way or other, but there was a return to what may have been an earlier practice in most early nineteenth-century codes. (*See Rule 13 for detailed discussion*.) The St. Andrews golfers, however, continued to restrict the conditions for lifting free of a difficulty, and it was their rules that eventually dominated thinking on this subject during the second half of the century.

In the St. Andrews codes of 1812, 1829, and 1842, a ball could not be lifted from a rabbit scrape, but if it lay in a burrow the player could "lift it, drop it behind the hazard, and play with an Iron without losing a stroke." This rule also applied if the ball lay in the other hole, "the supernumerary hole," on each double green on the Old Course.

A ball half-covered with water could be lifted, teed, and played "from behind the hazard, losing a stroke." This rule was specifically applied in 1842 to a ball in the Swilcan Burn on the first hole. In no other case was lifting allowed.

THE GODDESS DISCORDIA WRITES A RULE

When the St. Andreans adopted a new and substantially revised code of rules in 1851, they experimented with a quite different approach:

> XIV.—Unplayable Balls.
>
> When the ball lies in a hole or in any place that the player considers it not playable, he shall, with the consent of his adversary, lift the ball, drop it behind the hazard, and lose a stroke. Should the adversary say, however, that he thinks the ball playable, then he (the adversary) plays the ball; if he gets the ball out of the place in two strokes, these two strokes count as if the player had played the ball; the player then plays the ball as if he himself had played it out; but, if the adversary does not get the ball out at two strokes, then, as stated above, it is lifted and dropped, a stroke being lost.

It's not difficult to imagine the discord brought about by this rule. Its rather tortured language was made a little more precise in 1852, when the phrase "if he gets the ball out of the place in two strokes" was replaced by the phrase "if he makes the ball playable in two strokes," but the rule remained otherwise unchanged. There was the obvious difficulty of whether both players could agree that the ball had indeed been made playable, and this must have led to a great deal of contention. A more reasonable approach prevailed by 1856, when a rule was substituted that provided for playing every ball where it lay in match play, and the right to lift and drop anywhere in stroke play. This formed the basis of the rule governing unplayable balls not only in the R&A code of 1858, but provided a useful approach to the general problem for many years to come:

> In Match playing every ball must be played, wherever it lies, or the hole to be given up, excepting when it lies on clothes, in water or in the bed of the burn, or in any of the holes, or short holes, made for golfing, in which latter case it may be lifted, dropt behind the hazard, and played with an iron, without losing a stroke. In Medal playing a ball may, under a penalty of two strokes, be lifted out of a difficulty of any description, and teed behind the hazard, and if in any of the golfing holes, it may be lifted, dropt, and played as above, without a penalty.

It's significant for the history of the rule that the penalty for lifting in stroke play was raised to two strokes and the ball could be teed.

186

WIDESPREAD MAYHEM

Before describing the further evolution of this rule, it's worth noting that although the St. Andrews golfers gave up the right to attack their opponent's ball in 1856, the practice was quite widespread at other clubs during most of the rest of the century. Actually, it wasn't the St. Andreans who originated this practice. Its first recorded occurrence is in the records of the Panmure Golf Club, adjacent to Carnoustie, which adopted the rules of golf "as laid down by" the R&A at its first meeting in 1845, but with the special additional rule:

> If a ball be so placed that the player says that it is not playable, and his opponent agrees to it, he shall drop it behind and lose a stroke, but if disputed the opposite player shall be bound to play it out in not more than three strokes, which shall stand against the player whose ball is so played, but if not taken out in three strokes, it shall be considered an unplayable ball and played as above.

It's difficult to say whether the similar 1851 R&A rule had its origins at Panmure, but the partial similarity of terminology would indicate a probable connection between them, even though the two clubs allowed the opponent a different number of whacks at the ball. A motion to discard this rule failed in 1862, but there is no record of when the Panmure golfers gave it up.

There is also some uncertainty about how long the rule lasted at the Dunbar Golf Club, in East Lothian, another club that had adopted it. Dunbar adopted an unplayable ball rule in 1867 that was almost identical with the St. Andrews rule of 1851 (except that the adversary was allowed "to get it out in one or two strokes"). The records suggest the Dunbar golfers played according to this rule until at least 1875, and perhaps longer. It was certainly all over in 1894, when they officially adopted the 1891 rules of the R&A.

C'est la guerre

The Liverpool Golf Club, which was formed in 1869, joined those other nineteenth-century golfers devoted to this special form of mayhem. On the Ides of March in 1870 they adopted a rule that not only revealed a knowledge of earlier unplayable ball practices at other clubs, but a desire to give them a definite Liverpudlian flavor as well:

> Every ball must be played where it lies or the hole given up, except when it lies in water, or in any of the holes made for golfing, or in a rabbit hole, or scrape, out of which it cannot be played; in which case it may be lifted, teed behind the hazard, and played with loss of one stroke. When a player declares his ball unplayable his opponent has the right to challenge, and on his adversary refusing to play it, may endeavour to take it out of the hazard. If he succeeds in three strokes, or less, the ball should be considered playable, and the number of strokes so played by the adversary shall count to the score of the proper

The St. Andrews golfers gave up the right to attack their opponent's ball in 1856.

187

player of the ball; but should the adversary fail to extricate the ball in three strokes, the number of strokes so played shall be added to his score, and the ball considered unplayable and treated accordingly.

This ingenious rule must have served to liven up many a match at Hoylake. The added special condition that any strokes the adversary made at the ball counted against his score, if he failed to extricate it, was a true stroke of genius and must have served to discourage any frivolous claims of playability. On the whole, though, playing on the opponent's ball goes against the basic idea of golf, which is that each side plays its own ball free of interference from the other. The Hoylake golfers finally realized this and in 1875 adopted a new code of rules that was a close adaptation of the new R&A code. Since then, normal golf has been played at Hoylake, which has been the site of many great matches and championships.

C'est la vie

Yet another ingenious version of this rule was in use by the Lanark Golf Club, to the southwest of Edinburgh. This club was founded in 1851, but since we have no early records we don't know what rules the club played by before 1883, when it adopted "Rules of The Lanark Golf Club and for The Game of Golf as Played by the Club." A freely adapted and condensed version of the 1882 R&A code, these rules contained this very succinct and undoubtedly very effective variant of the rule:

> An unplayable ball, except in a hazard, may be lifted and dropped over the shoulder, the player losing a stroke. If the opponent objects, he shall be allowed three strokes to play it out; in the event of succeeding he wins the hole; if he fails he loses it.

It isn't known how long this rule was in effect at Lanark, but it was perhaps the last gasp of this quaint form of hostility on the links.

LESS MAYHEM, MORE CONFUSION

The rule adopted by the R&A in 1858 that mandated playing the ball where it lay (under penalty of loss of hole, with certain exceptions) in match play, or lifting and teeing (under penalty of two strokes) in stroke play, remained essentially unchanged until 1920. Since 1882 a lost ball had been penalized by loss of hole in match play, but in 1920 the R&A returned to its original penalty of stroke-and-distance in both match and stroke play. The new code combined these two cases into one rule: "Lost and Unplayable Ball." The player was now permitted to play stroke-and-distance in match play if he deemed his ball to be unplayable. This rule was also included in the code adopted in 1933 by both the R&A and the USGA. Both these 1920 and 1933 codes allowed the player to lift his ball "from any place on the course" in stroke play. He could then either play stroke-and-distance or tee the ball behind the spot from which it was lifted under penalty of two strokes.

This was the rather confused situation when the R&A and the USGA, each working on its own, set about revising the rules after the Second World War. The 1946 USGA code and the 1950 R&A code treated lost ball, ball out of bounds, and unplayable ball quite differently. The USGA included lost ball and unplayable ball under the same rule, with stroke-and-distance in both cases in match play and either stroke-and-distance or—still under two strokes penalty—teeing behind in stroke play for an unplayable ball. The condition that the ball could be teed even when not on the teeing ground was continued in this otherwise quite revolutionary code, although by this time it was an obvious and glaring anachronism. New methods of teeing the ball had made it obsolete by the 1930s. (*See Rule 11: Teeing Ground, page 97.*) In this 1946 USGA code, a ball out of bounds was treated in a separate rule and was penalized by loss of distance only.

SORTING IT OUT

The 1950 R&A code involved a sweeping reduction of penalties in these cases. They were treated in three separate rules, but the same penalty was applied: loss of distance only. An unplayable ball could also be dropped within two club lengths for a penalty of one stroke. (*See also Bernard Darwin's Preface to this code in Appendix 5 for discussion of this point.*) Both these postwar codes attempted to define unplayable ball, but the results were very different. The USGA was quite modern in its approach:

> The player is the sole judge as to when his ball is unplayable. It may be declared unplayable at any place on the course.

This obviously served eventually as the basis for our present definition. The 1950 R&A code also allowed the player to be the sole judge, but under rather limiting conditions:

> The ball is "unplayable" if the player consider he cannot make a stroke at it and dislodge it into a playable position.

These obviously unworkable conditions, allowing too much latitude for individual judgment and ability, were quickly abandoned, and they never appeared in any later code.

The wholesale reduction of penalties in the 1950 R&A code was also unworkable, and Robert Harris's dire predictions were fulfilled many times over. (*See Part II, Chapter 5.*) This was the situation when the joint R&A-USGA conference was called in 1951 to resolve these and other conflicts and differences in the rules of the game as it was being played in different parts of the world. It's important to note that the contingencies of lost ball and unplayable ball had been treated essentially the same after 1920.

DENOUEMENT

This identical treatment of unplayable ball and lost ball was continued in the first uniform R&A-USGA code of 1952, and it was even augmented with the inclusion of ball out of bounds under the same rule. In all three cases the next stroke could be played under penalty of stroke-and-distance in all forms of play, and, in the case of unplayable ball, the ball could also be dropped behind or within two club lengths under penalty, now once again, of two strokes. This two-stroke penalty remained in force for another sixteen years in the codes adopted by the R&A. When the USGA experimented with the penalties for lost ball and ball out of bounds in 1960, important changes were also made in the unplayable ball rule, with reduction in the penalty to one stroke and elimination of the possibility of playing a provisional ball. *(See Rule 27: Ball Lost or Out of Bounds.)* Joseph Dey explained the rationale behind these changes in his 1959 article on the experimental USGA code:

> In the USGA experimental amendments for 1960, the one-stroke relief from an unplayable lie will bring it into line with the water hazard Rule.
>
> These two Rules will thus have two identical optional methods of getting out of trouble. Consequently, a provisional ball will be unnecessary and will be prohibited for a ball unplayable or in a water hazard, under the USGA trial code.

John M. Winters, Jr., Chairman of the USGA Rules of Golf Committee in 1960 provided a little more background on the reasons for these changes in an article in 1961. Referring to the water hazard rule, he explained:

> It had proven fair and workable over many years with its two optional methods of relief, allowing for playing a ball, under penalty of one stroke, either:
>
> (a) Behind the water hazard (or within two club-lengths of a lateral water hazard margin);
>
> - or -
>
> (b) At the place where the original ball was played (stroke and distance).

> It seemed reasonable to give the same relief for a ball unplayable elsewhere than in a water hazard. Therefore, a trial Rule last year brought this into the USGA code (independent of the British). It seems to have worked well and is being tried again in 1961.

By 1968 the R&A had also adopted these changes. Throughout the world since then, a ball declared unplayable has been penalized the same as a ball unplayable in a water hazard, with a provisional ball not allowed in either case. "Unplayable ball" was still included as a section of the same rule as ball lost or out of bounds after 1968, but it was placed in its own separate rule in 1984.

Hush! hush! hush! Here comes the bogey man!

—1890S MUSIC-HALL SONG

Other Forms of Play

RULES 29 THROUGH 32

The original form of golf seems to have been match play, despite the fact that the competition for the Silver Club in 1744, which prompted the first set of written rules, was some combination of stroke and match play. (*See Rules 2 and 3: Match Play and Stroke Play.*) The early codes of rules included very few references to stroke play and, during the eighteenth century, no specific mention of any form of match play other than single match play.

The Edinburgh Burgess golfers seem to have been the group most interested in other forms of play in the early days of the game. They were, at any rate, the first to mention them. Their 1814 code included the rule:

> In a match of more than two players, if a ball is struck twice or oftener successively by one player, that side of the match loses the hole.

MORE PLAYERS

This rule obviously refers to threesome and foursome play and corresponds exactly to present Rule 29-2. The Burgess golfers once again addressed the problem in 1838, but now they referred only to foursome play:

> In a double match, if a ball be struck twice, or oftener successively by the same player, he and his partner shall lose the hole.

Perhaps some of the Burgess golfers were also tennis players and adopted the term *double match* from that game. It's certainly an appropriate term, balancing nicely the term *single match* also used in tennis. It seems to have appealed to other golfers as well. Both the Royal Perth Golfing Society and the Honourable Company adopted it in the lost ball rules in their 1839 codes and the R&A followed their lead in 1842:

> If a ball is lost, the player (or his partner, if a double match) returns to the spot where the ball was struck, tees another ball, and loses both the distance and the stroke.

The original form of golf seems to have been match play.

Perhaps some of the Burgess golfers were also tennis players and adopted the term *double match* from that game.

The lost ball rules in all codes before 1839 had referred only to "the player." This 1842 reference to foursome play appeared in the lost ball rules in all later R&A codes until they suddenly began playing lost ball—lost hole in match play in 1882, making it unnecessary to mention anyone returning anywhere. *(See Rule 27: Ball Lost or Out of Bounds, page 176.)*

HOW MANY DID YOU SAY?

The situation was complicated by the fact that Rule 1 in the 1842 R&A code gave a rather detailed description of the game, beginning:

> The game of Golf is played by two persons, or by four (two a side) playing alternately.

Later in the rule, reference was made to "a match of four" and, after 1858, to both "a match of four" and "a double match." The R&A codes in 1882 and 1888 substituted "a match with two on a side" for "a match of four," but retained "a double match" in the same rule.

TERMS NICELY CLARIFIED

This was all perhaps a bit too confusing even for the St. Andreans, because they rephrased the description of the game in their 1891 code:

> The Game of Golf is played by two or more sides, each playing its own ball. A side may consist of one or more persons.

Later in this code they refer to "a match with two or more on a side." Willie Park, Jr., in his commentary on this code in 1896 wrote that this description refers "to foursome play." Clearly, there must have been competing terms in use for this form of play during the late nineteenth century. The newly appointed Rules of Golf Committee settled the matter in the 1899 R&A code when it provided definitions for the different forms of play that have continued to this day:

> If one player play against another, the match is called "a single." If two play against two, it is called "a foursome." A single player may play against two, when the match is called "a threesome," or three players may play against each other, each playing his own ball, when the match is call "a three-ball match."

The R&A first started to include separate sections describing rules for other forms of play in 1902, with a section on rules for three-ball matches. A ruling in the USGA edition of this 1902 code allowed those rules to be applied to four-ball matches as well. In addition, the USGA allowed—by another ruling—the rules for stroke play to be applied to bogey competitions, thus giving early recognition to that new form of play. It was 1920 before the R&A gave official recognition to it, even though Colonel Bogey had been gracing British courses for nearly thirty years by that time.

THE BOGEY MAN

The idea behind bogey first developed in 1891 at the Coventry Golf Club in England. Hugh Rotherham, a Coventry member, conceived the idea of playing a competition against what he called a "ground score" (what is referred to in our current Rule 32 as a "fixed score"), representing error-free play. After the first such competition was played on May 13 of 1891, the idea spread quickly. Dr. Thomas Browne, honorary secretary of the golf club in Great Yarmouth, on the coast east of Coventry, adopted it at his club. A popular music-hall song of the time referred to "the bogey man," and this term was adopted as the name of the formidable opponent the ground score had become.

During the spring of 1892, Dr. Browne paid a visit to the United Services Golf Club at Gosport, on the south coast of England. He introduced the bogey man to Captain Seely Vidal, the secretary there, who was pleased to have him join the club, but who pointed out that all members had to have military rank. He felt that such a sterling player could be no less than a colonel, and the genesis of Colonel Bogey was complete.

A NEW TERM

It was also during the 1890s that the concept of par developed, although its development is less clearly understood than that of bogey. Originally it seems also to have meant an ideal fixed score, similar to bogey, but it gradually came to mean a slightly better result than bogey, especially in the United States. The USGA switched from talking about "Bogey Competitions" to "Par Competitions" in 1946, and in 1950 the R&A adopted the term "Bogey or Par Competitions." In their first joint code of 1952 the R&A and USGA settled on this latter term. It was also in 1952 that a rule governing four-ball stroke play was first adopted. Foursome stroke play had been recognized for the first time in the 1933 code.

The many years that Colonel Bogey wandered in the wilderness before being granted formal recognition were nevertheless shorter than the period of neglect to which yet another English inventor of a new form of competition was subjected. Dr. Frank Stableford of Wallasey Golf Club, near Liverpool, developed his point scoring system in 1931, but his idea languished thirty-

---

TRUE TOE-TAPPIN'

Colonel Bogey became such a popular figure that Kenneth J. Alford composed the "Colonel Bogey March" in his honor in 1914, when Alford was bandmaster of the Argyll and Sutherland Highlanders in Edinburgh. Its sprightly main melody became world famous after the Second World War when it was featured in the motion picture *Bridge on the River Kwai*.

seven years before being officially welcomed into the tent by the rules-legislating bodies in 1968. The first Stableford competition was played over Dr. Frank's home course on 16 May 1932. This form of play has been steadily growing in popularity ever since.

No new forms of play have been recognized since 1968. The latest rage—the Skins game—remains for the time being in the outer darkness of non-recognition.

The Committee;
Disputes and Decisions

The Committee

A committee of the sort described in our present Rule 33 is a twentieth-century phenomenon that was mentioned for the first time in the code of 1902, and then only in passing in one of the Special Rules for Stroke Competitions:

> Competitors shall not discontinue play nor delay to start on account of bad weather, nor for any other reason whatever, except such as is satisfactory to the Committee of the Club in charge of the competition.

This somewhat offhand status of the Committee was, however, rectified in the very next code of rules adopted by the R&A and USGA in 1908. A definition was provided at the head of the section on rules for stroke competitions:

> Wherever the word Committee is used in these Rules, it refers to the Committee in charge of the Competition.

The functions of the Committee were briefly defined in the rules that followed. These included
- arranging the starting order of the competitors,
- making decisions about the condition of the course,
- settling questions of penalties, and
- deciding disputes.

The Committee's decision on disputes in stroke competitions was to be final, but an appeal to the Rules of Golf Committee could be made.

GOVERNING COMPETITIONS PAINLESSLY

These few rules remained essentially unchanged until after the Second World War. Many of the Decisions issued by the Rules of Golf Committee during the first decades of the twentieth century dealt with problems of the organization of competitions, an indication that the rules defining the functions of the Committee weren't adequate. This was corrected in the R&A experimental code of 1950, which included a separate rule delineating the role of the Committee in basically the same terms and to almost the same extent as in

Rule 33 of our present code. Six sections laid out the basic functions of the Committee:

1. Conditions (under which the competition was to be played);
2. Order and Times of Starting;
3. Decision of Ties;
4. The Course;
5. Handicapping;
6. Scoring Cards-Stroke Play.

At the same time the decision-making function of the Committee was moved to the rule covering the handling of disputes (present Rule 34).

In the 1952 joint USGA-R&A code, three sections were added dealing with

a. Defining Bounds and Margins (now a subsection under the section on The Course),
b. Modification of Penalty (now Rule 33-7),
c. Local Rules.

Only minor changes in wording have been made since then.

Disputes and Decisions

The origin of Rule 34 predates even the first code of rules by almost a month. The resolution passed by the Edinburgh town council on 7 March 1744 specified that the winner of the proposed competition should, in addition to being "stiled Captain of the Goff," have other rights and duties, including "the determination of disputes among goffers, with the assistance of two or three of the players . . . ." This remained the essential form of the rule during the rest of the eighteenth and most of the nineteenth century.

Actually, neither the Gentlemen Golfers nor the Society of St. Andrews Golfers included any mention of disputes and how to resolve them in their first, nearly identical, codes of rules in 1744 and 1754. In 1775 the Gentlemen Golfers established a slightly different court of appeals:

> Any disputes arising between the parties on the Green shall be determined by the Captain for the time being, if present, or by the latest Captain who may be on the ground.

The following year the Company of Golfers at Bruntsfield (now the Royal Burgess Golfing Society) adopted something closer to the original edict of the Edinburgh town fathers:

> All Disputes arising between Parties on the Green, are to be determined by the Captain and any two or more of the Council.

197

The Council here referred to would correspond to a modern golf club's executive committee or board of directors. No other eighteenth-century code of rules addressed the problem of disputes.

LINES OF AUTHORITY

In their 1809 code of rules, the Gentlemen Golfers, by now calling themselves the Honourable Company of Golfers, referred the settling of disputes to "the Captain or senior counsellor present." The St. Andrews golfers broadened the judging body in 1812 to ensure that a dispute could always be resolved:

> Any disputes respecting the play shall be determined by the Captain or Senior Member present, and if none of the Members are present, by the Captain and his annual Council for the time.

This wording remained the basic form of the rule in the various codes of the R&A throughout most of the nineteenth century, with the addition in 1851 of the condition that if no Members were present "it shall be settled by a committee appointed by the parties interested."

This rule was the first hesitant attempt to establish a Rules of Golf Committee. It was followed in 1888 by the mention of a specific committee:

> Any dispute respecting the play shall be determined by the green committee, with power to add to their number.

It was the green committee that was the ultimate court of appeals during the 1890s, but the appointment of the Rules of Golf Committee in 1897 opened a new era.

AMICABLE NEGOTIATIONS

The mandate of the Rules of Golf Committee was to be the final authority in matters of interpretation of the rules. The first R&A code adopted after its formation, in 1899, recognized this:

> If a dispute arise on any point, the players have the right of determining the party or parties to whom it shall be referred, but should they not agree, either side may refer it to the Rules of Golf Committee, whose decision shall be final. If the point in dispute be not covered by the Rules of Golf, the arbiters must decide it by equity.

The final sentence of this rule had appeared first in the 1891 R&A code. Since then, the importance of equity has grown steadily. *(See also the final paragraphs of Rule 1: The Game.)*

A ruling added to the rule in the code adopted by the USGA in 1900 specified:

> Such decisions may be finally referred to the executive Committee of the United States Golf Association.

The winner should be charged with the determination of disputes among golfers.

THE EXECUTIVE COMMITTEE OF THE USGA, 1916.

The first mention of a referee appeared in 1902.

The USGA established its own Rules of Golf Committee in 1922. Appeals can now be made to it by golfers under its jurisdiction.

The rule that first appeared in the 1899 R&A code has changed little in essence since the turn of the century, although it has been rephrased considerably. The first mention of a referee appeared in 1902, and his authority to make a final decision was recognized in 1920.

The requirement that players of a match make a claim before playing from the next teeing ground (or, in the case of the last hole of the round, before they leave the putting green) was introduced in 1908 as part of the rule on disputes. Moving it to its present position in Rule 2-5 in 1984 has produced partial overlapping with Rule 34-1.

PART IV

Appendices

Golf is a world encircling game. One of its

charms is that no matter where you go, whether

America, Asia, Africa, Australia, Europe or Scotland,

the game is the same, with only such local rules

as are necessary to govern the local situation.

—CHARLES B. MACDONALD, 1927

Local Rules

The first official local rules in the history of golf were written into the 1888 R&A code. This came about through the debate about the rules in *The Field* during the 1880s, and through Horace Hutchinson's motion in May 1888 to extract "local accidents" from the rules and group them under a separate heading. (*See Part II, Chapter 4, for a more complete discussion*.) Before 1888, local situations were covered in the main body of the rules themselves, both in the rules drawn up by the St. Andrews golfers and by other clubs. St. Andrews local rules were included at the end of the text of the code adopted by the R&A in 1888, but the 1891 and later R&A codes left them out.

Paul Pumfrey summed up the difficulties this situation led to in his centenary study of the Lincoln Golf Club, founded in 1891:

> The Royal and Ancient rules governed play, but unusual conditions made the introduction of local rules essential. There was much "offensive matter" on the common from the grazing animals and the Carholme Road was a part of the course with its horse drawn traffic frequently interfering with play. Race meetings and agricultural shows sometimes meant that holes had to be realigned, and the very fact that the public had access to the area often made play most frustrating.

The R&A made no attempt to provide any guidelines for drafting local rules until the Midland Golf Association drew up a set of "general local rules" in 1908. The R&A recommended that other clubs and associations adopt them. The actual content of some of these recommended local rules is surprising to present-day golfers:

1. If a player's ball lies in or under a bush or a tree, or in a ditch, or within a club's length of the nearest point of a hedge or fence, the player shall be allowed to drop a ball behind such an obstruction under the penalty of one stroke. Where it is impossible to drop a ball behind such an obstruction, the player shall be allowed to drop a ball within two club lengths of it at the side at which the ball entered, but not nearer the hole, under penalty of one stroke. All boundary hedges and fences are to be considered out of bounds.

2. A ball lying on or touching a mole hill, or dung which cannot well be removed with a club, may be lifted and dropped behind without penalty.

3. A ball lying on a putting-green other than that of the hole being played shall be lifted and dropped without penalty on the course as near as possible to the place where it lay, but not nearer the hole.

Points 2 and 3 of these recommended local rules are now covered under present Rule 25: Abnormal Ground Conditions and Wrong Putting Green. *(See also the article on Rule 25 for discussion of them.)* When considering point 1, it must be kept in mind that in 1908 the unplayable ball rule involved a two-stroke penalty in stroke play and loss of hole in match play. Looked at from this standpoint, a one-stroke penalty in both forms of play is a considerable relief. What is most surprising here is the classification of trees as obstructions to be dealt with by local rules. This was upheld in a Decision in 1909:

In a stroke competition a competitor's ball lodged in a tree. What should be done in the circumstances?

Answer.—If the competitor's ball is found in a tree, Stroke Rule 11 (Unplayable ball rule) can be applied. Such obstructions as trees should, however, be made the subject of local rule, *vide* "Recommendations for Local Rules."

It was perhaps the fact that golf had developed primarily on windswept coastal courses inhospitable to such frivolous embellishments as trees that led to this rather bizarre view of them as obstructions. Our present viewpoint is much more enlightened. We respect trees as the natural objects they are, with every right to adorn our courses and become an integral part of the game's challenge. However, a ball lodging in a tree, as in that 1909 Decision, may still be treated as an unplayable ball if it can be identified. *(See present Decisions 27/14, 27/15, and 28/11.)*

There was little change in the recommendations for local rules before the USGA and the R&A drafted their independent codes after the Second World War. Even in the code of 1933 (the last before the war), trees were still considered obstructions to be handled by means of local rules. Both the R&A and the USGA made at least partially similar recommendations for local rules when they began legislating after the war.

The USGA appended some recommendations for local rules to its 1946 unilateral code:

> When necessary local rules should be made for rabbit scrapes, hoof marks, mole-hills and other damage caused to the course by animals; for ground under repair in hazards; for parts of the course under cultivation on which play is prohibited; for snow and ice when they are not casual water under Rule 16; for mud which may interfere with the proper playing of the game; and for the preservation of the course.

In addition, special local rules were recommended for problems possibly involved in dropping when the player took relief from water hazards, and to allow a provisional ball for a ball in a water hazard. This last point is especially interesting, since playing a provisional ball for a ball possibly lost in a water hazard became part of the regular rules in 1952 and lasted into the early 1960s. *(See Rule 26: Water Hazards.)*

The R&A's experimental code of 1950 made it a responsibility of the "Committee in charge of the Course" to provide local rules:

> They shall make Local Rules for such abnormal local conditions as the existence of mud, accumulation of leaves, damage caused to the course by animals, or other conditions which could be held to interfere with the proper playing of the Game, or which are necessary for the preservation of the course.

Although the main body of rules was identical in the codes that the R&A and the USGA adopted in 1952, their approach to local rules was quite different. The R&A was content to list the abnormal conditions from its 1950 code, while the USGA set out a much fuller list of items to consider, including rather detailed recommendations for treating an embedded ball, both on the putting green and through the green. Through the 1960s and 1970s the USGA gradually expanded its recommendations for local rules, while the R&A's treatment remained quite modest. Since 1984, however, the USGA and the R&A have treated local rules and recommendations for them in a much more similar, though not identical, manner.

Somewhat different attitudes toward application of local rules have also developed over the years. It's common in Europe to allow players to remove stones from bunkers, although this is prohibited in the United States. On the other hand, lifting an embedded ball through the green is generally allowed by local rule in the United States, but only in "closely mown" areas in Europe. This can obviously lead to difficulties unless players carefully keep in mind where they are at all times.

A local rule generally practiced in professional tournaments has in recent years caused comment among television viewers who see professionals given free drops clear of such objects as grandstands and scoreboards. This is allowed in the case of such "temporary immovable obstructions" and is an exception, recommended by both the R&A and USGA, to Rule 24-2 that forbids relief from "intervention on the line of play."

Craig Stadler had a bad year in 1987. In addition to having run afoul of Rule 13 for building a stance when he knelt on a towel in San Diego, only a few months later he lifted an embedded ball in the rough to the right of the fifth fairway at Muirfield during the first day of the British Open. Fortunately, in this case his error was pointed out before he had signed his card, so he escaped with a two-stroke penalty. Actually, in this case he should have escaped without penalty. It was later reported that, although Stadler didn't know it at the time, his ball became embedded because someone had stood on it, and it should have been replaced.

Nick Faldo ran into trouble in a bunker during the third round of the Alfred Dunhill Masters in Bali in the autumn of 1994. Used to removing stones from bunkers in Europe, he did so, not realizing there was no local rule allowing it. He was leading the tournament by six strokes after twelve holes during the final round the next day when he was called off the course. A fellow competitor who had just been penalized for removing a stone in a bunker defended his action by pointing out that Faldo had done the same the day before. Since Faldo had signed his card for the third round without two penalty strokes for the infraction, he was disqualified.

There is an obvious lesson to be learned from these two cases: all golfers, amateurs as well as professionals, should always carefully study Local Rules.

The Dates of Adoption of Individual Rules

In the following list two dates are given for each rule: the first is the date when the rule, or an earlier form of the rule, first appeared in a code of rules, and the second (in parentheses) is the date when it assumed a form essentially the same as it has in the most recently adopted code (1996).

Rule	Date	Rule	Date
Rule 1-1	1891 (1984)	Rule 6-1	1950 (1950)
1-2	1964 (1964)	6-2	1950 (1984)
1-3	1933 (1933)	6-3	1908 (1984)
1-4	1891 (1950)	6-4	1960 (1960)
		6-5	1968 (1968)
Rule 2-1	1842 (1908)	6-6	1816 (1952)
2-2	1891 (1902)	6-7	1950 (1952)
2-3	1882 (1984)	6-8	1891 (1960)
2-4	1882 (1988)		
2-5	1908 (1984)	Rule 7-1	1829 (1960)
2-6	1899 (1899)	7-2	1946 (1996)
Rule 3-1	1759 (1759)	Rule 8-1	1783 (1839)
3-2	1851 (1851)	8-2	1744 (1908)
3-3	1946 (1980)		
3-4	1960 (1960)	Rule 9-1	1950 (1950)
3-5	1899 (1899)	9-2	1913 (1992)
		9-3	1980 (1980)
Rule 4-1	1909 (1984)		
4-2	1960 (1988)	Rule 10-1a	1839 (1899)
4-3	1968 (1984)	10-1b	1744 (1744)
4-4	1950 (1992)	10-1c	1839 (1839)
		10-2a	1908 (1952)
Rule 5-1	1920 (1990)	10-2b	1744 (1744)
5-2	1968 (1968)	10-2c	1952 (1952)
5-3	1858 (1984)	10-3	1946 (1972)
		10-4	1952 (1952)

Rule	11-1	1744 (1984)	Rule	18-1	1899 (1960)
	11-2	1988 (1988)		18-2	1899 (1972)
	11-3	1899 (1952)		18-3	1908 (1952)
	11-4	1875 (1980)		18-4	1899 (1960)
	11-5	1992 (1992)		18-5	1946 (1984)
Rule	12-1	1809 (1952)	Rule	19-1	1744 (1899)
	12-2	1908 (1984)		19-2	1812 (1842)
				19-3	1775 (1980)
Rule	13-1	1775 (1952)		19-4	1891 (1891)
	13-2	1773 (1952)		19-5	1950 (1988)
	13-3	1783 (1933)			
	13-4	1773 (1992)	Rule	20-1	1956 (1984)
				20-2a	1809 (1984)
Rule	14-1	1883 (1883)		20-2b	1933 (1992)
	14-2	1968 (1968)		20-2c	1899 (1996)
	14-3	1960 (1976)		20-3	1839 (1984)
	14-4	1839 (1899)		20-4	1952 (1964)
	14-5	1908 (1908)		20-5	1908 (1984)
	14-6	1908 (1980)		20-6	1960 (1984)
				20-7	1972 (1984)
Rule	15-1	1744 (1988)			
	15-2	1809 (1952)	Rule	21	1946 (1988)
	15-3	1908 (1952)			
			Rule	22	1744 (1984)
Rule	16-1a	1882 (1960)			
	16-1b	1960 (1970)	Rule	23	1744 (1960)
	16-1c	1960 (1984)			
	16-1d	1952 (1952)	Rule	24	1838 (1980)
	16-1e	1968 (1968)			
	16-1f	1976 (1976)	Rule	25-1	1775 (1980)
	16-1g	1882 (1984)		25-2	1773 (1980)
	16-2	1899 (1988)		25-3	1908 (1952)
Rule	17-1	1875 (1956)	Rule	26-1	1744 (1964)
	17-2	1960 (1960)		26-2	1984 (1988)
	17-3	1902 (1968)			
	17-4	1875 (1875)	Rule	27-1	1744 (1962)
				27-2	1902 (1972)

Rule	**28**	1807 (1968)	**Rule**	**32**	1902 (1968)

Rule	**28**	1807 (1968)
Rule	**29**	1814 (1952)
Rule	**30**	1902 (1984)
Rule	**31**	1952 (1984)

Rule	**32**	1902 (1968)
Rule	**33**	1902 (1952)
Rule	**34-1**	1908 (1984)
	34-2	1902 (1920)
	34-3	1744 (1920)

AUTHOR KEN CHAPMAN IN THE LIBRARY AT THE R&A

The Major Codes of Rules from 1744 to the Present

A. Codes of Rules of The Society of St. Andrews Golfers (before 1834) and
The Royal and Ancient Golf Club (after 1834)

Year of Code	Date of Adoption	Dates of Minor Revisions
1754	14th May 1754	1759, 1777, 1789
1812	1st May 1812	
1829	30th September 1829	1833, 1834, 1838
1842	(no precise date)	1846, 1847, 1848
1851	15th October 1851	1852, 1856
1858	5th May 1858	1859, 1865, 1869, 1873
1875	(no precise date)	1876, 1881
1882	2nd May 1882	1888
1891	29th September 1891	1895

Rules of Golf Committee appointed, 28th September 1897

1899	26th September 1899	
1902	23rd September 1902	1904
1908	29th September 1908	1909, 1910, 1911, 1913
1920	27th September 1920	1929
1933	26th September 1933	1939, 1946

Edition	Effective Date
15th	1st January 1950
16th	1st January 1952
17th	1st January 1954
18th	1st January 1956
19th	1st January 1960
20th	1st January 1964
21st	1st January 1968
(—	1st January 1970)
22nd	1st January 1972
23rd	1st January 1976
24th	1st January 1980
25th	1st April 1984
26th	1st January 1988
27th	1st January 1992
28th	1st January 1996

B. Codes of Rules of the United States Golf Association

Year of Code	Date of Adoption	
1897	June 10, 1897	same as R&A 1891 with USGA rulings
1900	February 28, 1900	same as R&A 1899 with USGA rulings
1903	February 17, 1903	same as R&A 1902 with USGA rulings
1905	February 28, 1905	same as R&A 1904 with USGA rulings
1909	February 17, 1909	same as R&A 1908 with interpretations Minor revisions: 1912, 1913, 1915, and yearly thereafter
1921	January 7, 1921	same as R&A 1920 with interpretations Minor revision: 1926
1933	November 23, 1933	same as R&A 1933 with interpretations Minor revisions: 1938, 1941
1946	September 12, 1946	complete reorganization

For 1952 and later, see the R&A 16th edition and subsequent editions (with minor revisions in 1960, 1961, and 1962).

This list of codes of rules of the Royal and Ancient Golf Club and the United States Golf Association is an attempt to present a complete catalog of all codes adopted by these rules-making bodies. It's possible that such a list can never be completely accurate.

Nowadays the rules-making process is extremely rigorous and systematic. Modern professional golf, with its huge amounts of prize money, has made this development unavoidable. Until quite recently, however, golf was primarily an avocation engaged in by amateurs for their own amusement, and a more informal approach to the issuing of codes of rules prevailed. For many years little attention was paid to questions of copyright, and rule books were sometimes issued by local printers acting on their own initiative. Not even all codes issued by the R&A were ever officially adopted (see 1842 and 1875). Changes in individual rules were voted on and recorded in the minutes, and after a number of changes had been adopted, the revised code was issued in printed form. This seems to have been rigorous enough for the demands of that day.

The situation became considerably more systematized after the appointment of the Rules of Golf Committee in 1897. The establishment of the USGA in 1894 and the wish of American golfers to play by rules suited to the conditions they experienced was for many years a disturbing factor. After 1915, the USGA adopted the practice of printing up a new edition of the rules each year including whatever changes they may have adopted. This practice has continued, but by agreement with the R&A no substantive changes are made between official four-year editions. In the list above, the dates of minor revisions made by the USGA after 1915 are included only when some change of importance was involved. The R&A has in recent years made it a practice to assign edition numbers to each new edition, but this practice hasn't been followed by the USGA, which merely assigns an effective date (usually 1 January) to each year's edition.

Even after the establishment of unanimity in 1952, with agreement to issue new editions only each four years, anomalies have occurred. Extensive linguistic polishing (but no substantive change) was carried out in 1954, and a separate edition number was assigned by the R&A to that code. On the other hand, an important substantive change was made in 1970 (the nullifying of the continuous putting rule in stroke play), but no new edition number was assigned. In 1960 the USGA began experimenting with respect to certain penalties, but this was abandoned in 1968, and general unanimity has prevailed since then. *(The details of this process are covered in Part II, Chapters 5 and 6.)* This hard-won unanimity now appears to be firmly and permanently established.

Early Codes of Rules

CODES ADOPTED BEFORE 1850

The following table lists the codes of clubs that adopted their earliest codes before 1850 and the relationships and later development of these codes, with date of adoption of R&A Rules, if known.

Annotations

A "close copy" refers to a nearly identical version of the original with only minor differences.

An "adaptation" is a version clearly based on the original but with significant changes.

The superscripts refer to the numbered examples that follow this table.

Abbreviations include:

    HC Honourable Company

    AB Aberdeen

    PR Perth

    EB Edinburgh Burgess

	Earliest Code	Later Developments
Gentlemen Golfers (Honourable Company of Edinburgh Golfers)	1744	1775[2] 1809[4] 1839 (an adaptation of R&A 1829) 1866 Formally adopted R&A Rules on 5 April 1883
St. Andrews, R&A	See separate list in Appendix 3.	
Edinburgh Burgess (Royal Burgess) Golfing Society	1773[1]	1776 (an adaptation of HC 1775) 1790 1802 1807 1814 1816 1838 1864

	Earliest Code	**Later Developments**
Aberdeen (Society of Golfers, Golf Club)	1783[3] (an adaptation of HC 1775)	1815 (an adaptation of AB 1783 and HC 1809) 1816 1847 Formally adopted R&A Rules on 24 April 1873
Crail Golfing Society	1786 (local rules only; basic rules were probably St. Andrews rules)	
Glasgow Golf Club	1810 (a close copy of HC 1809)	
Manchester Golf Club	1818 (a close copy of HC 1809)	
Bruntsfield Links Golfing Society	1819 (a close copy of EB 1814 and EB 1816)	
Thistle Golf Club	1824 (a close copy of HC 1809)	1866 (a close copy of R&A 1858)
(Royal) Perth Golfing Society	1825 (an adaptation of HC 1809)	1839 (an adaptation of R&A 1829) 1864
(Royal) Blackheath Golf Club	1828[6] (an adaptation of AB 1783)	1844 (a close copy of PR 1839) 1860 1868 1874 1879 Formally adopted R&A Rules on 4 April 1889
Burntisland Golf Club	1828 (an adaptation of HC 1809 and PR 1825)	
(Royal) Musselburgh Golf Club	1829 (an adaptation of R&A 1812 and HC 1809)	1834 (an adaptation of R&A 1829) 1871

	Earliest Code	Later Developments
(Royal) Montrose Golf Club (Royal Albert Golf Club, Montrose)	1830[8] (an adaptation of HC 1809 and AB 1815)	1851 (a close copy of R&A 1842)
Panmure Golf Club	1845 (a close copy of R&A 1842 with the addition of a special unplayable ball rule)	

TEXTS OF SELECTED EARLY CODES

(See Part II, Chapter 2, "The Thirteen Articles," for the 1744 code of the Gentlemen Golfers of Leith and 1754 code of the Society of St. Andrews Golfers.)

Example 1

Code of the Society of Golfers, in and about Edinburgh, at Bruntsfield Links (now the Royal Burgess Golfing Society)

Adopted: 8 April 1773

I. In order to preserve the holes, no Golfer or Cadie shall be allowed to make any Tee within ten yards of the hole, and no Ball shall be teed nearer the Hole than two Club lengths, nor farther from it than four.

II. In case two or more parties meet at the hole, the party who playes first must be allowed to play their second strokes before the party who plays after them shall be allowed to strike off their first Ball. And if the first party's Ball be in a hazard, the said party shall stand aside till the second pass them.

III. To prevent Disputes in taking up Balls from water, every Ball taken from water or Tee, either upon the Green or a hazard such ball shall be teed behind and lose one, excepting in the case of a made hazard, when the ball is to be dropped behind by the opposite party and played with an iron club.

IV. Any Golfer losing his Ball either by accident or in a hazard, shall go to the place from whence he last struck and lose one: But in case the Ball is seen fairly on the Green, and afterwards stolen, or run away with by a dog, then a new Ball must be drop't where the former one was last seen, and no loss ensue.

v. Every Golfer addressing himself to his Ball shall not have liberty to put down Earth, sand or anything else, nor in drawing his stroke take anything away from behind his Ball except a Stone or a Bone.

vi. No Golfer is to change his Ball either in the Green or hazards except agreed on by both parties, and then the opposite party is take up the one Ball and lay down the other.

vii. If any Golfer shall be at a loss to know his own Ball from his opposite, he shall not hit any of the Balls till they both agree.

viii. If a Ball shall be so played as to stick fast to the ground, the said Ball shall be loosened by the opposite party to the owner of the Ball so fastened.

ix. When a Ball is struck into the Whins or any part where it may be covered, so much of the fogg grass, &, must be set aside, that the player may have a view of his ball before he playes, but no whins must be laid aside excepting such as he shall set his foot upon when playing the Ball.

x. No Golfer shall under any pretence whatever give any old Balls to the Cadies, if they do, they shall for every such Ball given away forfeit sixpence to the Treasurer.

xi. That no member of this Society pay the Cadies more than one penny p. round.

Example 2

Laws to be observed by the Members of The Golfing Company in playing Golf

(now the Honourable Company of Edinburgh Golfers)

Adopted: 22 April 1775

1. You must tee your Ball not nearer the Hole than two Club lengths, nor farther distant than four.

2. Your Tee must be on the ground.

3. You are not to change the Ball you strike off the Tee before that Hole is played out.

4. You are not to remove stones, bones, or any break club, in order to play your Ball except upon the fair Green.

5. If your Ball is half covered or more with water, you are at liberty to take it out, tee it behind the Hazard, and play it with any Club, allowing your adversary a stroke: And if on Tee, you may take it up, and tee behind the Tee, losing one, or play it off the Tee, in the option of the Player.

6. If your Ball lye in a made Hazard, or in any of the Water-tracts for draining the Links, when the cut of the Spade appears at the place where the Ball lyes, it may be taken out, dropped behind the Hazard, and played with an iron club without losing a stroke; or, in the option of

the Player, the Ball to be tee'd, and lose one: And in no case, but what is mentioned in this and the immediately preceding law, can a Ball be lifted, but must be played where it lyes.

7. If your Balls be found anywhere touching or within six inches of one another, you are to lift the first Ball until the other is played.

8. At Holing, you are to play your Ball honestly for the Hole and not play on your Adversary's Ball not lying in your way to the Hole.

9. If you lose your Ball, you are to drop another as near as can be judged to the place where your Ball was lost, and allow your Adversary a stroke for the misfortune.

10. At Holing, you are not to mark the direction to the Hole.

11. If a Ball be stopped by accident, it must be played where it lyes; and if stopped by the adversary, his cadie, or servant, the party who stops the Ball to lose one.

12. If, in striking, your club breaks, it is nevertheless to be accounted a stroke, if you strike the ground, or pass the Ball with the club.

13. The Ball farthest from the Hole must be first played.

14. In playing, you are to strike off from the Braehead-hole, and play from it to the Sawmill, for the First hole; from the Sawmill, to the North Mid-hole, for the Second Hole; to the East Hole for the Third; to the South Mid-hole, for the Fourth; and to the Thorntree-Hole, for the Fifth, where the First Round ends; and every other Round is to begin at the Thorntree-hole, playing from that to the Sawmill-hole, and from thence to the North mid-hole, etcetera, as above, until you come again to the Thorntree-hole, where every Round ends.

15. Any disputes arising between the parties on the Green shall be determined by the Captain for the time being, if present, or by the latest Captain who may be on the ground.

Example 3

Laws of Golf to be observed by the Society of Golfers at Aberdeen

Adopted: 9 May 1783

I. The Distance from the Hole, in Teeing, shall not exceed two Lengths of a Club, either in Advance or Aside, and the Tee shall be on the Ground.

II. While a Stroke is playing none of the Party shall walk about, make any motion, or attempt to take off the Player's attention, by speaking or otherwise.

III. The Party gaining a Hole shall have the Privilege of striking off first, as long as the opposite Party do not make a good Hole—the Ball furthest from the Hole shall be always first played.

iv. If two Balls happen to ly so near to one another as Six Inches, or less, the Ball nearest the Hole shall be taken up, till the other is played.

v. Untill the Hole be quitted no Ball shall be changed nor handled on any pretence, unless in compliance with the Fourth Law, or that the ball happen to ly on Ice, or half sunk in Water; in which Cases the Player shall have it in his option either to tee his Ball on the Green, or behind the Ice or Water, or play as it lyes; If tee'd, the opposite Party shall reckon one against the Player.

vi. No Stones, Bones, or other Break-clubs shall be removed in a Hazard, nor on the fair Green.

vii. If one Ball happen to Strike against another, or if the Player accidentally strike the Opponents and his Ball at the same time, both parties must take their balls as they happen to ly after such Accidents.

viii. No person shall be at Liberty to vary or better his Stance in playing, by breaking the Surface of the Green, by placing or removing Stones, Sand, or any other Substance; damping his feet with Water excepted.

ix. In playing on the Green, or out of Sand, loose Ground or long Grass, no means shall be used to beat down the Ground or Grass, or to draw away or make any mark in the Sand or Soil, whereby to improve the ly of the Ball.

x. If a Stroke is made, and the Club pass the Ball and strike the Ground, it shall be reckoned against the Player; though the Ball be mist, or the Club happen to be broke.

xi. A Ball lost in playing shall in all Cases forfeit the Hole, unless when struck into Water; as to which vide Law V.

xii. The Party whose Ball is amissing shall be allowed Five Minutes to search for it, after coming to the Spot where the Ball appeared to drop.

xiii. If a Dog happens to carry off or damage a Ball in the course of playing, the party to whom it belongs shall be entitled to use another, and lay it as near to the Spot where taken from as can be guessed.

xiv. If a Stroke is made and the Ball be stopt by any Person not in the Game, it shall be played as it may chance to ly, altho' in a Hazard; the Parties being obliged to submit to the Accident, whether for or against the Player.

xv. If a Ball, in playing thro' the Green, be stopt by the Player's partner or their Club-bearers, it shall be played where it chance to ly, and the Stroke reckoned as if no such Accident had happened.

xvi. If a Ball, in playing thro' the Green, be stopt by any of the opposite Party or their Club-bearers, no stroke shall be reckoned against the player and he shall also be at liberty to lay the Ball fair.

xvii. If any of the Players or their Club-bearers, by standing at or near the hole, stop a Ball, whether from a Putter or any other Club, the Hole shall be lost to the Party so stopping; with this exception only, that after a Ball passes the Hole, and is stopped by any of the opposite Party, the Hole shall not thereby be lost to such party; But the Player shall have it in his option either to play the Stroke over again, or take the Ball as it may happen to ly.

xviii. At holing the Player is to aim honestly for the Hole and not at his Opponent's Ball not lying in the way.

xix. The Player shall not be at liberty to draw a Line, or make any Mark as a Direction for holing, nor shall his Partner stand at the Hole, or direct him in aiming.

xx. No Stones, loose Sand, or other Impediments shall be removed when putting at the Hole.

xxi. When the Hole is distinctly in view of the Player, no Person shall be allowed to stand at it for a Direction.

xxii. If both the Balls happen to be holed by the same Stroke, such Stroke shall reckon in Favour of the Player's Opponent, and be the same as if his Ball had been previously in the Hole.

xxiii. It is understood that Partners may consult with, and give verbal Directions to one another; how to play; but nothing further.

Example 4

Golf Rules to be observed by the Honourable Company of Golfers

Adopted: 27 May 1809

1. You must tee your ball not nearer the hole than two club-lengths, nor further from it than four, and the tee must be on the ground.

2. The ball furthest from the hole must be played first.

3. You are not to change the ball struck from the tee before the hole is played out, and if at a loss to know the one ball from the other, neither of them to be uplifted till both parties agree.

4. You are not to remove stones, bones, or any break-club in order to play your ball, except upon the fair green, but if a ball stick fast in the ground it may be loosened.

5. The player, in every case, shall be entitled to lift his ball, drop it behind, at such distance as he thinks proper, behind the hazard, and lose one stroke; but where he cannot get behind the hazard without going off the green, he shall be entitled to drop his ball on the green, on a line with the place where it lay, except it lies on any of the roads bounding the links.

6. If a ball is half covered, or more, with water on the green, the player is at liberty to take it out, drop it behind the hazard, and play it with an iron without losing a stroke; and when the ball is completely covered with

fog or grass, so much thereof may be set aside that the player shall have a view of his ball before he plays.

7. If a ball lies in any of the water-tracks on the green, it may be taken out, dropped behind the track, and played with an iron without losing a stroke.

8. When the balls lie within six inches of one another, the ball nearest the hole to be lifted till the other is played.

9. If a ball be stopped by accident it must be played where it lies, but if stopped by the adversary or his cady, the party who stops the ball to lose the hole.

10. If a ball is lost on the green, the player shall drop another behind the place where the other was lost, and lose one.

11. If, in striking, the club breaks, it is, nevertheless, to be accounted a stroke, if you either strike the ground or pass the ball.

12. At holing you are not to mark the direction to the hole; you are to play your ball honestly for the hole, and not play on your adversary's ball, not lying on your way to the hole; but all loose impediments may be removed within six club-lengths of the hole.

13. In all cases where a ball is to be dropped, the party dropping shall front the hole to which he is playing, and drop the ball behind him over his head.

14. Any disputes respecting the play shall be determined by the Captain or senior counsellor present.

Example 5

Regulations for the Game of Golf adopted by the St. Andrews Society of Golfers

Adopted: Friday, 1 May 1812

I. The Balls must be teed not nearer the hole than two club-lengths, nor further from it than four.

II. The Ball farthest from the hole must be played first.

III. The Ball struck from the tee must not be changed before the hole is played out, and if the parties are at a loss to know the one Ball from the other, neither shall be lifted till both parties agree.

IV. Stones, Bones, or any break-club within a club-length of the Ball may be removed when the Ball lies on grass, but nothing can be removed if it lie on Sand or in a bunker, if however it Stick fast in the ground, it may be loosened.

V. If a Ball lie in a Rabbit-scrape, the Player shall not be at liberty to take it out, but must play it as from any common hazard, if however it lie in one of the burrows, he may lift it, drop it behind the hazard, and play with an Iron without losing a stroke.

vi. If the Ball is half covered or more with water, the Player may take it out, tee it, and play from behind the hazard, losing a stroke.

vii. If the Ball lie in the supernumerary hole on the hole-across green, it may be dropped behind the hazard, and played with an Iron, without losing a stroke.

viii. When the Balls lie within six inches of one another, the Ball nearest the hole must be lifted till the other is played, but on the putting green it shall not be lifted, although within six inches, unless it be directly between the other and the hole.

ix. Whatever happens to a Ball by accident, must be reckoned a Rub of the green, if however the Player's Ball strike his adversary or his Cady, the adversary loses the hole: If it strike his own Cady, the Player loses the hole: If the Player strike his adversary's Ball with his Club, the Player loses the hole.

x. If a Ball is lost, the stroke goes for nothing, the Player returns to the spot whence the Ball was struck, tees it, and loses a stroke.

xi. If in striking, the Club breaks, it is nevertheless to be accounted a stroke, if the Player either strike the ground or pass the Ball.

xii. In holing, you are not to place any mark to direct you to the hole, you are to play your Ball fairly and honestly for the hole, and not on your adversary's Ball not lying in your way to the hole.

xiii. All loose impediments of whatever kind, may be removed upon the putting green.

xiv. In all cases where a Ball is to be dropped, the party dropping shall front the hole to which he is playing, and drop the Ball behind him over his head.

xv. When a Ball is completely covered with fog, bent, whins, etc. so much thereof shall be set aside as that the Player shall have a full view of his Ball before he plays.

xvi. When the Balls touch each other, one of them must be lifted until the other is played.

xviiI. Any disputes respecting the play shall be determined by the Captain or Senior Member present, and if none of the Members are present, by the Captain and his annual Council for the time.

Example 6

Laws of Golf. Revised and amended by the Committee of the Blackheath Golf Club in 1828

i. The distance from the Hole, in Teeing, shall not exceed four club Lengths, nor be nearer it than two, and the Tee must be on the ground.

ii. The Ball farthest from the Hole played for must be first played.

III. Whilst a Stroke is played, none of the Party shall walk about, making any motion, or attempting to take off the Player's attention by speaking or otherwise.

IV. The Party gaining a Hole shall strike off first.

V. The Ball shall not be changed or handled, on any pretence, whilst playing except when by accident it is driven into water or mud, in which case the Player may take it out, and throw it behind the hazard, losing a stroke.

VI. No Stones, Bones, or other Break-clubs shall be removed.

VII. If the Player by mistake strikes his Opponent's Ball in playing through the Green, the Stroke shall not be reckoned against either, and the Ball must be played as it may chance to lie.

VIII. No person shall be at liberty to better his position in playing, by breaking the surface of the Green, placing or removing stones; but should the Ball be driven into Furze, he shall be at liberty to break down as much of it as will enable him to see the Ball before striking.

IX In playing, no mark shall be used to beat down or make any mark in the sand or soil, whereby to improve the lie of the Ball.

X. If a stroke be made, and the Club passes the Ball, or strikes the Ground, it shall be reckoned against the Player, although the Ball be missed, or the Club broken.

XI. The Party whose Ball is amissing shall be allowed five minutes to search for it, after coming to the spot where the Ball appeared to drop. If not then found, the Hole is lost.

XII. But should it be evident to both Parties that the Ball must of necessity have been carried off by some person or animal, the loser shall be entitled to throw down another, as near the spot as the Player can guess.

XIII. If the Ball be stopped by accident, it must be played as it may chance to lie.

XIV. But if stopped by the opposite Party, or their Club-bearers, no stroke shall be reckoned against the Player, and he shall also be at liberty to lay the Ball Fair.

XV. At Holing, you are not to mark the direction to the Hole, the Ball must be played honestly for the Hole, and not on the adversary's Ball not lying in the way.

XVI. Nothing whatever shall be removed when putting at the Hole, except on the play for the Medal, when all loose impediments, within six club-lengths of the Hole may be removed.

XVII. When the Hole is distinctly in view, no person shall stand at it for a direction.

xviii. When several Parties are on the Green, the second Party shall not strike off before each of the advanced Party has played his second stroke.

xix. If the Player Holes the Opponent's Ball, it shall be reckoned in favour of the Opponent, and be the same as if his Ball had been previously Holed.

Example 7

Rules of the St. Andrews Club

Adopted: 30 September 1829

i. The balls must be teed not nearer the hole than two club-lengths nor further from it than four.

ii. The ball farthest from the hole must be played first.

iii. The ball struck from the tee must not be changed before the hole is played out; and if the parties are at a loss to know one ball from the other, neither shall be lifted till both parties agree.

iv. Stones, bones, or any other break-club within a club-length of the ball may be removed when the ball lies on grass, but nothing can be removed if it lie on sand, or in a bunker; no other loose impediment, such as turf, bent, whins, or anything whatever can be removed on the driving course, nor is any obstruction to be bent down or levelled with the club.

v. When a ball is completely covered with fog, bent, whins, etc., so much thereof shall be set aside as that the player shall have a full view of his ball before he plays; a ball which is stuck fast in the ground may be loosened.

vi. All loose impediments of whatever kind may be removed on the putting green, which is considered not to exceed 20 yards from the hole.

vii. If the ball lie in a rabbit-scrape the player shall not be at liberty to take it out, but must play it as from any common hazard; if, however, it be in one of the burrows, he may lift it, drop it behind the hazard, and play with an iron without losing a stroke.

viii. When the balls touch each other, one of them must be lifted till the other is played.

ix. When the balls lie within six inches of one another, the ball nearest the hole must be lifted till the other is played, but on the putting green it shall not be lifted although within six inches, unless it lie directly between the other and the hole; the six inches to be measured from the surface of each ball.

x. If the ball is half covered or more with water, the player may take it out, tee it, and play from behind the hazard, losing a stroke.

xi. If the ball lie in the supernumerary hole on the Hole Across Green, it may be dropped behind the hazard and played with an iron without losing a stroke. The same rule applies to the short holes at the first hole.

xii. Whatever happens to a ball by accident must be reckoned a rub of the green; if, however, the player's ball strike his adversary, or his caddie, or his clubs, the adversary loses the hole; if it strike his own caddie or hit his clubs, the player loses the hole. If the player strike his adversary's ball with his club, the player loses the hole.

xiii. If a ball be lost, the stroke goes for nothing; the player returns to the spot whence the ball was struck, tees it, and loses a stroke. If the original ball is found before the party playing a new one has come to the ground where it was lost, the first continues the one to be played.

xiv If, in striking the club breaks, it is nevertheless to be accounted a stroke if the player either strike the ground or pass the ball.

xv. On holing, you are not to place any mark, nor draw any line, to direct you to the hole; you are to play your ball fairly and honestly for the hole, and not on your adversary's ball not lying in your way to the hole. Either party may smooth sand lying round the hole.

xvi. In all cases where a ball is to be dropped the party dropping shall front the hole to which he is playing, and drop the ball behind him over his head.

xvii. New holes shall always be made on the day a medal is played for, and no competitor shall play at these holes before he starts for the prize.

xviii. Any disputes respecting the play shall be determined by the Captain or Senior member present, and if none of the members are present, by the Captain and his annual Council for the time.

Example 8

Rules of the Game of Golf established by the Montrose Golf Club
Adopted: 26 April 1830

i. The Ball must be teed not nearer the hole than two Club-lengths, nor farther from it than four; and the tee must be on the ground.

ii. The Ball farthest from the hole, after being struck from the tee, must be first played.

ii. The Ball struck from the tee must not be changed before the hole is played out; and, if at a loss to distinguish one Ball from another neither of them is to be lifted till the parties agree.

iv. Break-clubs, such as stones, bones &c. are not to be removed in order to play a Ball, except on the putting green, and that only within six Club-lengths of the hole.

v. When it is impossible to play the Ball, the player shall be entitled to lift and drop it at such a distance as he thinks proper, behind the hazard and lose one stroke, but where he cannot get behind the hazard, without going off the green, he shall be entitled to drop his Ball on the green, in a line with the place where it lay.

vi. Should a Ball get into any hole on the putting green that comes within the denomination of made-holes it shall not be considered a hazard; but in such case, the player is entitled to lift the Ball and drop it behind the hole, and play without losing a stroke.

vii. If a Ball on the green is half covered with water or filth, the player is at liberty to take it out, drop it behind the hazard, and play with an iron or putter without losing a stroke, and where the Ball is completely covered with fog, furze, or grass, so much thereof may be set aside as that the player shall have a view of his Ball before he plays.

viii. When two Balls only are playing, the Ball, betwixt the other and the hole on the putting green, is not to be lifted; but when more than two Balls are playing, or when the match is to be decided by the number of strokes, as in playing for medals or prizes, if one Ball lie on the putting green, betwixt another and the hole, the Ball nearest the hole shall be lifted till the other is played.

ix. If a Ball be stopped by accident, it shall notwithstanding, be reckoned a stroke; but the hole shall be declared lost to the party who may, by himself or his cady, stop or interupt the Ball of his opponent.

x. If a Ball is lost, the player shall drop another behind the place where it was lost and lose one stroke.

xi. Every attempt to strike shall be considered a stroke, whether or not the Club break, touch the ground or pass the Ball.

xii. At putting, the direction of the hole is not to be marked, but the Ball is to be played honestly for the hole;—all loose impediments, however, may be removed, if within six Club-lengths of the hole.

xiii. When several parties are playing over the ground, no stroke shall be played from the tee till each of the advanced party has played his second stroke; and, should the party following advance on the latter, they must call out before playing their Ball.

xiv. In all cases where a Ball is to be dropped, the party dropping shall front the hole to which he is playing, and drop the Ball over his head.

xv. Parties are at liberty to ask advice for direction from their partners, or cadies, in playing, but not from onlookers, whose observations on the play are not to be listened to; and while the one party is prohibited from walking before the other, it is understood, that no spectator shall interfere in the most distant manner with the game while playing.

XVI. Disputes, relative to the reckoning of any hole, must be settled before the parties strike off for next hole.

XVII. All Disputes respecting the play shall be referred to the Captain and his Council, whose determination shall be binding on the parties.

CODES ADOPTED AFTER 1850

Prestwick Golf Club   1858 (a close copy of R&A 1858)

East Lothian Golf Club   1859 (an adaptation of R&A 1858)

King James VI   1860 (an adaptation of R&A 1858)
Golf Club (Perth)

North Devon and West   1864 (an adaptation of R&A 1858
of England Golf Club   and Blackheath 1860)
(Westward Ho!)

Innerleven Golf Club   1869 (a close copy of R&A 1858)

Otago Golf Club   1871 (a close copy of R&A 1857)
(New Zealand)

(Royal) Liverpool   1875 (an adaptation of R&A 1875)
Golf Club (Hoylake)   1895 (a close copy of R&A 1891)

(Note: Wallasey Golf Club adopted "Hoylake Rules" when it was founded in 1891.)

Monifieth Golf Club   1875 (an adaptation of R&A 1857)

Lanark Golf Club   1883 (an adaptation of R&A 1882)

(Royal) Wimbledon   1883 (an adaptation of R&A 1882)
Golf Club   Formally adopted R&A Rules
                        in April 1898

(Note: Wimbledon Rules were adopted by Littleston Golf Club when it was founded in 1888, and by Epsom Golf Club when it was founded in 1889.)

(Royal) Isle of Wight   1885 (an adaptation of R&A 1882
Golf Club (Bembridge)   and Blackheath 1879)

(Note: Tenby Golf Club, Wales, adopted Royal Isle of Wight Rules when it was founded in 1888.)

(Royal) Lytham and   1886 (an adaptation
St. Annes Golf Club   of R&A 1882)
                        Formally adopted R&A Rules in 1894

(Note: Wilmslow Golf Club adopted Lytham and St. Annes Rules when it was founded in 1889 and played by them through 1891.)

Historical
Documents

1. Letter of 5 June 1896 from W. Rutherford, Hon. Sec. of St. George's Golf Club, to the Captain of the Royal and Ancient Golf Club. The text of this letter is found only in the form of a copy of it prepared by C. S. Grace, Hon. Sec. of the R&A, and circulated in accordance with the wishes of a meeting of the Committee of Management on 8 June 1896. This copy is preserved in a ledger containing a number of old documents of the R&A from that period.

3 Plowden Buildings,
Temple, E. C., 5th June 1896.

John Oswald, Esq.
Captain of the Royal and Ancient Golf Club, St. Andrews.

Dear Sir,
You will remember that, at the Informal Meeting which the Delegates of the Amateur Championship, held at the St George's Golf Club on the 21st ult., immediately after their business meeting was over, I was asked to write to you, the Delegate and Captain of the Royal and Ancient Golf Club, a letter embodying certain views as to which all the Delegates present at the meeting were unanimous. This accordingly I now do.

Immediately after our Whitsuntide Meeting was over, I was called away on urgent business, and as I had not my notes taken at the Informal Meeting of the Delegates with me, and did not wish to write this letter without my notes, I have been forced into a delay which I hope this explanation will excuse.

The first opinion, which emerged from the discussion relating to various proposals as to a Golf Union, of which all the Delegates present had heard, was that no support should be given to any scheme tending to set up, or to attempt to set up, an authority rival to the Royal and Ancient Club.

The second opinion was, that it would be well if the Royal and Ancient Club could be persuaded to consider whether it would not be possible to evolve some scheme that would enable important Clubs to explicitly recognise the authority of the Royal and Ancient, instead of only tacitly as at present.

The Meeting then went on to consider on what idea such a scheme might be based. Eventually the Delegates unanimously agreed that the following was good, and hoped that you might be able to get it favourably considered by the Committee of your Club.

1. That the Royal and Ancient Club should appoint from members of the Royal and Ancient Club a Special Committee. That such Committee should consist of X Members (to be a quorum); $\frac{1}{2}$X to be elected as being representatives of the Royal and Ancient Golf Club, $\frac{1}{2}$X to be elected as being representatives of some other great Clubs. The Chairman to be one of the representatives of the Royal and Ancient Club, and to have a casting vote.

2. That the powers of such Committee should be limited to dealing with proposals relating to the Rules and Customs of the Game of Golf.

3. That no Rule of the game should be repealed or altered, and no New Rule should be made, unless approved by a majority of the Members of, and present and voting at a Meeting of, such Committee, and unless subsequently confirmed by the next General Meeting of the Royal and Ancient Club.

4. That on all questions relating to the interpretation of the Rules and Customs of the game, as applied to particular cases, such Committee should be the ultimate court of appeal.

5. That such Committee should meet twice a year, at ___ in the months of ___, and ___.

I have not a note of the names of the Delegates present when the above was approved, or of the Clubs they represented. Perhaps you can get this from CAPTAIN BURN. I do not wish to write anything from memory.

> I remain, Dear Sir,
> Yours faithfully,
> (Signed) W. Rutherford.

(C. S. Grace, Hon. Sec. of the R&A sent two letters in reply to this letter:)

> Royal and Ancient Golf Club of St. Andrews,
> The Club House, St. Andrews, 23rd June 1896.

W. Rutherford, Esq., Hon. Secy.
St. George's Golf Club,
3 Plowden Buildings, Temple, E. C.

Dear Sir

I beg to inform you that your letter of the 5th inst., addressed to Mr Oswald, the Captain of this Club, embodying certain views expressed at an Informal Meeting of the Delegates of the Amateur Championship, held at Sandwich on 21st ult., has been carefully considered by the Committee of Management of this Club. I am desired by the Committee to say that they approve generally of the suggestions contained in your letter, and I hope to be in a position to write you further on the subject in the course of next week.

> I am, Dear Sir,
> Yours faithfully.
> (Signed) C. S. Grace
> Hon. Secy.

Royal and Ancient Golf Club of St. Andrews,
The Club House, St. Andrews, 10th July 1896.

W. Rutherford, Esq.
3 Plowden Buildings, Temple, London.

Dear Sir,

Referring to my letter of 23rd ult., I am desired by the Committee of Management to say that they have now considered the suggestions contained in your letter of 5th ult., addressed to Mr Oswald, the Captain of this Club, embodying certain views expressed at an Informal Meeting of the Delegates of the Amateur Championship, held at Sandwich on 21st May, and they are prepared to submit for the consideration of the Club at a General Meeting, a scheme for the formation of a Special Committee to deal with questions on the Rules of Golf on the following lines, viz.:-

1. That a Committee be formed to deal with all proposals relating to the Rules and Customs of the Game of Golf.

2. That the Committee consist of fourteen members (eight to be a quorum). That the Royal and Ancient Golf Club shall nominate seven members of that Club, and that the following seven Clubs be invited to nominate one member each, viz.:—Honourable Company of Edinburgh Golfers, Prestwick, Royal Blackheath, Royal North Devon, Royal Liverpool, St. George's, and Royal Portrush. The Chairman (who shall also be Convener) shall be one of the Representatives of the Royal and Ancient, and shall have a casting vote.

3. That such Committee shall meet twice a year at St. Andrews in the weeks of the Spring and Autumn Meetings of the Royal and Ancient.

4. That no Rule of the Game shall be repealed or altered, and no new Rule shall be made unless approved by a majority of the Members of and present and voting at a meeting of such Committee, and unless subsequently confirmed by a General Meeting of the Royal and Ancient in conformity with the Rules of that Club.

5. That on all questions relating to the interpretation of the Rules and Customs of the game as applied to particular cases, such Committee shall be the ultimate Court of Appeal.

As the above proposals are the outcome of an Informal Meeting of Delegates at Sandwich, the Committee of Management suggest that you should communicate copies of this correspondence to the Secretaries of the Clubs represented on that occasion, and obtain a formal endorsement of the opinions expressed by their Delegates—such communications for the present to be treated as private and confidential. The Committee of Management would then be in a position to bring these proposals before the Club, and to take the sense of a General Meeting upon the same.

I am, Dear Sir,
Yours faithfully,
(Signed) C. S. Grace,
Hon. Secy.

2. Letter of 10 December 1896 from The Edinburgh Burgess Golfing Society to The Royal and Ancient Golf Club. The text of this letter is found entered in the minute books of both the Royal Burgess Golf Society (Council Meeting, 16 December 1896) and the R&A (Spring General Meeting, 4 May 1897).

11 York Buildings
Edinb. 10th Dec. 1896.

Royal and Ancient Golf Club
St. Andrews

Dear Sirs,

The proposal submitted to the Royal and Ancient Golf Club at their Autumn Meeting, for the formation of a Special Committee representative of that club and seven other clubs to deal with all matters relating to the rules and customs of the game of Golf, has been brought under the notice of the Edinburgh Burgess Golfing Society.

This club have considered the scheme so far as the details have been made public, and I am directed to express their disapproval thereof.

This club has hitherto acknowledged the position occupied by the Royal and Ancient Golf Club and they are still willing to do so, but they consider that if any change in the existing state of matters is considered necessary, provision ought to be made for the older Scotch clubs being represented, and you are no doubt aware that the Edinburgh Burgess Golfing Society is the most ancient Golf Club in Scotland, having been instituted in 1735.

Will you be so good as to bring this letter under the notice of the Royal and Ancient Golf Club.

I am
Yours faithfully
"Arthur S. Muir"
Hon. Secy.

(Mail seems to have traveled with enviable speed in 1896, since a reply to this letter was sent from St. Andrews the following day):

St. Andrews
11th Dec. 1896

Dear Sir,

I have received your letter of yesterday and shall submit it to the next General Meeting of this club. In the meantime I am sending a copy of it to the chairman of the committee appointed to consider the scheme to which you refer.

Yours faithfully
"C. S. Grace"
Hon. Secy.

3. Letter of 24 April 1897 from The Royal Albert Golf Club, Montrose, to The Royal and Ancient Golf Club. This letter is found only in the minute book of the R&A (Spring General Meeting, 4 May 1897). There is a peculiar hiatus in the minutes of the Royal Albert Golf Club from July 1896 to April 1897. A meeting of the club was held on 22 April 1897, but no reference is made in the minutes of that meeting to the letter below, sent two days later. It's clear from the letter's contents, however, that there had been some communication between the Royal Albert Golf Club and the R&A before it was drafted.

Royal Albert Golf Club, Montrose
April 24th/97

C. S. Grace, Hon. Secy.
Royal and Ancient Golf Club
St. Andrews

Dear Sir,

I am instructed to intimate to your Committee that this Club is strongly opposed to the appointment of a permanent Committee consisting of representatives of other Clubs as well as Members of the Royal and Ancient Club, to deal with questions relating to the rules and customs of golf.

This Club holds that these matters should rest with the Royal and Ancient Club and is therefore in favour of the amendment to be proposed to that effect.

If, however, it should be decided to import representatives of other Clubs into the permanent Committee, this Club, as one of the oldest in the country, claims representation.

I shall be much obliged by your submitting the letter to your meeting on the 4th proxo.

I am &c. (signed)
V. Stone, Hon. Secy.

4. Letter from Charles B. Macdonald to the Rules of Golf Committee of the R&A concerning "mallet-headed type" putters (as it is entered in the minutes of a meeting of the Rules of Golf Committee on 22 September 1910).

New York
June 10th, 1910

Rules of Golf Committee
Royal and Ancient Golf Club
St. Andrews, Scotland.

Dear Sir:

I received the notice of the Spring Meeting of the Royal and Ancient Golf Club, at St. Andrews, and particularly noted the motion by the Rules of Golf Committee, No. 12:-

'That the Rules of Golf Committee be empowered to add to the clause on form and make of golf clubs, words which will declare that all clubs with heads of the mallet type, are "a substantial departure from the traditional and accepted form and make of golf clubs."'

Later I have had notice that the motion was carried practically unanimously as stated.

Upon receiving the notice of the Spring Meeting I naturally concluded that this motion was brought before the Royal and Ancient Golf Club on account of the comments regarding Decision No. 47 of the Nga Motu Golf Club, New Zealand, which asked the question: 'With regard to form and make of golf clubs is it permissible to use a small croquet mallet to putt with?' The answer to this was: 'A croquet mallet is not a golf club and is inadmissible.'

From the data and information at hand which I received as a member of the Committee, it never occurred to me that this motion covered anything but that of clubs which are generally known as 'mallets'. By that I mean the kind of a mallet a carpenter uses, a croquet mallet, etc., etc.—that is, where there is a right-angled centered shaft with two heads to strike with. Further, the motion itself states that the mallet type are 'a substantial departure from the accepted form and make of golf clubs'. Now, Schenectady putters and wry-neck clubs have been an accepted form and make of golf club for over ten years. Much as golfers of the old school felt that they were an innovation, they were accepted generally. I believe fifty per cent. of the golfers in the United States play with a Schenectady. As for the United States Golf Association, the carrying of this motion, conveying with it the interpretation made by Captain Burn by cable that Schenectady and wry-neck clubs were included under the 'mallet-headed type', caused a great sensation, even to a point of the parting of the ways. Had action immediately been taken by the United States Golf Association, I fear they would have repudiated their allegiance to the Royal and Ancient Golf Club. However, Section 10 of their by-laws reads as follows:

'The competitions shall be played in accordance with the Rules of Golf, as adopted by the Royal and Ancient Golf Club of St. Andrews, Scotland, with the rulings and interpretations as adopted by the United States Golf Association, together with such local rules as are in force and published on the Green over which the Competition takes place.'

Being consulted, I pointed out to members of the Committee that when they met they could embody the new rule as passed by the Royal and Ancient Golf Club and interpret it so as not to bar the Schenectady putter, taking the definition of a mallet as universally understood and interpreted in this country. This will I think obviate a distinct breach.

If Captain Burn is to be sustained in his interpretation of the mallet type of club it occurs to me that the Rules of Golf Committee must make a ruling as a body on that subject. For my part, I do not think that the Schenectady is a mallet. Neither is a wry-neck putter. Neither of these clubs really makes the slightest difference in a man's play. It is only his character of mind. There are a few people in this country stupid enough to think, owing to Travis's uncalled for and undignified criticism of his treatment at Sandwich, that this is the line of retaliation. That can be dismissed without a thought. Travis is now putting with a Braid aluminum, and, if anything, putting better than ever.

The Royal and Ancient Golf Club maintains an allegiance throughout the world in golf that no other sport has anything like or comparable with it. A regime so honorably and effectively administered in a game that encircles the world, appealing to all classes, should to my mind be conserved with the utmost care and delicacy, and it would be a source of the deepest regret should that allegiance be jeopardized by so small and unnecessary a matter as the interpretation of the word 'mallet', which means nothing to the game itself.

Believe me,
Yours faithfully,
Charles B. Macdonald

The following reply to Macdonald's letter was drafted by the Rules of Golf Committee:

26th September 1910

C. B. Macdonald, Esq.
11 Broadway
New York

Dear Sir,

In reply to your letter of June 10th, I am requested by the Rules of Golf Committee to inform you that it was impossible to ignore the very strong feeling in this country against the use of clubs in which the traditional manner of having the leverage of the head beyond the shaft is departed from.

The term "mallet-headed" has long been used, not in a dictionary sense, but to denote clubs in which the shaft is let into the head anywhere except at the heel.

The telegram you refer to, which was answered by Captain Burn, asked no question with regard to wry-necked clubs, some of which are fair clubs, but many of which are merely constructed to acquire the same balance as is obtained by inserting the shaft towards the centre of the head. The Committee believes that it is working for the best interests of the game in debarring such clubs, and has the support of the Royal and Ancient Golf Club, and the mass of the best golfers in Great Britain.

The Committee deeply regrets that American golfers are not in sympathy with the views of the Royal and Ancient Club on this subject.

I am, etc.

5. Bernard Darwin's preface to the 1950 R&A experimental code.

PREFACE

THE RULES OF GOLF have been revised by the Royal and Ancient Golf Club of St. Andrews with the object of simplifying their interpretation. The revision is based largely on experience gained from questions asked and decisions given during the past fifteen years.

The Etiquette of the Game has been placed immediately before the Rules in order to emphasise the duty of players to familiarise themselves with the long-established customs and usage of the game.

The Rules have been laid out in sections of co-related subjects and the match and stroke play Rules have been amalgamated where possible: where there is different treatment in the two forms of play this has been brought out in separate clauses under the same rule.

A section incorporating the Rules which apply peculiarly to competitions has been introduced and includes directions which committees and players should find helpful. It is strongly recommended that players taking part in a competition should carry a copy of the Rules.

The most important individual change made is in regard to the reduction in penalty for the ball lost, out of bounds, or unplayable, and the consequent general reduction in penalties which this change has entailed. A referendum was held among members of The Royal and Ancient Golf Club as to whether the penalty in each case should be as before, loss of stroke and distance, or loss of distance only. The opinion of the governing bodies at home and overseas was also requested on this point. In each case there was a majority in favour of distance only. It was therefore decided to give effect to the majority's view, and, at the same time, for the sake of consistency, to reduce the penalties in the other Rules proportionately. The penalty for all breaches of Rule, except those which must be regarded as deliberate and therefore inexcusable, is now one stroke in both match and stroke play. For deliberate breach of a Rule the penalty is loss of hole in match play and disqualification in stroke play. The penalty of loss of hole in match play remains where a player's action could affect the subsequent play of his opponent.

Apart from the adjustment to the penalties there are certain new definitions and Rules to the most important of which particular attention is drawn:—

Ball, unplayable. This definition gives a guide to players as to the conditions which justify them in considering the ball unplayable. In this connection it is pointed out that a player may not now deem a ball unplayable and tee a ball behind under a penalty of two strokes in stroke play. A new clause has been added to the unplayable ball Rule which permits the player if he considers his ball unplayable, in accordance with the definition, to drop a ball under penalty of one stroke in both match and stroke play.

Playing the wrong ball. This Rule has been amended and wrong information given by an opponent or an opponent's caddie does not absolve the player from the responsibility of playing his own ball.

Ball at rest, moved during search. A player is no longer penalised if he, or his caddie, moves his or his partner's ball during a search.

Ball lost, or out of bounds. The player, if he considers his ball may be lost or out of bounds is now allowed to play only one "provisional" ball before going forward.

Ball unplayable. The playing of a provisional ball is not now permitted. After the player has established by examination that his ball is in an unplayable lie he has the choice of dropping under penalty of one stroke or of going back for loss of distance.

Nearer ball interfering with play on the putting green. In stroke play when a ball lying on the putting green interferes with the play of another ball, the ball nearer the hole must be played first. This Rule has been introduced in order to avoid much unnecessary lifting of balls on the green with its resulting waste of time.

Practice on days of stroke competitions. On stroke competition days practice is prohibited on the course or courses over which the competition is being held, except when there is an area of the course defined as practice ground, in which case competitors who practise on the course are restricted to that area.

Undue delay. This Rule has been introduced to check the growing abuse of unduly slow play. It is recommended that the penalty should not be enforced without prior warning being given to the offender.

Discontinuance of play. This Rule now applies to match as well as stroke play, since the discontinuance of play in the former may entirely upset the time-table of a competition. Stoppage of play has not hitherto been allowed in case of bad weather unless authorised by the committee. Players now may stop play if there is danger from lightning—a danger which has been increased by the use of steel-shafted clubs.

It has been decided not to alter the Rule as to what is commonly known as the Stymie, since the majority of the governing bodies consulted were in favour of retaining the existing Rule.

These Rules will remain unaltered for two years. At the end of that period they will be reconsidered and amended if necessary. It is hoped that this will result in a code which will require no further alteration for many years.

> BERNARD DARWIN (Chairman),
> The Rules of Golf Committee,
> The Royal and Ancient Golf Club of St. Andrews.

6. Preface to the 1952 uniform R&A-USGA code of rules

PREFACE

This edition of the Rules of Golf is the result of a joint revision by the Royal and Ancient Golf Club of St. Andrews, Scotland, and the United States Golf Association.

For some years a growing desire for uniform Rules has manifested itself and this has now been achieved after special committee conferences in which representatives of Canada and Australia participated also.

It has been customary for both the R&A and the USGA to revise their Rules periodically and individually in the light of experience. However, there has been no regular machinery for co-ordinating their respective views. As a result, differences have crept into the Rules.

Departures from uniformity are no new phenomenon, for in early days each prominent club in the United Kingdom had its own Rules. Nevertheless, as the game spread, it became recognized that uniformity would be advantageous to all, and towards the end of the last century the Royal and Ancient Golf Club, as a result of requests from the main clubs in the British Isles, published the first uniform set of Rules.

The history of the present code dates to the end of the recent world war. The USGA revised its Rules and the R&A were in the process of doing the same. Because there had been intimations of a deep interest in standardization of Rules, USGA representatives were invited to visit St. Andrews and conferences took place there in the Spring of 1951. In a most cordial atmosphere, the negotiating committees achieved agreement on this unified code, which subsequently was ratified by the Executive Committee of the USGA and by the membership of the R&A.

The Main Aims

At the conferences three primary considerations were kept to the fore:

First, the perspective was to be world-wide to meet the varying conditions under which the game is now played.

Second, to achieve this objective, there would clearly have to be "give and take" over items of differing importance to different countries.

Third, the negotiating representatives reminded themselves that, if legislation lags too far behind public opinion, the legislation loses effect.

These considerations account for some of the new code's unusual features reflected by both inclusions and omissions.

The Putter

At the beginning of the century, there were no essential differences in the respective Rules of the R&A and the USGA. The first major departure from uniformity occurred with the introduction of the Schenectady putter in the United States. This was not accepted by the R&A as a traditional form of golf club, but play with this type of club continued in the United States.

Now, after nearly fifty years, it is agreed that this type has become traditional and universal use will be permitted hereafter.

The Stymie

There were only a few other divergencies in the Rules of play up to the late 1930s, when the USGA experimentally introduced its variation of the stymie Rule. By giving relief when balls were within six inches of the hole or within six inches of each other, it did away with an unpopular feature—the unnegotiable stymie. This type of stymie often resulted from a missed putt on the part of the opponent. The American Rule survived its experimental stage and until now has been in effect in the United States, although it was not adopted in other countries.

Some five years ago, the R&A took a referendum on the stymie amongst the governing bodies of various countries. The result suggested a more or less equal division of opinion for retention, abolition, and two other alternatives; i.e., the United States version on the one hand and abolition of stymies laid by the opponent on the other. The latter alternative means almost total abolition, as relative few stymies are laid by the player himself.

With opinion so widely divided on the issue of the stymie, there seemed little chance of achieving uniformity in a world-wide code by retaining it or adopting either of the other alternatives. Abolition of the stymie was therefore recommended and adopted.

The Ball

There has been and still remains a difference in the size of the ball. This matter has been regarded in a somewhat different light from that of the Rules of actual play. Playing conditions differ in many parts of the world, and the ruling bodies held to the opinion that the smaller British ball is no more suitable for play in the United States than the larger American ball is suitable for play in Great Britain. It is hoped that in the future it may be possible to find some basis for standardizing the ball.

In the meanwhile, and in this code, the size of the British ball is specified as not less than 1.620 inches in diameter and that of the American ball as not less than 1.680 inches, with weight coinciding at 1.620 ounces. To give playing equality in international team competition, the USGA has legalized the smaller ball for use in such contests in its country.

The Penalties

On the introduction of the 1950 Royal and Ancient revised code, there arose another major difference when the R&A, as an experiment, made many changes in penalties. The USGA continued with substantially the traditional scale. The R&A had taken a referendum as regards the penalties for out of bounds, unplayable ball and lost ball, and they accepted the majority view that the penalty for all these contingencies should be reduced from stroke and distance to loss of distance only.

Playing experience, however, soon showed that the removal of the penalty stroke (which was the equivalent of the stroke the player theoretically played to get out of the adverse situation and still in fact had to play to get out of a bunker) was not equitable, and that the penalty of distance only (which was variable, as it was the distance the player struck the ball) was not an adequate penalty. Consequently, the R&A decided to return to the traditional penalties, and so were of one mind with the USGA when penalties for the uniform code came up for consideration.

These four items—the putter, the stymie, the ball, and the penalties—seemed likely to be the most controversial items in the achievement of a unified code, but in each instance viewpoints were harmonized in the interests of uniformity.

Maintenance of Uniformity

In framing this code, attention has been particularly directed to clarifying the Rules, consolidating them wherever possible, and rationalizing the headings so that reference is simplified.

There is one final point. A unified set of Rules having been achieved, it is recognized that it can only be kept uniform by mutual agreement not to alter it unilaterally. If questions of alteration arise, the Royal and Ancient and the United States Golf Association will consult with each other and with the governing bodies in other countries, and will use all possible means to ensure the maintenance of uniformity.

> Isaac B. Grainger
> Chairman, Rules of Golf Committee
> United States Golf Association
>
> Harold Gardiner-Hill
> Chairman, Rules of Golf Committee
> Royal and Ancient Golf Club of St. Andrews

Bibliography

Included in this list are the titles of all articles and books quoted or referred to, plus some general works containing relevant material, as well as a few of the more important club histories containing references to early rules.

Anderson, J. "The Rules of Golf Committee." *The Golfing Annual 1897–1898.* London 1898: 1–6.

Anderson, John G. "A Plan for Unity of Golf Rules." *The American Golfer* (December 1921): 19–30.

Baird, Archie. *Golf on Gullane Hill.* Edinburgh, 1982.

Boatwright, P. J., Jr. "Worldwide Decisions Book Complements Revised Rules." *USGA Golf Journal* (May/June 1984): 12 13.

Browning, Robert. *A History of Golf.* London, 1955. cf. Chapter Twenty-seven: "The Evolution of the Rules."

Browning, Robert H. K. "Some Everyday Points in the Rules." Lesson XXVII in Whitcombe, Charles. *Golf.* London, 1949.

C. H. "The 'Burning Questions' in Golf." *The Golfing Annual 1889–1890.* London, (1890): 19 23.

Clapcott, Charles B. *The Rules of the Ten Oldest Golf Clubs from 1754 to 1848 together with The Rules of the Royal and Ancient Golf Club of St. Andrews for the years 1858, 1875 and 1888.* Edinburgh, 1935.

Clark, Robert. *Golf: A Royal and Ancient Game.* Edinburgh, 1875.

Cousins, Geoffrey. *Golfers at Law.* London, 1958.

Cousins, Geoffrey. *The Handbook of Golf.* London, 1969. cf. Chapter VIII: "Alterations to Rules."

Cruden, Stewart. *Bruntsfield Links Golfing Society: A Short History.* Edinburgh, 1991. cf. pp.8–9: "Rules and Regulations".

Cruickshank, Charles. *The History of the Royal Wimbledon Golf Club 1865–1986.* Wimbledon, 1986. cf. Chapter Thirteen: "Rules."

Cundell, John. *Rules of The Thistle Golf Club.* Ballantyne, 1824. (A Facsimile of the 1824 Edition with a New Foreword by Joseph C. Dey. USGA, Far Hills, N.J., 1983.)

Davies, Peter. *The Historical Dictionary of Golfing Terms, From 1500 to the Present.* New York, 1992.

Dey, Joseph C. "A World Code of Rules." *USGA Journal and Turf Management* (June 1951): 5–6.

Dey, Joseph C. "Relaxation in Rules: A New Year's Gift." *USGA Journal and Turf Management* (November 1959): 5.

Everard, H. S. C. *A History of the Royal & Ancient Golf Club of St. Andrews from 1754–1900*. Edinburgh and London, 1907. cf. especially Chapter XXVII: "Rules of Golf Committee."

Farnie, H. B. *The Golfer's Manual*. Cupar, 1857 (reprinted London 1947). cf. "Appendix: A Code of Golfing Laws."

Farrar, Guy B. *The Royal Liverpool Golf Club, A History 1869–1932*. Birkenhead, 1933.

Francis, Richard S. *Golf, Its Rules and Decisions*. N.Y., 1937. Revised edition 1939. cf. pp.5–19: "The Rules of Golf Committee."

Gardiner-Hill, H. "The History of the Rules of Golf." Chapter II in Darwin, B., et al., *The History of Golf in Britain*. 1952.

Geddes, Olive M. *A Swing Through Time. Golf in Scotland 1457–1743*. Edinburgh, 1992.

Goodban, J. W. D. *Royal North Devon Golf Club, A Centenary Anthology 1864–1964*. Bideford, 1964. cf. pp. 17–23: "Rules and Regulations of the North Devon Golf Club" (with discussion by Bernard Darwin).

Grainger, Isaac B. "Stroke and Distance for Out of Bounds." *USGA Journal and Turf Management* (August, 1951): 16–24.

Hamilton, David. *Early Aberdeen Golf: Golfing Small-talk in 1636*. Glasgow, 1985.

Hannigan, Frank. "World Rules Uniformity Re-established by USGA." *USGA Journal and Turf Management* (February 1962): 4–5.

Harris, Robert. *Sixty Years of Golf*. London, 1953. cf. Chapter IV: "Rules and Regulations."

Harris, Robert. *Proposed New Rules of Golf, A Threat to the Game as a Sport*. (Privately Printed) 1949.

Henderson, I., and Stirk, D. *Golf in the Making*. Winchester, 1979.

Henderson, I., and Stirk, D. *Royal Blackheath*. London, 1981. cf. Chapter 10: "Rules of Golf at Blackheath."

Henderson, J. Lindsay. *The Records of the Panmure Golf Club*. Dundee, 1926.

Hilton, Harold H., and Smith, Garden G., ed., *The Royal and Ancient Game of Golf*. London, 1912.

Hughes, W. E. *Chronicles of Blackheath Golfers*. London, 1897. cf. pp. 216–240: "Regulations and Rules."

Hutchinson, Horace G. *Golf*. The Badminton Library. 1890.

Hutchinson, Horace G. "An Appeal from America." *Golf* (12 February 1897): 395 (cf. also Macdonald, C. S., op.cit., pp.102–103).

Johnston, Alastair J. *The Clapcott Papers*. Edinburgh, 1985.

Johnston, Alastair J., and Johnston, James F. *The Chronicles of Golf: 1457 to 1857*. Cleveland, 1993.

Jones, Bobby (Robert Tyre, Jr.). *Golf Is My Game*. N.Y., 1959. cf. Chapter 18: "The Stymie—Let's Have It Back."

Kerr, John. *The Golf Book of East Lothian*. Edinburgh, 1896.

Kerr, John. *The History of Curling*. Edinburgh, 1890.

Lauthier, Joseph. *New Rules for the Game of Mail*. Tr. by James Cunningham; Introduction by Andrew Lang. St. Andrews, 1910.

Lawson, J. Stewart. *The Original Rules of Golf*. Muirfield, 1981.

Lawson, J. Stewart. "Evolution of the Rules of Golf." In *Golfer's Handbook 1984–1994*. London, 1984–1994.

Leitch, Cecil. *Golf*. London, 1922. cf. Chapter XVI: "The Rules—Their Meaning and Application."

Lewis, Peter N. "Bounding Billy Bounces to Britain. The Arrival of the Rubber-Cored Ball, 1901–1903." *Golfiana* 3, no. 4 (1991).

Lewis, Peter N. "Mechanical Contrivances & Mallet Heads. Standardizing Clubs in Britain 1907–1910." *Golfiana* 3, no. 3 (1991).

Lewis, Peter. "The History of the Golf Ball in Britain." *Golf-The Scientific Way*, ed. Alastair Cochran. Aston, 1995.

Lewis, Peter. "The Birth of the Rules of Golf Committee 1895–97." *Through the Green—Journal of the British Golf Collectors' Society*. March 1995.

Low, John L. "Golf and the Man." In Hilton, Harold H., and Smith, Garden G., ed., *The Royal and Ancient Game of Golf*. London, 1912, pp. 57–71.

Macdonald, Charles Blair. *Scotland's Gift: Golf. Reminiscences, 1872–1927*. New York and London, 1928.

Mair, Lewine. *One Hundred Years of Women's Golf*. Edinburgh, 1992.

Mair, Norman. *Muirfield—Home of the Honourable Company (1744–1994)*. Edinburgh and London, 1994.

McDonnell, Michael. "Toward a Uniform Ball." *USGA Golf Journal* (September 1983): 21–23.

Mearns, J. A. G. *200 Years of Golf, 1780–1980, Royal Aberdeen Golf Club*. Aberdeen, 1980.

Milton, John T. *A History of Royal Eastbourne Golf Club 1887–1987*. Eastbourne, 1987.

Park, W., Jr. *The Game of Golf*. London, 1896. cf. Chapter XI: "The Laws of Golf". (comparison of 1891/1895 R&A and 1883 Royal Wimbledon codes).

Pottinger, George. *Muirfield and The Honourable Company*. Edinburgh & London, 1972. cf. Chapter II: "The Thirteen Articles."

Pumfrey, Paul. *Lincoln Golf Club Centenary 1891–1991*. Lincoln, 1991.

Purves, W. Laidlaw. "The Laws of Golf." *The Golfing Annual 1888–1889*. London (1889): 4–19.

Robbie, J. Cameron. *The Chronicle of the Royal Burgess Golfing Society of Edinburgh, 1735–1935*. Edinburgh, 1936. cf. Appendix VIII: "Principle Rules and Regulations."

Rumjahn, Doris. *Remember Some Golf Rules in Rhyme*. Liverpool, 1990.

Russell, Jean M. *Old Manchester Golf Club 1818–1988*. Manchester, 1988.

Scott, Tom. *The Story of Golf*. London, 1972. cf. Chapter 5: "The Rules."

Simpson, Walter G. "The Laws of Golf." *The Golfing Annual 1887–1888*. London (1888): 1–47.

(pp.16–23: Appendix I. Rules of The Royal and Ancient Golf Club (St. Andrews); the Adaptations of them by The Honourable Company of Edinburgh

Golfers for the Musselburgh Green; and the Alterations and Adaptations by The Royal North Devon and West of England Golf Club for the Westward Ho! Green.

pp. 24–47: Appendix II. Correspondence which has taken place during the past two years in the columns of "The Field" on this vital question.)

Smith, David B. *Curling: an Illustrated History*. Edinburgh, 1981.

Taylor, William Duncan. *Wallasey Golf Club 1891–1953*. Wallasey, 1953.

Travis, Walter J. "An Epoch in Putters." *The American Golfer*, (November 1910): 32–34.

Tufts, Richard S. *The Principles Behind the Rules of Golf*. Pinehurst, North Carolina, 1960.

Ward-Thomas, Pat. *The Royal and Ancient*. Edinburgh, 1980. cf. Chapter Nine: "The Rules of Golf."

Watson, Tom with Hannigan, Frank. *The Rules of Golf, Illustrated and Explained*. New York, 1980, 1984, 1988, 1992, 1996.

Williams, William J., Jr. "Reorganizing the Rules of Golf." *USGA Golf Journal* (January/February 1981): 4–7.

Williams, William J., Jr. "Can the Rules of Golf Be Simplified." *USGA Golf Journal* (March/April 1982): 14–19.

Williams, William J., Jr., and Boatwright, P. J., Jr. "The New Rules of Golf." *USGA Golf Journal* (Nov./Dec. 1983): 14–20.

Winters, John M., Jr. "The Trial Rules for 1961: How They Were Developed." *USGA Golf Journal and Turf Management* (February 1961): 4–7.

Index

The indexes to the Rules of Golf and Decisions on the Rules of Golf are both useful additional references for locating specific topics within the Rules.

Photo Credits

Brown Brothers, cover photos and pages ii, x, xiv, 6, 24, 40, 56, 65, 73, 92, 94, 115, 123, 148, 168, 200, and 240. Corbis-Bettmann, pages 3, 8, 10, 12, 20, 29, 38, 48, 70, 80, 84, 86, 88, 108, 127, 128, 150, 171, 173, 182, and 199. Pages vi and 58, courtesy of Dover Publications. The Granger Collection, pages 26, 93, 106, and 112. Page 208 courtesy of Helka Chapman. Pages 52 and 101 © Ken May/Rolling Greens. Pages 16, 28, 66, and 97 © Leo Kelly. Page 139 © Visualarity/Canadian National Railways. Page 135 © Larry Petrillo/USGA.